Q&A Series
Contract Law

FIFTH EDITION

Cavendish
Publishing
Limited

London • Sydney • Portland, Oregon

Q&A Series
Contract Law

FIFTH EDITION

Richard Stone, LLB, LLM, Barrister
Professor of Law, University of Lincoln
Visiting Professor, University College Northampton

Cavendish
Publishing
Limited

London • Sydney • Portland, Oregon

Fifth edition first published in Great Britain 2003 by
Cavendish Publishing Limited, The Glass House,
Wharton Street, London WC1X 9PX, United Kingdom
Telephone: + 44 (0)20 7278 8000   Facsimile: + 44 (0)20 7278 8080
Email: info@cavendishpublishing.com
Website: www.cavendishpublishing.com

Published in the United States by Cavendish Publishing
c/o International Specialized Book Services,
5804 NE Hassalo Street, Portland,
Oregon 97213-3644, USA

Published in Australia by Cavendish Publishing (Australia) Pty Ltd
3/303 Barrenjoey Road, Newport, NSW 2106, Australia

© Stone, Richard	2003
First edition	1992
Second edition	1995
Third edition	1998
Fourth edition	2001
Fifth edition	2003

British Library Cataloguing in Publication Data

Stone, Richard, 1951–
Contract law – 5th ed – (Q&A series)
1 Contracts – England 2 Contracts – Wales
I Title
346.4'2'02

Library of Congress Cataloguing in Publication Data
Data available

ISBN 1-85941-734-5

1 3 5 7 9 10 8 6 4 2

Printed and bound in Great Britain

PREFACE

Contract must be one of the most widely studied areas of English law. As well as being one of the 'core' subjects for professional purposes, it is often studied by those taking law options within a more general course, at degree level or below. One reason for this is that contract law provides a good, and in some cases essential, grounding for the study of many other legal subjects, such as commercial law, company law, consumer law, employment law and land law. Master contract, and you will have a firm basis for the study of many other courses. It is also a typical 'common law' subject, which means that its rules and principles have developed largely through the decisions of the courts, rather than through statutory intervention. A comparison between the size of the Table of Cases and that of the Table of Statutes in this book illustrates the point.

This book was written with a view to helping all those studying contract. I am pleased that previous editions seem to have been well received by students. This edition contains five completely new questions and answers, and has been fully revised throughout to take account of developments in the law. The most important of these are the House of Lords decisions in *Royal Bank of Scotland v Etridge (No 2)* (2001) and *Farley v Skinner* (2001), and the Court of Appeal decision in *Great Peace Shipping Ltd v Tsavliris Salvage (International) Ltd* (2002). The first of these has thoroughly reviewed the law and procedures relating to undue influence. The second has restated the approach to be adopted in relation to the recovery of non-pecuniary losses resulting from a breach of contract. The third (the *Great Peace* case) has resulted in a significant restriction on the remedies available where the parties have contracted on the basis of a mistaken assumption. In the area of contract formation, the Consumer Protection (Distance Selling) Regulations 2000 and the European Directive on Electronic Commerce 2000 are both important, and are fully considered. In this context, the developing area of contracting over the internet is looked at in detail in Chapter 1.

The purpose of this book remains the same. It is not a substitute for attending lectures, or reading textbooks or law reports. It is hoped that it will prove a valuable supplement to those activities. Students often find that, having attended lectures, or read the books, they have difficulty in deciding what is relevant and irrelevant, what is important and less important, what needs to be committed to memory, and what can be safely regarded as background. This is a particular difficulty when students are taught contract early in their legal studies, as is usually the case. One of the objectives of this book is to help students who face such difficulties. The answers to the questions contained in this book provide a distillation of the essential points on the topics which they cover. They help to highlight the most important elements, and indicate the fundamental rules and principles which need to be learnt.

The second objective is to illustrate, by example, how to answer questions on contract law. The answer plans are important here, as well as the answers themselves. Each of the answers is around 1,500–1,700 words long, which is probably an average length for a first year law degree essay. Exam answers may well be a little shorter and less detailed, but the overall approach should be the same. Note, however, that the answers given are not, and are not intended to be, perfect. There is probably no such thing. Nor are they the only way in which the questions given could be answered. They are, however, examples of the kind of well structured answer which will be likely to receive good marks. They will also help to answer, it is hoped, some of the perennial student concerns, such as 'how far should I give the facts of cases?', and 'how many cases do I need to cite?'. It is not easy to answer such questions in the abstract. The answers here give concrete examples of how the material should be handled.

The questions themselves are frequently adaptations of questions used in past examination papers, and are of the style used in many degree courses, including the London External LLB. Non-degree courses will often adopt a similar approach. The law is stated as it stood on 1 December 2002.

I hope that you find this book useful as a supplement to your study of the law of contract. It will not remove the need to read the textbooks and the cases, but it will help you to make better use of the information you have acquired from these sources and, I hope, achieve success in your examinations.

Richard Stone
Oadby, Leicester
1 December 2002

CONTENTS

Table of Cases   *ix*
Table of Statutes   *xxiii*
Table of Legislation   *xxv*

1	Offer and Acceptance	1
2	Intention and Consideration	25
3	Privity	51
4	Capacity	67
5	Contents of the Contract	81
6	Exclusion Clauses	97
7	Mistake and Misrepresentation	117
8	Duress and Undue Influence	135
9	Illegality	157
10	Frustration	177
11	Performance and Breach	193
12	Remedies	209
13	Quasi-Contract and Restitution	225
14	Agency	235
15	Sale of Goods	251

Index   261

TABLE OF CASES

A to Z Bazaars (Pty) Ltd v Minister of Agriculture
(1974) (4) SA 392(C) 23

Adams v Lindsell (1818) 1 B & Ald 681; 106 ER 250 ....1, 3, 4, 6, 8, 16, 22

Addis v Gramophone [1909] AC 488 222

Adler v Dickson [1955] 1 QB 158; [1954] 3 All ER 397 110

Aiken v Short (1856) 1 H & N 210 228

Ailsa Craig Fishing Co v Malvern Fishing Co
[1983] 1 WLR 964; 1 All ER 449 109

Aldridge v Johnson (1857) 7 E & B 885 255

Alec Lobb (Garages) Ltd v Total Oil (Great Britain) Ltd
[1985] 1 All ER 303 174

Alfred McAlpine Construction Ltd v Panatown Ltd
[2000] 3 WLR 946 ....58, 60, 61

Allcard v Skinner (1887) 36 Ch D 145 149

Aluminium Industrie Vaasen BV
v Romalpa Aluminium Ltd [1976] 1 WLR 676 ....255, 256

Andrews v Hopkinson [1957] 1 QB 229 243

Anglia Television v Reed [1972] 1 QB 60; [1971] 3 All ER 690 ....210, 212

Appleby v Myers (1867) LR 2 CP 651;
[1961–73] All ER Rep 452 ....179, 181, 183, 184,
186, 187

Appleton v Campbell (1826) 2 C & P 347 160

Arcos Ltd v Ronaasen & Son [1933] AC 470 ....197, 202, 260

Armagas v Mundogas [1986] AC 717; 2 All ER 385 ....240, 245–47

Armhouse Lee Ltd v Chappell (1996) The Times, 7 August 161

Ashdown v Samuel Williams [1957] 1 QB 409; 1 All ER 35 111

Ashington Piggeries v Christopher Hill [1972] AC 441 ....203, 258, 260

Ashmore and Others v Corporation of Lloyd's (No 2)
(1992) The Times, 17 July 85

Associated Japanese Bank (International) v Credit du Nord SA
[1988] 3 All ER 902; [1989] 1 WLR 255 125

Aswan v Lupdine [1987] 1 WLR 1;
[1986] 2 Lloyd's Rep 347 260

Atkinson v Denby (1862) 7 H & N 934 165

Atlas Express Ltd v Kafco (Importers and Distributors) Ltd
[1989] QB 833; 1 All ER 641 ....40, 137, 141, 143, 146

Attorney General v Blake (2000) 31 SLR 43 ....209, 213

Attwood v Lamont [1920] 3 KB 571 ....168, 173

Attwood v Small (1838) 6 Cl & F 232; 7 ER 684 90

BMTA v Salvadori [1949] Ch 556 56
BP Exploration Co (Libya) Ltd v Hunt (No 2)
  [1982] 1 All ER 925 ....177, 179–81, 184,
                                                                                      186, 188, 189
Baker v White (1690) 2 Vern 615; 23 ER 740 163
Balfour Beatty Construction (Scotland) Ltd
  v Scottish Power plc (1994) The Times, 23 March 218
Balfour v Balfour [1919] 2 KB 571 ....25, 28, 45
Bank of Credit and Commerce International SA
  v Aboody [1990] 1 QB 923; [1989] 2 WLR 759 ....138, 142, 144
Bannerman v White (1861) 10 CBNS 844; 142 ER 685 ....87, 93
Barclays Bank v Fairclough Building Ltd [1994] 3 WLR 1057 212
Barclays Bank v O'Brien [1993] 3 WLR 786 ....142, 145, 148, 150,
                                                                                      152–55
Barton v Armstrong [1976] AC 104; [1975] 2 WLR 1050 ....142, 148
Bell v Lever Bros [1932] AC 161 ....117, 121, 123, 125,
                                                                                      130, 134
Beswick v Beswick [1968] AC 58; [1967] 2 All ER 1197 ....52, 54, 55, 63, 65, 66, 216
Bettini v Gye (1876) 1 QBD 183; [1874–80] All ER Rep 242 198
Bisset v Wilkinson [1927] AC 177; [1926] All ER Rep 343 ....88, 119, 131, 132
Bolton v Mahadeva [1972] 2 All ER 1322; 1 WLR 1009 201
Bowmakers v Barnet Instruments
  [1945] KB 65; [1944] 2 All ER 579 166
Brace v Calder [1895] 2 QB 253 214
Braymist Ltd v Wise Finance Co Ltd (2002) 242
Brimnes, The [1975] QB 929; [1974] 3 All ER 88 ....5, 16
Brinkibon Ltd v Stahag Stahl GmbH
  [1983] 2 AC 34; [1982] 1 All ER 293 ....5, 16
British Reinforced Concrete Engineering Co Ltd
  v Schelff [1921] Ch 563 167
British Steel Corporation v Cleveland Bridge and
  Engineering Company [1984] 1 All ER 504 ....230, 231, 233
British Westinghouse Electric Manufacturing Co Ltd
  v Underground Electric Railways Co of London Ltd
  [1912] AC 673 ....212, 218, 220, 221
Bull v Pitney-Bowes [1966] 3 All ER 384; [1967] 1 WLR 273 ....163, 175
Bunge Corporation v Tradax Export SA
  [1981] 1 WLR 711; 2 All ER 513 ....195, 198
Burrell v Jones (1819) 3 B & Ald 47 244
Butler Machine Tool Ltd v Ex-Cell-O [1979] 1 All ER 965 10–12

Butterworth v Kingsway Motors [1954] 1 WLR 1286 . . . . .228, 233

Byrne v van Tienhoven (1880) 5 CPD 344 . . . . .5, 9, 16

C & P Haulage v Middleton [1983] 1 WLR 1461; 3 All ER 94 213

CCC Films (London) Ltd v Impact Quadrant Films Ltd
    [1985] QB 16; [1984] 3 All ER 298 214

CIBC Mortgages v Pitt [1993] 4 All ER 433 . . . . .138, 148, 151

CTN Cash and Carry v Gallaher [1994] 4 All ER 714 . . . . .137, 139, 142–44

Cammell Laird & Co Ltd
    v Manganese Bronze & Brass Co Ltd [1934] AC 402 259

Caparo Industries v Dickman [1990] 2 WLR 358 . . . . .247, 248

Carlill v Carbolic Smoke Ball Co [1893] 1 QB 256 . . . . .7, 10, 20

Carlos Federspiel & Co SA v Charles Twigg & Co Ltd
    [1957] 1 Lloyd's Rep 240 255

Casey's Patents, Re, Stewart v Casey [1892] 1 Ch 104 30

Cehave NV v Bremer Handelsgesellschaft mbH,
    The Hansa Nord [1976] QB 44; [1975] 3 WLR 447 198

Central London Property Trust v High Trees House
    [1947] KB 130 . . . . .26, 33, 34, 37–39,
                                                                    41, 42, 47, 48

Chandler v Webster [1904] 1 KB 493 . . . . .179, 184, 185, 189

Chapelton v Barry [1940] 1 KB 532; 1 All ER 356 111

Chaplin v Hicks [1911] 2 KB 786 . . . . .216, 219

Chappell & Co v Nestlé & Co [1960] AC 87;
    [1959] 2 All ER 701 . . . . .25, 29

Chapple v Cooper (1844) 3 M & W 252 . . . . .69, 73, 78

Chesterton v Barone [1987] 1 EGLR 15 244

Clarke v Newland [1991] 1 All ER 397 . . . . .163, 168, 174

Clarkson Booker Ltd v Andjel [1964] 2 QB 775 244

Clements v London & NW Rly [1894] 2 QB 482 78

Collen v Wright (1857) 8 E & B 647; 120 ER 241 . . . . .243, 245, 248

Collins v Associated Greyhound Racecourses Ltd
    [1930] 1 Ch 1 242

Collins v Godefroy (1831) 1 B & Ald 950; 120 ER 241 46

Combe v Combe [1951] 2 KB 215; 1 All ER 767 . . . . .26, 34, 41

Condor v Barron Knights [1966] 1 WLR 87 179

Cooper v Phibbs (1867) LR 2 HL 149 . . . . .119, 232

Co-operative Insurance Society Ltd v Argyll Stores
    (Holdings) Ltd [1998] AC 1; [1997] 2 WLR 898 217

Courtney & Fairbain v Tolaini Bros (Hotels) Ltd
[1975] 1 WLR 297 ....91, 92, 233
Couturier v Hastie (1852) 8 Exch 40; (1856) 5 HLC 673 120
Cowern v Nield [1912] 2 KB 419 80
Craven-Ellis v Canons Ltd [1936] 2 KB 403 ....229, 230
Credit Lyonnais Bank Nederland NV v Burch
[1997] 1 All ER 144 154
Cremdean v Nash (1977) 244 EG 547, CA 114
Cricklewood Property Investment Trust
v Leighton's Investment Trusts Ltd [1945] AC 221 180
Cundy v Lindsay (1878) 3 App Cas 459 128
Cutter v Powell (1795) 6 Term Rep 320;
[1775–1802] All ER Rep 159 ....193, 199, 200

D & C Builders v Rees [1966] 2 QB 617;
[1965] 3 All ER 837 ....26, 34, 35, 38, 39, 41,
44, 45, 47, 48
Darlington Borough Council v Wiltshire Northern Ltd
[1995] 3 All ER 895 60
Daulia Ltd v Four Millbank Nominees
[1978] Ch 231; [1978] 2 All ER 557 ....7, 9, 21
Daun v Simmins (1879) 41 LT 783 237
Davis Contractors Ltd v Fareham UDC [1956] 3 WLR 37 ....181, 182, 188
De Francesco v Barnum (1889) 45 Ch D 430 ....69, 78
De Mattos v Gibson (1858) 4 D & J 276 57
Dennant v Skinner [1948] 2 KB 164 253
Denne v Light (1857) 8 DM & G 774; 44 ER 588 217
Denny, Mott & Dickson v James Fraser
[1944] AC 265; 1 All ER 678 ....179, 188, 190
Derry v Peek (1889) 14 App Cas 337 ....128, 133
Dick Bentley Productions v Harold Smith (Motors)
[1965] 1 WLR 623 ....87, 88, 94
Dickinson v Dodds (1876) 2 Ch D 463 ....8, 22
Diesen v Samson 1971 SLT 49 222
Director of Public Prosecution for Northern Ireland
v Lynch [1975] AC 653; 1 All ER 913 140
Doyle v Olby (Ironmongers) Ltd
[1969] 2 QB 158; 2 All ER 119 120
Dunlop v Selfridge [1915] AC 79 ....52, 54, 63
Dunmore v Alexander (1830) 9 Shaw 190 22

East v Maurer [1991] 2 All ER 733 133

Edgington v Fitzmaurice (1885) 24 Ch D 459 .88, 94, 119, 120, 132

Edmonds v Lawson [2000] 2 WLR 1091 29

Edwards v Carter [1893] AC 360 69

Edwards v Skyways [1964] 1 WLR 349 . . . . .25, 28, 45

Entores v Miles Far East Communication
  [1955] 2 QB 327; 2 All ER 493 . . . . .5, 16, 17

Errington v Errington and Woods
  [1952] 1 KB 290; 1 All ER 149 . . . . .8, 21

Esso Petroleum v Harpers Garage
  [1968] AC 269; [1967] 1 All ER 699 170–72

Esso v Mardon [1976] QB 801; 2 All ER 5 . . . . .89, 94

Eurymedon, The [1975] AC 154; [1974] 1 All ER 1015 . . . . .13, 30, 45, 48, 55,
                                                                                   107, 111, 235

Exall v Partridge (1799) 8 TR 308 229

Faccenda Chicken Ltd v Fowler
  [1987] Ch 117; [1986] 1 All ER 617 175

Farley v Skinner [2001] 3 WLR 899 . . . . .209, 220–24

Fawcett v Smethurst (1914) 84 LJ KB 473 75

Felthouse v Bindley (1862) 11 CBNS 869; 142 ER 1037 . . . . .1, 21

Fenner v Blake [1900] 1 QB 427 36

Fibrosa Spolka Akcyjna v Fairbairn Lawson
  Combe Barbour Ltd [1943] AC 32; [1942] 2 All ER 122 . . . . .177–79, 181, 183–86,
                                                                            189, 192, 226, 227,
                                                                            231, 232

Financings Ltd v Baldock [1963] 2 QB 104; 1 All ER 443 198

First Energy (UK) Ltd v Hungarian International Bank Ltd
  [1993] 2 Lloyd's Rep 194 . . . . .245, 247

Fitch v Dewes [1921] 2 AC 158 162

Flavell, Re (1883) 25 Ch D 89 55

Fleet v Murton (1871) LR 7 QB 126 244

Foakes v Beer (1884) 9 App Cas 605 . . . . .26, 32, 36–39, 44,
                                                                                    45, 47, 48

Foley v Classique Coaches [1934] 2 KB 1 174

Forsikringsaktieselskapet Vesta v Butcher (No 1)
  [1986] 2 All ER 488; [1989] 2 WLR 290 212

Freeman & Lockyer v Buckhurst Park Properties
  (Mangal) Ltd [1964] 2 QB 480; 1 All ER 630 . . . . .236–38, 245, 246

Gamerco SA v ICM/Fair Warning Agency
[1995] 1 WLR 1126 . . . . .180, 185, 189

Gibbons v Proctor (1891) 64 LT 594 . . . . .19, 20

Gibson v Manchester City Council [1979] 1 All ER 972 12

Glasbrook Bros v Glamorgan County Council [1925] AC 270 45–47

Goddard v O'Brien (1882) 9 QBD 37 49

Goldsoll v Goldman [1915] 1 Ch 292 . . . . .168, 169

Goldsworthy v Brickell [1987] 1 All ER 853 147

Gore v Gibson (1843) 13 M & W 623 77

Gran Gelato v Richcliff (Group) [1992] 2 WLR 867 214

Great Northern Rly Co v Witham (1873) LR 9 CP 16 9

Great Peace Shipping Ltd
v Tsavliris Salvage (International) Ltd [2002] 3 WLR 1617 . . . . .117, 121, 126

Grieg v Insole [1978] 3 All ER 449; 1 WLR 302 161

Griffiths v Peter Conway [1939] 1 All ER 685 259

Grist v Bailey [1967] Ch 532; [1966] 2 All ER 875 126

Gurtner v Beaton [1993] 2 Lloyd's Rep 369 240

Hadley v Baxendale (1854) 9 Exch 341; 156 ER 145 . . . . .211, 215, 218

Hannah Blumenthal, The [1983] 1 All ER 34 9

Hardman v Booth (1863) 1 H & C 803 . . . . .129, 130

Harlingdon & Leinster Ltd v Christopher Hull Fine Art Ltd
[1990] 1 All ER 737 . . . . .257, 258

Harnett v Yielding (1805) 2 Sch & Lef 549 216

Harris v Sheffield United FC Ltd
[1987] 2 All ER 838 49

Harvey v Facey (1893) AC 552 . . . . .7, 9

Healey v Howlett & Sons [1917] 1 KB 337 . . . . .254, 260

Hedley Byrne v Heller [1964] AC 465; [1963] 2 All ER 575 . . . . .81, 86, 118, 133, 247

Henthorn v Fraser [1892] 2 Ch 27;
[1891–94] All ER Rep 908 . . . . .4, 22

Hermann v Charlesworth [1905] 2 KB 123 163

Herne Bay Steam Boat Company
v Hutton [1903] 2 KB 683 . . . . .177, 179, 182, 188, 190

Heron II, The [1969] 1 AC 350; [1967] 3 All ER 686 . . . . .209, 211, 218, 223

Hertford Foods Ltd v Lidl UK GmbH
(2001) 145 SJ 650 12

Hill v Parsons [1972] 1 Ch 305; [1971] 3 All ER 1345 217

Hoenig v Isaacs [1952] 2 All ER 176 ....193, 199–201, 203

Holwell Securities Ltd v Hughes [1974] 1 All ER 161 ....4, 8

Hong Kong Fir Shipping Co Ltd v Kawasaki Kisen
Kaisha Ltd [1962] 2 QB 26; 1 All ER 474 ....194–98, 204, 206, 207

Hughes v Liverpool Victoria Legal Friendly Society
[1916] 2 KB 482 165

Hughes v Metropolitan Rly Co (1877) 2 App Cas 439 ....26, 33, 34, 37, 38

Hutton v Warren (1836) 1 M & W 466; 150 ER 517 83

Hyde v Wrench (1840) 3 Beav 334; 49 ER 132 ....3, 11

Imperial Loan Co v Stone [1892] 1 QB 599 77

Ingram v Little [1961] 1 QB 31; [1960] 3 All ER 332 ....121, 122, 129, 130

Inntrepreneur Pub Co (GL), The v East Crown Ltd
[2000] 2 Lloyd's Rep 611 114

Interfoto Picture Library v Stiletto Visual Programmes
[1989] QB 433; [1988] 1 All ER 348 ....82, 109

JEB Fasteners v Bloom [1983] 1 All ER 583 88

Jackson v Horizon Holidays
[1975] 3 All ER 92; 1 WLR 1468 ....55, 58, 59, 61, 66, 221–23

Jarvis v Swan Tours [1973] 1 QB 233 222

Junior Books v Veitchi [1983] AC 520; [1982] 3 All ER 201 52

Kearley v Thomson (1890) 24 QBD 742 ....165, 169

Kelly v Solari (1841) 9 M & W 54 ....228, 231, 232

Kelner v Baxter (1866) LR 2 CP 174 242

King's Norton Metal Co Ltd v Edridge (1897) 14 TLR 98 120

Kiriri Cotton Co Ltd v Dewani
[1960] AC 192; [1960] 1 All ER 177 166

Kleinwort Benson Ltd v Lincoln City Council
[1998] 3 WLR 1095 ....226, 228

Krell v Henry [1903] 2 KB 740 ....177, 184, 185

L'Estrange v Graucob [1934] 2 KB 394 ....100, 108, 113

Lacey (William) (Hounslow) Ltd v Davis [1957] 1 WLR 932 ....230, 233

Lambert v Lewis [1982] AC 225 111

Lampleigh v Braithwait (1615) Hob 105; 80 ER 255 30

Larner v LCC [1949] 2 KB 683 228

Lefkowitz v Great Minneapolis Surplus Stores (1957) USA 15
Leigh & Sillivan Ltd v Aliakmon Shipping Co Ltd
(The Aliakmon) [1986] 2 WLR 902 256
Leonidas D, The [1985] 1 WLR 925 23
Les Affréteurs Réunis v Walford [1919] AC 801 65
Lewis v Averay [1973] 2 All ER 229; 1 WLR 510 ....119, 121, 128, 129
Linden Gardens v Lenesta Sludge Disposals
[1993] 3 WLR 408 ....55, 58, 60, 61
Littlewoods Organisation v Harris [1978] 1 All ER 1026;
[1977] 1 WLR 1472 ....163, 168, 174, 175
Liverpool CC v Irwin [1977] AC 236; [1976] 2 All ER 39 82–85
Lloyd's v Harper (1880) 16 Ch D 290 ....57, 58
Lloyds Bank v Bundy [1975] QB 326;
[1974] 3 All ER 757 ....136, 138, 140, 142,
                                                               145, 149, 151, 153
Lombard North Central plc v Butterworth
[1987] QB 527; 1 All ER 267..198
Long v Lloyd [1958] 2 All ER 402..133
Lord Strathcona SS Co Ltd v Dominion Coal [1926] AC 108 56
Lucas (T) & Co v Mitchell [1974] Ch 129 173
Lumley v Gye (1853) 2 E & B 216...52, 56
Lumley v Wagner (1852) 1 De GM & G 604; 42 ER 687 57

McArdle, Re [1951] 1 All ER 905 30
McCutcheon v McBrayne
[1964] 1 All ER 430; 1 WLR 125 100
McRae v Commonwealth Disposals Commission
(1951) 84 CLR 377 119
Macclesfield Corporation v Great Central Rly
[1911] 2 KB 528 229
Malins v Freeman (1837) 2 Keen 25 ....126, 134
Maredelamto Compania Naviera SA
v Bergbau-Handel GmbH, The Mihalis Angelos
[1970] 3 WLR 601; [1970] 3 All ER 125 ....197, 198
Marion White Ltd v Francis [1972] 1 WLR 1423 173
Maritime National Fish Ltd v Ocean Trawlers Ltd
[1935] AC 524 ....177, 182, 188, 191
Mason v Provident Clothing [1913] AC 724 162
Matthews v Baxter (1873) LR 8 Ex 132 80
Merritt v Merritt [1970] 2 All ER 760 31

Metropolitan Police District Receiver
v Croydon Corporation [1957] 2 QB 154; 1 All ER 78 229

Metropolitan Water Board v Dick Kerr [1918] AC 119 182

Mitchell, George v Finney Lock Seeds
[1983] 2 AC 803; 2 All ER 737 . . . . .100, 101, 115

Monmouthshire CC v Smith
[1957] 2 QB 154; [1957] 1 All ER 78 230

Moorcock, The (1889) 14 PD 64; [1886–90] All ER Rep 530 81–85

Moore & Co and Landauer & Co, Re [1921] 2 KB 519 . . . . .202, 260

Museprime Properties v Adhill [1990] 2 EG 196;
(1990) 61 P & CR 111 . . . . .120, 131, 133

Nash v Inman [1908] 2 KB 1 . . . . .69, 70, 74, 76, 78

National Carriers Ltd v Panalpina (Northern) Ltd
[1981] 2 WLR 45 . . . . .179, 180

National Westminster Bank plc v Morgan
[1985] AC 686; 1 All ER 821 . . . . .136, 138, 140, 145, 146

Nema, The [1982] AC 724; [1981] 2 All ER 1030 179

Newborne v Sensolid [1954] 1 QB 45 242

Nordenfelt v Maxim Nordenfelt [1894] AC 535 . . . . .161, 166, 167

North Ocean Shipping Co v Hyundai Construction Co and
Hyundai Shipbuilding and Heavy Industries Co,
The Atlantic Baron [1978] 3 All ER 1170;
[1979] 1 Lloyd's Rep 89 143

Norwich Union Fire Insurance Society Ltd v Price Ltd
[1934] AC 455 228

Nurdin and Peacock Ltd v DB Ramsden & Co Ltd
[1999] 1 EGLR 119 228

Olley v Marlborough Court
[1949] 1 KB 532; 1 All ER 127 . . . . .100, 111

Oscar Chess v Williams [1957] 1 All ER 325; 1 WLR 370 87

Overseas Medical Supplies Ltd
v Orient Transport Services Ltd [1999] 2 Lloyd's Rep 273 . . . . .101, 102, 115

Pao On v Lau Yiu Long [1980] AC 614;
[1979] 3 All ER 65 . . . . .25, 30, 45, 48, 137, 143

Paradine v Jane (1647) Aleyn 26; 82 ER 897 184

Parker v South Eastern Rly (1877) 2 CPD 416 . . . . .100, 108

Parkinson v College of Ambulance [1925] 2 KB 1 165

Pars Technology Ltd v City Link Transport Holdings Ltd (1999) 13

Parsons v Uttley Ingham [1978] QB 791; 1 All ER 525 . . . . .214, 219

Partridge v Crittenden [1968] 2 All ER 421 . . . . .15, 20, 23

Patel v Ali [1984] Ch 383; [1983] 2 All ER 421 219

Payne v Cave (1789) 3 Term Rep 148 16

Payzu v Saunders [1919] 2 KB 581 214

Pearce v Brooks (1866) LR 1 Ex 213 159–61

Penn v Bristol and West Building Society
    [1997] 1 WLR 1356 . . . . .245, 248

Peters v Fleming (1840) 6 M & W 42 78

Phillips v Brooks [1919] 2 KB 243 130

Phonogram v Lane [1982] QB 938; [1981] 3 All ER 182 242

Photo Production v Securicor [1980] AC 827; 1 All ER 556 98

Pinnel's Case (1602) 5 Co Rep 117a; 77 ER 237 . . . . .26, 32, 37, 39, 45, 47

Pitt v PHH Asset Management [1993] 4 All ER 961 91–93

Planché v Colburn (1831) 8 Bing 14 229

Port Line v Ben Line [1958] 2 QB 146; 1 All ER 787 56

Post Chaser, The [1981] 2 Lloyd's Rep 695 . . . . .34, 41, 49

Poussard v Spiers (1876) 1 QBD 410 198

Powell v London Borough of Brent [1988] ICR 176;
    [1987] IRLR 446, CA 217

Price v Strange [1978] Ch 337; [1977] 3 All ER 371 217

Priest v Last [1903] 2 KB 148 259

Pym v Campbell (1856) 6 E & B 370 . . . . .7, 9

Quenerduaine v Cole (1883) 32 WR 185 4

R & B Customs Brokers v UDT
    [1988] 1 All ER 847; 1 WLR 321 . . . . .103–06, 113, 115, 116

R v Clarke (1927) 40 CLR 227 . . . . .19, 20

Raffles v Wichelhaus (1864) 2 H & C 906; 159 ER 375 . . . . .120, 123–25, 134

Rama Corporation Ltd v Proved Tin and
    General Investments [1952] 2 QB 147; [1954] 1 All ER 554 240

Ramsgate Victoria Hotel Co Ltd
    v Montefiore (1866) LR 1 Ex 109 6

Reardon Smith Line Ltd v Hansen Tangen
    [1976] 3 All ER 570; 1 WLR 989 . . . . .203, 258

Redgrave v Hurd (1881) 20 Ch D 1 132

Rice v Great Yarmouth BC (2000) The Times, 26 July 198, 204–06

Riverlate Properties v Paul [1975] Ch 133 134

Roberts v Gray [1913] 1 KB 520 ....74, 76, 79

Robinson v Harman (1848) 1 Ex 850; 154 ER 363 ....210, 211, 214, 218, 221

Routledge v Grant (1828) 4 Bing 653; 130 ER 920 ....8, 92

Routledge v McKay [1954] 1 All ER 855; 1 WLR 615 ....87, 94

Rowland v Divall [1923] 2 KB 500 ....227, 232–34

Royal Bank of Scotland plc v Etridge (No 2)
    [2001] 3 WLR 1021 ....138, 142, 145, 146, 148,
                                                            150–52, 154–56

Royscot Trust Ltd v Rogerson [1991] 3 All ER 294 ....90, 120, 133

Ruxley Electronics and Construction Ltd v Forsyth;
    Laddingford Enclosures Ltd v Forsyth
    [1996] AC 344; [1995] 3 WLR 118...................................210, 213, 224

Ryder v Wombwell (1868) LR 4 Exch 32 78

Schenkers Ltd v Overland Shoes Ltd [1998] 1 Lloyd's Rep 498 ....102, 115

Schuler AG v Wickman Machine Tool Sales Ltd
    [1974] AC 235; [1973] 2 All ER 39 ....196, 204–06

Scotson v Pegg (1861) 6 H & N 295; 158 ER 121 49

Scriven Bros v Hindley [1913] 3 KB 564 ....126, 132, 134

Selectmove, Re [1995] 1 WLR 474 ....39, 48

Shadwell v Shadwell (1860) 9 CBNS 159; 142 ER 62 ....29, 45, 48

Shanklin Pier v Detel Products [1951] 2 KB 854; 2 All ER 471 ....55, 65, 89, 92, 95

Shell v Lostock Garages Ltd [1977] 1 All ER 481 ....84, 85, 170, 172, 174, 217

Shirlaw v Southern Foundries Ltd [1939] 2 KB 206 84

Siboen, The and The Sibotre [1976] 1 Lloyd's Rep 293 146

Sibree v Tripp (1846) 15 M & W 23 47

Simpson v London and North Western Rly Co
    (1876) 1 QBD 274 211

Sims v Bond (1833) 5 B & Ad 389 244

Skilton v Sullivan (1994) The Times, 25 March 169

Smith New Court Securities Ltd
    v Scrimgeour Vickers (Asset Management) Ltd
    [1996] 4 All ER 769; [1994] 1 WLR 1271 ....90, 120

Smith v Bush [1990] 1 AC 831; [1989] 2 All ER 514 97

Smith v Hughes (1871) LR 6 QB 597 ....123, 124, 134

Smith v Land & House Property Corporation
    (1884) 28 Ch D 7 ....88, 131, 132

Solle v Butcher [1950] 1 KB 671; [1949] 2 All ER 1107 ....121, 126

Somma v Hazlehurst [1978] 2 All ER 1011; 1 WLR 1014 163

Southern Water Authority v Carey [1985] 2 All ER 1077 ....107, 111

Spurling v Bradshaw [1956] 2 All ER 121; 1 WLR 461 ....100, 108

Stevenson v Rogers [1999] 2 WLR 1064 ....104, 116

Stewart Gill Ltd v Horatio Myer & Co Ltd
    [1992] 2 All ER 257 ....102, 116

Stilk v Myrick (1809) 2 Camp 317; 170 ER 1168 ....25, 40–44

Summers v Solomon (1857) 7 E & B 879 ....236, 239

Sumpter v Hedges [1898] 1 QB 673 ....199, 200

Super Servant Two, The [1990] 1 Lloyd's Rep 1 ....177, 183, 188, 191

Swan, The [1968] 1 Lloyd's Rep 5 ....241, 244

Swiss Bank Corporation v Lloyds Bank
    [1979] Ch 548; 2 All ER 853 57

Tamplin v James (1879) 15 Ch D 215 126

Taylor v Bowers (1876) 1 QBD 291 165

Taylor v Caldwell (1863) 3 B & S 826; 122 ER 309 ....179, 180, 184, 188, 189

Taylor v Chester (1869) LR 4 QB 309 169

Thompson v LM & S Rly [1930] 1 KB 41 108

Thornton v Shoe Lane Parking
    [1971] 2 QB 163; 1 All ER 686 108

Tinsley v Milligan [1993] 3 All ER 65 166

Tool Metal Manufacturing Company Ltd
    v Tungsten Electric Company Ltd [1955] 2 All ER 657 ....34, 35, 38, 42

Trentham Ltd v Archital Luxfer [1993] 1 Lloyd's Rep 25 ....5, 10, 12, 230

Tsakiroglou v Noblee Thorl
    [1962] AC 93; [1961] 2 All ER 179 190

Thomas Witter Ltd v TBP Industries [1996] 2 All ER 573 114

Tulk v Moxhay (1848) 2 Ph 774; 41 ER 1143 ....52, 53, 56

Tweddle v Atkinson (1861) 1 B & S 393; 121 ER 762 ....52, 54, 63

United Bank of Kuwait v Hamoud, City Trust
    v Levy [1988] 1 WLR 1051 239

Universe Tankships Inc of Monrovia
    v International Transport Workers Federation
    and Laughton [1983] AC 366; [1982] 2 All ER 67 ....137, 140

Vesta v Butcher (1986)
 See Forsikringsaktieselskapet Vesta v Butcher—

Victoria Laundry (Windsor) Ltd v Newman Industries
 [1949] 2 KB 528; 1 All ER 997 ....211, 212, 218, 219

Vitol SA v Norelf Ltd [1996] 3 All ER 193 21

Walford v Miles [1992] 1 All ER 453 ....91–93, 234

Walters v Morgan (1861) 3 DF & J 718 217

Watteau v Fenwick [1893] 1 QB 346 236–38

Waugh v Clifford [1982] 1 Ch 374; 1 All ER 1095 ....240, 246

Wells v Buckland Sand & Silica
 [1965] 2 QB 170; [1964] 1 All ER 41 ....90, 95

Wenckheim v Arndt (1873) 1 JR 73 23

Whincup v Hughes (1871) LR 6 CP 78 ....213, 232

White v Bluett (1853) 23 LJ Ex 36 29

White v John Warwick
 [1953] 2 All ER 857; [1972] 1 WLR 1285 ....100, 109

Williams v Carwardine (1833) 5 C & P 566 20

Williams v Roffey Bros & Nicholls (Contractors) Ltd
 [1991] 1 QB 1; [1990] 1 All ER 512;
 (1989) 139 NLJ 1712 ....25, 33, 40–43, 48, 203

With v O'Flanagan [1936] Ch 575 ....90, 131, 132

Woodar Investment Development Ltd
 v Wimpey Construction (UK) Ltd
 [1980] 1 All ER 571; 1 WLR 277 ....58–60, 66, 223

Wroth v Tyler [1974] Ch 30; [1973] 1 All ER 897 212

Wyatt v Kreglinger & Fernau [1933] 1 KB 793 ....163, 175

Yonge v Toynbee [1910] 1 KB 215 ....243, 248

TABLE OF STATUTES

Betting and Loans (Infants)
Act 1892—
s 5 71

Civil Liability (Contribution)
Act 1978 ....234, 243

Companies Act 1985—
s 36C 235
s 36C(1) 242

Competition Act 1998 157

Consumer Credit Act 1974—
s 56 244

Contracts (Rights of Third Parties)
Act 1999 ....51–56, 58,
61–66, 110, 111
s 1 ....54, 63, 95
s 1(1)(a), (b) 66, 110
s 1(2) 57, 63, 110
s 1(3) 64
s 2 ....54, 55
s 3 55
s 3(6) 110
s 7 55

Infants Relief Act 1874 ....69, 70

Judicature Act 1873 39

Judicature Act 1875 39

Law of Property Act 1925—
s 56 65

Law Reform (Contributory
Negligence) Act 1945 212

Law Reform (Frustrated
Contracts) Act 1943 177–80,
182–86, 188, 189, 192
s 1(2) 177, 180, 181, 183–86,
189, 191
s 1(3) 177, 179, 181, 182,
184, 186–91
s 2(3) 180

Mental Health Act 1983 77

Minors' Contracts Act 1987 ....67–71, 80
s 1 ....69, 70
ss 2, 3 ....70, 79
s 3(1) 75

Misrepresentation
Act 1967 ....82, 118, 131, 249
s 2 114
s 2(1) 88, 89, 94, 120,
133, 134, 214
s 3 114

Police Act 1996—
s 25(1) 49

Rent Act 1977 ....166, 169
s 125 1

Sale of Goods Act 1893 ....76, 80, 86
s 13 203

Sale of Goods Act 1979 ....67, 78, 79,
82–85, 105, 106,
112–14, 116, 194, 195,
197, 198, 205, 251–53,
255–58
s 3 ....71, 75, 78
s 3(2) 79
s 3(3) 80
s 11(4) 259
ss 12–15 ....81, 84, 251, 252
s 12 ....85, 86, 105, 251, 253
s 13 ....84, 111, 112, 116, 197,
198, 203, 251, 252,
257, 258
s 14 ....85, 92, 104, 198, 257
s 14(2) 85, 112, 116, 251,
252, 257–59
s 14(2A) 258
s 14(2B) 251, 258
s 14(3) 85, 251, 252, 257–59
s 15 ....85, 251
s 15A 198, 202, 258
ss 16–20 ....251, 252

Sale of Goods Act 1979 (Contd)—
    ss 16–18 . . . . .253, 257, 259
    s 16 . . . . .252–54, 259
    s 17 . . . . .252, 253, 260
    s 18 . . . . .252–54, 260
    s 19 255
    s 20 . . . . .253, 255
    ss 21–25 260
    s 21 256
    s 32 260
    s 49 . . . . .253, 256
    s 51 . . . . .257, 258, 260

Supply of Goods (Implied
Terms) Act 1973 102

Supply of Goods and Services
Act 1982 . . . . .90, 102, 199
    s 3 201
    s 5A 202
    s 15(1) 230

Unfair Contract Terms
Act 1977 . . . . .97–107, 109,
                  110, 113–15
    s 1 98
    s 1(3) 97, 101, 106, 111, 113
    s 2 . . . . .97, 98, 101, 105,
                109, 111, 114
    s 2(1) 101, 109
    s 2(2) 101, 110, 111
    s 3 . . . . .97, 98, 103, 105,
                    113, 114
    s 3(2)(a) 116
    s 5 105
    s 6 . . . . .85, 97, 98, 102–05,
                   114, 115
    s 7 . . . . .103, 105
    s 8 . . . . .113, 114
    s 9 98
    s 11 . . . . .97, 98, 101, 105, 110,
                   114, 115
    s 11(1) 115
    s 11(4) 115, 116
    s 12 . . . . .103, 104
    s 12(1)(c), (2) 106
    s 13 . . . . .97, 115
    Sched 2 . . . . .97, 98, 101, 111, 115

TABLE OF LEGISLATION

Statutory instruments (UK)

Consumer Protection (Distance Selling) Regulations 2000 .14, 16, 17
Unfair Terms in Consumer Contracts Regulations 1999 . . . . .97–99, 101–07,
109–11, 113
    reg 2 103
    regs 5, 7, 8 104
    Sched 2 104

European Directives

Directive on Electronic Commerce (COM (1999) 427/EU) 15, 18

Treaties and Conventions

EC Treaty—
    Art 81 157
Vienna Convention on the International Sale of Goods 13

CHAPTER 1

OFFER AND ACCEPTANCE

Introduction

There can be few contract exam papers which do not contain a question on offer and acceptance. Students will often make this one of their 'banker' questions, but you will need to make sure that you are prepared to deal with any of the forms in which a question about offer and acceptance may be asked. The topics which are covered within this general heading are quite varied, but are nevertheless fairly predictable. General issues which will need to be understood include:

- the nature of an offer and an acceptance – is an advertisement an offer? What if an 'acceptance' does not match the offer precisely? The effect of a 'counter offer';
- the relationship between offer and acceptance on the one hand and 'agreement' on the other – the objective approach to determining the existence of a contract; and
- the differences between unilateral and bilateral contracts.

As will be seen from the questions in this chapter, problems concerning the communication of offer and acceptance are often asked. In particular, students will need to be familiar with:

- the 'postal rule' (*Adams v Lindsell*) – the types of communication to which it applies, and the situations where it does not apply;
- silence as acceptance – the rule in *Felthouse v Bindley*, and possible exceptions to it;
- the problems, many of them unresolved by the courts, of electronic communications, such as faxes, email and internet contracts. Does the postal rule apply to them? If not, when and where do they take effect?; and
- the rules governing revocation of an offer, in both bilateral and unilateral contracts – can there be revocation once performance of a unilateral contract has started?

Finally, it should be remembered that a question involving offer and acceptance may also sometimes require you to touch on other issues. You may find, for example, that an offer and acceptance question (though this is not the case with those contained in this chapter) will also involve discussion of intention to create legal relations, consideration or mistake.

Checklist

You should be familiar with the following areas:

- The meaning of offer: the distinction from an 'invitation to treat'.
- The meaning of acceptance: the distinction from a 'counter offer', and the possibility of acceptance by conduct or silence.
- Subjective and objective approaches to agreement.
- The differences between unilateral and bilateral contracts.
- The postal rule and its limitations.
- Revocation of offers.
- Recall of acceptance.

Question 1

On 1 November, Albatross plc sent a letter to Budgie Ltd, with whom they had been negotiating, offering them a contract to service all Albatross's birdseed processors each month for the next five years at a cost of £10,000 per annum. The letter said that Budgie should reply by return of post. Unfortunately, the letter contained an error in the address and was not delivered to Budgie until 6 November. Budgie replied at once accepting. This letter was posted at 11 am on 6 November. In the meantime, on 4 November, Albatross had received an offer from Canary Ltd to do the servicing work for £9,000 per annum. Albatross, having heard nothing from Budgie, telephoned Canary on 5 November and offered them the contract at £8,000. Canary accepted. Albatross sent a fax to Budgie on 6 November telling them that the offer of 1 November was withdrawn. This fax was received on Budgie's fax machine at 10.45 am on 6 November, but not read by anyone until 5 pm on the same day.

Advise Albatross, Budgie and Canary.

Answer plan

This question is of a common type, raising issues about the communication of offers and acceptances, and which of two parties is entitled to enforce a contract. In answering such a question, where the timing of events may be very important, it is a good idea to make a chronological plan – for example, here:

1 Nov –	Albatross offer to Budgie, letter posted
4 Nov –	Canary offer to Albatross, £9,000
5 Nov –	Albatross counter offer to Canary, £8,000, accepted by Canary
6 Nov –	1 Nov offer arrives
	10.45 am Albatross's fax withdrawing offer to Budgie
	11 am Budgie's acceptance posted
	5 pm Albatross's fax read

This should make it easier to pinpoint the issues for discussion. Particular areas to be considered here are:

- offers and counter offers;
- the operation of the postal rule (*Adams v Lindsell* (1818));
- the time of communication of electronic messages, such as faxes; and
- the revocation of an offer.

Answer

This problem raises the issue of whether Albatross are committed to one contract, or two. The answer to this will depend on the precise time at which each contract was formed. This in turn depends on the point at which communications between the parties take effect, particularly acceptances and revocations of offers.

The English law on the formation of contracts has at its centre the need for there to be an offer and a matching acceptance.[1] The offer must set out, or refer to, all the important terms of the contract; the acceptance must indicate agreement to all these. If it does not do so, not only will it not be a valid acceptance, but it will be regarded as a counter offer which prevents the original offer from being accepted later (*Hyde v Wrench* (1840)). An offer can generally be withdrawn at any time before acceptance is complete.

In the problem, there are three offers, two of which are made by Albatross. One is contained in the letter to Budgie of 1 November, and the other in the phone call to Canary on 5 November (this is strictly speaking a counter offer). The third offer is made by Canary in the letter received by Albatross on 4 November. This offer is rejected by Albatross's counter offer, and so need not be discussed further.

Which of the other two offers was accepted? In both cases, there was a purported acceptance. Albatross's first offer is accepted by Budgie in the letter posted on 6 November. Canary accept Albatross's offer during the telephone conversation on 5 November. There seems no reason to doubt the effectiveness of this acceptance, so Albatross would appear to have made a binding contract for the servicing of their machines with Canary. Have they also made such a contract with Budgie?

The issue here is the time at which communications are effective when conducted by post or fax. Looking first at Albatross's offer to Budgie, this was posted on 1 November, but did not arrive until 6 November.[2] Offers have to be actually communicated to the recipient to be effective, so this offer took effect on 6 November. Budgie posted a reply accepting on the same day. We are not told when this was received, but this may well not matter, if the special postal rule as regards acceptances applies.

The postal rule derives from the case of *Adams v Lindsell* (1818). In this case, a letter offering some wool for sale was sent to the plaintiffs, but unfortunately, as in the problem, it was misdirected and delayed. The plaintiffs posted a letter of acceptance as soon as they received the offer. After this letter was posted, but before it was delivered, the defendants had sold the wool elsewhere. The plaintiffs brought an action for non-delivery. The court decided that the acceptance should be regarded as having taken effect when posted. The main reason for adopting this rule was that of business efficiency. It was thought that businesses would be able to operate more effectively if, having posted an acceptance of a contract, they could then proceed on the basis that a valid contract existed immediately, rather than having to wait to receive confirmation that the acceptance had been delivered. Later cases have confirmed that the *Adams v Lindsell* rule should apply whenever it was reasonable for the offeror to expect the acceptance to be made by post (for example, *Henthorn v Fraser* (1892)). This expectation can be removed by express instructions from the offeror (as in *Holwell Securities v Hughes* (1974), where a requirement for 'notice in writing' displaced the postal rule) or be implicit in the means of communication (for example, *Quenerduaine v Cole* (1883), where an offer by telegram was held to imply a requirement for an acceptance by equally speedy means).

From the facts given here, there is no reason to say that the postal rule should be displaced. The offer was made through the post, and specifically asks for a reply by 'return of post'. There is no indication that actual notice of acceptance was specified. What of the fact that the letter was delivered five days after posting? This was the result of the letter being wrongly addressed by Albatross, so they should take responsibility for that. Indeed, the same had happened in *Adams v Lindsell*, so it is clear that, despite the fact that the acceptance was not sent until several days after Albatross would have expected, the acceptance must be taken to have been effective at 11 am on 6 November. If this were the only relevant communication, then Albatross and Budgie would be bound to a contract created at that point. Albatross, however, had tried to withdraw their offer at 10.45 am on 6 November. The effectiveness of this attempted withdrawal must now be considered.

The first point to note is that the postal rule has no application here for two reasons. First, there is clear authority from the case of *Byrne v van Tienhoven* (1880) that the rule does not apply to revocation of offers. Secondly, the case of *Entores v Miles Far East Communication* (1955) established that the postal rule did not apply to 'instantaneous communications' such as telex. It is submitted that this should also apply to communications by fax.[3]

If the postal rule does not apply, when exactly is a faxed revocation effective? In particular for our purposes, does it need to be read by the recipient to be effective, or is it sufficient that it is received on his fax machine?

Two cases since *Entores* have addressed this issue in respect of telexes. In *The Brimnes* (1975),[4] the Court of Appeal agreed with the judge that the telex took effect when it was received on the recipient's telex machine, provided that this was within office hours. In *Brinkibon Ltd v Stahag Stahl* (1983), Lord Wilberforce suggested a more flexible approach, looking at all the circumstances.[5] On balance, it seems likely that the courts would say that Albatross's fax withdrawing their offer was effective at 10.45 am on 6 November (assuming that 6 November was a normal working day).

If this is the answer given by the court, then Albatross are in a good position. They have their contract at £8,000 with Canary, and have managed to escape from their contract with Budgie. Budgie's only hope is to try to argue that the revocation of an offer by fax should not be effective until it is actually communicated. If that is so, then Albatross's attempted revocation will be ineffective and Budgie's acceptance will stand. Albatross will then be in the position of having made contracts with both Budgie and Canary, and being unable to fulfil both of them. They run the risk of having to pay substantial damages for breaking one of the contracts. Canary are in the best position. Their contract was clearly formed on 5 November. They can stand aside and leave Albatross and Budgie to sort out their differences, confident in the knowledge that their contract with Albatross is without doubt enforceable.

Notes

1   Note, however, the suggestion in *Trentham Ltd v Archital Luxfer* (1993) by the Court of Appeal that offer and acceptance may not always be necessary.

2   An offer will lapse after the expiry of a reasonable time: *Ramsgate Victoria Hotel Co Ltd v Montefiore* (1866). Could it be argued that this has happened here, because of the delay?

3   This is not accepted by Treitel, who suggests that electronic communications may occupy an intermediary position, whereby, for example, an illegible message of acceptance might still be regarded as effective: see Treitel, *The Law of Contract*, 10th edn, 1999, p 26 and Stone, *The Modern Law of Contract*, 5th edn, 2002, pp 51–56.

4   Note that this case was not concerned with the formation of a contract, but the exercise of a right to withdraw a vessel from a charter.

5   He said: 'No universal rule can cover all such cases; they must be resolved by reference to the intentions of the parties, by sound business practice and, in some cases, by a judgment where the risks should lie.'

Question 2

Michael in Manchester wrote to Laura in Loughborough offering to sell Laura his Rolls Royce car for £20,000. On receiving Michael's offer, Laura telephoned him in order to accept. Michael, however, said that since such a large sum of money was involved he wanted written confirmation of the acceptance from Laura. He said that if Laura got her letter of acceptance to him by 11 am the next day (Tuesday), he would go ahead with the sale at £20,000. Laura at once wrote and posted a letter of acceptance which Michael received at 9 am on the Tuesday morning. In the meantime, however, Michael had received a better offer for his car, and wrote to Laura withdrawing his offer to her. This letter was posted at 5 pm on the Monday evening, and was received by Laura at 8.30 am on Tuesday.

Discuss.

Would it make any difference to your answer if the letter from Michael to Laura withdrawing his offer had been received by her at 9.30 am instead of 8.30 am?

Answer plan

The important thing to note about this problem is that, although there are communications via the post, the postal rule (from *Adams v Lindsell* (1818)) has little role to play. The main issue relates to unilateral contracts, and whether an offer in a unilateral contract can be withdrawn once the other party has started to perform. Note also that the instruction at the end of the problem is simply 'Discuss', so you are not here looking at the problem from the point of view of any particular party, but should discuss all the issues raised by the facts.

The topics which will need covering include:

* acceptance by telephone;
* avoidance of the postal rule;
* the nature and definition of a unilateral contract; and
* revocation of offers in unilateral contracts.

Answer

The negotiations between Michael and Laura over the sale of Michael's Rolls Royce clearly reach an agreement, in the sense that at a certain point both are willing to go through with the transaction at an agreed price. Does this mean, however, that they have a contract? Not necessarily, for the English law of contract, rather than simply looking for a 'meeting of the minds' between two parties, generally looks for the formalisation of this into a matching 'offer' and 'acceptance'.[1] Indeed, it may well happen that in some cases, by the time an offer and acceptance have been exchanged, one of the parties is no longer in agreement, and would like to back out, but is prevented from doing so by the rules of offer and acceptance. This may be the position that Michael finds himself in at the end of this problem.

The exchanges between Michael and Laura are started by Michael's first letter, offering his car for sale at £20,000. It seems reasonable to treat this as a definite offer, rather than an invitation to treat, or an expression of willingness to contract (as in *Harvey v Facey* (1893)).[2] In any case, the status of the original letter does not matter because Michael and Laura clearly reach agreement on the terms of the contract during their telephone conversation.[3] Before the matter is finalised, however, Michael introduces a new stipulation. That is, he requires confirmation of Laura's acceptance in writing. It might be possible to regard this as a condition precedent for the contract taking effect (as in *Pym v Campbell* (1856)).[4] It is submitted that the court would be more likely to treat this as giving rise to a particular type of contract – a 'unilateral contract' – as it did in the rather similar situation in *Daulia Ltd v Four Millbank Nominees* (1978).[5]

Unilateral contracts are sometimes called 'if' contracts, in that rather than both parties committing themselves, one party makes an offer in the form 'if you do this, then I promise to do that'. A famous example of a unilateral contract is *Carlill v Carbolic Smoke Ball Co* (1893), where the company, by its advertisement for its 'smoke ball', was deemed to have made an offer in the form 'if you use our smoke ball as directed, and still catch influenza, we will pay you £100'. So, in the problem, Michael is saying 'if you get your letter of confirmation to me by 11 am on Tuesday, I will sell you my car for £20,000'. The contract is unilateral in that, although Michael is committing himself to the sale if Laura does what he has requested, Laura has no obligation. She can supply the written confirmation if she wishes, but she is perfectly free to change her mind and do nothing. In which case, Michael will have no claim against her.

As it happens, Laura decides to go ahead with the contract, and writes and posts the letter which Michael has requested. This letter is an acceptance, and the usual rule when a letter of acceptance is sent in reply to an offer made by letter is that the acceptance takes effect on posting (*Adams v Lindsell* (1818)). This postal rule has no application here, however, since the case of *Holwell Securities v Hughes* (1974) makes it clear that the rule can be avoided by a specific request for written notice. Moreover, in the context of the unilateral contract, the actual delivery of the letter to Michael is of crucial importance.

Even though the postal rule does not apply, Laura would at first sight appear to have a binding contract, in that her letter is received by Michael two hours before the 11 am deadline. At this point, however, a complication arises. Michael has changed his mind about the contract, and has tried to withdraw. His letter of revocation is received by Laura half an hour before her letter of acceptance is received by Michael. Is his withdrawal effective?

The normal rule about revocation of offers is that they will be effective provided they are communicated before the acceptance has taken effect (for example, *Dickinson v Dodds* (1876)),[6] and that this is so even if the offeror has said that the offer will be kept open for a particular time (*Routledge v Grant* (1828)). This is so because no consideration has generally been given in exchange for the promise to keep the offer open, and it is therefore unenforceable.

How does this apply to unilateral contracts? If applied strictly it would mean that the offeror could withdraw the offer even when the offeree was on the brink of completing the requested task. This is because the offer is not accepted, and therefore there is no complete contract until the offeree has done everything asked for. Thus, in a traditional example, the offeree who has been offered £100 if he walks from London to York could be met by a valid revocation of the offer when only a mile from his destination.[7] Application of this to the problem would mean that Laura had no contract with Michael. The rule is one which gives great potential for injustice, and in two cases the courts have indicated that it should not be applied strictly. First, in *Errington v Errington* (1952), a father had promised his son and daughter-in-law that if they paid the mortgage instalments on a house he would transfer it to them. Lord Denning took the view that once the young couple had started to make the payments that offer could not be withdrawn. Similarly, in *Daulia Ltd v Four Millbank Nominees* (on facts close to those in the problem), it was regarded as settled by at least some members of the Court of Appeal[8] that, once performance of a unilateral contract had begun, the power to revoke the offer was lost. The conceptual basis for this ruling is unclear, and in neither case was the statement of principle part of the *ratio*, but it perhaps indicates the likely approach of the courts, at least where the offeror has notice that the offeree is trying to accept.[9] Applying this to the problem would lead to the conclusion that Michael is unable to withdraw his offer, provided that Laura indicated in their telephone conversation that she would be sending the written confirmation, and that Laura is therefore entitled to enforce the contract for sale at £20,000.

As regards the alternative situation, Laura is in an even stronger position. Revocations of offers must be communicated to be effective (*Byrne v van Tienhoven* (1880)), and so Michael's letter clearly arrives too late to prevent the contract coming into existence. Once again, Laura can insist on buying the car at £20,000.[10]

Notes

1   In other words, the courts are applying an objective rather than a subjective test for the existence of an agreement. See, for example, *The Hannah Blumenthal* (1983).

2   In *Harvey v Facey* (1893), a telegram indicating the lowest price at which a person was prepared to sell a property was not regarded as an offer.

3   It might be possible to argue here that Laura got her acceptance of Michael's offer in before he raised the question of writing, so that all that happens subsequently is irrelevant. It is submitted that it is unlikely that a court would approach it in this way, particularly since Laura is using a different method to accept from that used for the offer.

4   A condition precedent is an event which must occur before the contract comes into existence. In *Pym v Campbell* (1856), for example, an agreement for the sale of a patent was conditional on a third party approving the invention. The approval was not given, and so there was no contract.

5   In this case, the defendants had promised to enter into a contract provided that the plaintiffs produced a full written agreement plus a deposit by a particular time.

6   In this case, the communication was via a third party.

7   This example was used in *Great Northern Rly Co v Witham* (1873).

8   See the judgment of Goff LJ at [1978] 2 All ER 557, p 561.

9   It may be different in a case where the offer is made to the world, as in *Carlill v Carbolic Smoke Ball Co* (1893).

10   Whether she can claim specific performance, or just damages, will depend on whether the car is regarded as being unique, or just one of a kind which could be purchased on the open market. See Stone, *The Modern Law of Contract*, 5th edn, 2002, pp 454–56.

Question 3

What is meant by 'the battle of the forms' in relation to the formation of contracts? Have the ways in which the courts have tried to deal with this problem led to satisfactory results?

Answer plan

Essay questions, while they may appear more straightforward than problems, often require just as much care in deciding exactly which issues you should concentrate on. Although it may be easy to identify the general area in which you should be writing, simply reproducing all your knowledge of that area will not gain you high marks. For that, you need to identify the precise 'angle' on the topic suggested by the question.

Here, the main topic is clearly the rules concerning the formation of contracts. The particular angle is the way in which those rules apply to 'battle of the forms' situations (that is, where businesses negotiate by the exchange of mutually inconsistent standard terms, and it is unclear which set is to apply to the eventual contract). It is this area that should form the main focus of your discussion. Two cases in particular will need close attention – namely, *Butler Machine Tool v Ex-Cell-O* (1979) and *Trentham v Archital Luxfer* (1993).

Your essay should contain the following points:

- explanation of 'the battle of the forms';
- outline of the rules of offer and acceptance;
- discussion of the approach adopted in *Butler Machine Tool v Ex-Cell-O* (1979);
- discussion of the alternative approach suggested by *Trentham v Archital Luxfer* (1993); and
- consideration of whether the current position in this area is 'satisfactory' (and perhaps of what alternatives there might be).

Answer

The traditional approach of the common law to the formation of contracts is to look for a matching 'offer' and 'acceptance'. This is sometimes referred to as a requirement that the two elements (offer and acceptance) must be a mirror image of each other. Any significant difference in the acceptance will mean that the offer is regarded as being rejected: *Hyde v Wrench* (1840).[1] The purported acceptance may constitute a 'counter offer', but no contract will be formed until it has in turn been unequivocally accepted. The 'battle of the forms' refers to a situation which sometimes arises when two businesses are negotiating towards a contract. Each business may well have its own standard terms which it prefers to use as the basis of its contracts. Letters which constitute the negotiation may well have the appearance of being an 'offer and acceptance'. If, however, each letter has attached to it a set of standard terms, and the two sets are inconsistent, it may be very difficult to determine whether there is in fact a contract between the parties.

This type of situation fell to be considered by the Court of Appeal in *Butler Machine Tool v Ex-Cell-O* (1979). In this case, the plaintiffs had offered an item of machinery to the defendants, using their (the plaintiffs') standard terms, which included a price variation clause. The defendants replied by sending an order in their standard form, which provided for a fixed price. This order enclosed an 'acknowledgment slip', to be filled out by the plaintiffs. The plaintiffs signed and returned the acknowledgment slip, but also referred in their accompanying letter to the terms of their original offer. There were no further relevant communications between the parties. When the machine was ready for delivery, the question arose as to whether the fixed price or the price variation clause was to apply. The Court of Appeal analysed the transaction using the traditional concepts of offer, counter offer and acceptance. The plaintiffs' original letter was an offer. The defendants' reply was not an acceptance, but because it put forward different terms (that is, in particular, a fixed rather than a variable price) it was therefore a counter offer. The plaintiffs' return of the signed acknowledgment slip was an acceptance of the defendants' counter offer. But what of the accompanying letter referring back to the original terms? The court treated this as not being of any legal significance, so that there was in the end a contract on the defendants' terms. This rather cavalier dismissal of what the plaintiffs no doubt saw as an important part of their communications is perhaps indicative of the courts' eagerness, in this type of situation, to find that some sort of contract has come into existence. A strict application of the offer and acceptance principles might well lead to the conclusion that there was no contract at all. But this might well be regarded as being unsatisfactory in a business context, where one or both of the parties may have spent time and money on the basis that a valid contract had been created.

A further example of this type of approach may be seen in *Hertford Foods Ltd v Lidl UK GmbH* (2001),[2] which concerned a contract for the sale of goods. Once again, inconsistent terms had been exchanged, but both parties thought that they had made a contract. In this case, the Court of Appeal was able to find that the parties had in fact reached agreement on the essential terms of the contract (that is, the goods to be sold and the price) before any of the standard terms had been put forward. Neither set of standard terms therefore applied. In particular, the claimant could not rely on a *force majeure* clause which appeared in its standard terms, but not in those of the defendant.

At times, some members of the Court of Appeal have attempted to confront the problem of the battle of the forms more directly. In *Butler Machine Tool v Ex-Cell-O* (1979), for example, Lord Denning would have preferred to find that the overall communications between the parties showed that there was an agreement and therefore a contract, without the need to divide this up strictly into offer and acceptance. He developed this argument further in *Gibson v Manchester City Council* (1979), but on this occasion his approach was specifically rejected by the House of Lords. More recently, a similar type of argument was put forward by Steyn LJ in *Trentham Ltd v Archital Luxfer* (1993). This concerned an agreement for the supply and installation of doors and windows as part of a construction contract. The work was done and paid for, but a dispute then arose, which required an analysis of whose terms governed the contract. Although there had been considerable correspondence and a number of telephone calls, there was no clear matching offer and acceptance. The trial judge held that there was acceptance by performance. Steyn LJ in the Court of Appeal agreed that this was a possible analysis, but went on to suggest that in a fully executed transaction, a contract could be found to have come into existence without the need for a precise analysis in terms of offer and acceptance. The other members of the court agreed with Steyn LJ's judgment. *Trentham*, despite the fact that it seems to revive an approach rejected by the House of Lords in *Gibson v Manchester City Council*, indicates the possibility for arguing that, at least in certain contexts, and in particular when a transaction has been completed, the courts should not be too concerned to find an offer and acceptance. Provided that there was clearly an agreement that there should be a contract between the parties (even if all the details have not been worked out), the courts should try, wherever possible, to give effect to that.

The problems of fitting all transactions into the precise 'slots' of offer and acceptance, in both the consumer and business contexts, has been recognised by the English courts at least since the comments to this effect by Lord Wilberforce in *The Eurymedon* (1975). Nevertheless, despite the recognition of the problem, the tendency has been to try to use the traditional concepts wherever possible. What are the advantages, if any, of this over the more broadly based approach to finding agreement advocated by Lord Denning and, to some extent, by Steyn LJ? One purported advantage might be that of certainty, which the courts often put forward as a reason for adopting a particular approach towards contracts. It is felt that businesses in particular will favour clarity about the legal rules which will apply to their transactions in general over flexibility which might lead to a more 'just' solution on particular facts. Such unpredictability is thought to be undesirable. The major disadvantage of the traditional approach is, however, that, applied strictly, it will be likely to lead in a 'battle of the forms' case to an answer which neither party would advocate – that is, that there was no contract at all. Hence the adoption of various strategies indicated in the various cases (outlined earlier in this essay) by which the courts have tried to find a contract, despite the difficulties of identifying a matching offer and acceptance. The desirability of mechanisms having this effect is illustrated by the fact that they appear in the Vienna Convention on the International Sale of Goods, the United States Uniform Commercial Code and the Principles of European Contract Law. These documents provide, for example, that an 'acceptance' which contains additional, but not material, alterations may still be effective as an acceptance, and that, in the case of the European Principles, where there are conflicting conditions, a contract may be made on such terms as are common to the offer and acceptance. To date, however, the English courts (and in particular the House of Lords) have not fully grasped the nettle of recognising that the 'battle of the forms' requires an explicit modification of the traditional offer and acceptance rules. Until they do, the English law in this area cannot really be said to be satisfactory.

Notes

1   You might also refer here to the case of *Pars Technology Ltd v City Link Transport Holdings Ltd* (1999) as an example of a case where the Court of Appeal did not allow a minor difference in terms to prevent a contract arising. See Stone, *The Modern Law of Contract*, 5th edn, 2002, p 39.

2   The case is unreported, but is discussed by Ross J in 'Setting the standards' (2001) 145 SJ 650. See also Stone, *The Modern Law of Contract*, 5th edn, 2002, p 41.

Question 4

Carl was browsing the internet when he came across a site, run by OperaClassics, which was offering a set of CDs of the complete Wagner *Ring* at the price of £120. In accordance with the information on the site, Carl immediately sent an email to OperaClassics ordering a set of the CDs, and giving his credit card details. About 30 minutes later he found another site, run by DirectOpera, which was offering the same set of CDs for £75. He selected this set and then moved to the website's 'checkout' page. Here he was asked to fill out a form, giving his details, including his credit card number. He was then presented with a page setting out the details of his order and asking him to click on the 'confirm order' icon if he wished to proceed. Carl did so. He then immediately sent a second email to OperaClassics cancelling his previous order. Five minutes later he received an email from OperaClassics in response to his original email, confirming that his order was being processed.

The next day Carl received an email from DirectOpera explaining that the price of £75 had been posted in error, and that the real price was £135. He also received a further email from OperaClassics stating that his second email had come too late; the processing of his order was continuing, and his credit card would be charged with £120.

Advise Carl, who wishes to hold DirectOpera to the price stated on the website, and does not wish to proceed with the transaction with OperaClassics.

Answer plan

This question requires you to apply the general principles governing the formation of contracts to the particular situation of contracting over the internet. The dealings with OperaClassics raise the issue of contracting by email; those with DirectOpera, the issue of contracting via a company's website.

The most important matters to be considered are:

- Are the advertisements contained in the websites 'offers' or 'invitations to treat'?
- If Carl's first email to OperaClassics was an offer, was his withdrawal communicated before it had been accepted?
- If there is a contract between Carl and OperaClassics, what is the effect of the Consumer Protection (Distance Selling) Regulations 2000?

- Was there a concluded contract with DirectOpera for a sale at £75? If so, what constituted the offer and the acceptance?

A further issue which might be considered is the possible effect of the European Directive on Electronic Commerce on the alleged contract with DirectOpera.

Answer

Carl has taken steps towards entering into contracts with two internet companies for the purchase of a set of CDs. He now wishes to enforce one of these contracts and escape from the other. In deciding how to advise him, it will be necessary to consider the ways in which the rules about formation of contracts, and in particular the rules of offer and acceptance, apply to internet transactions. There are no reported cases specifically dealing with the area of internet contracts, so it will be a question of applying the relevant general principles to the situations set out in the problem.

In both situations the starting point is the advertisement of goods on a website, at a stated price. The initial question is, therefore, whether these advertisements constitute 'offers' capable of 'acceptance', or whether they are simply 'invitations to treat'. A relevant authority is *Partridge v Crittenden* (1968), in which an advertisement was placed in a newspaper advertising bramblefinches for sale at 25 shillings each. It was held that this advertisement was not an 'offer' but simply an invitation to treat. Assuming that the placer of the advertisement only had a limited supply of the bramblefinches, he could not have intended to be bound to anyone who responded to the advertisement. Such responses would thus constitute offers to buy, which the advertiser would be free to accept or reject as he chose. A contrast can be drawn with the American case of *Lefkowitz v Great Minneapolis Surplus Stores* (1957), where an advertisement stated that three mink coats were available at a shop at a special price – 'first come, first served'. This was held to constitute an offer, which could be accepted by being one of the first three people to claim a coat. In the case of both OperaClassics and DirectOpera, the form of the advertisement seems to be in line with that in *Partridge v Crittenden* rather than in *Lefkowitz v Great Minneapolis Surplus Stores*. The advertisements should therefore be viewed as invitations to treat rather than offers.

Turning now to Carl's dealings with OperaClassics, it is clear that Carl's initial email is an offer to buy the CDs at the advertised price. This is accepted by OperaClassics in their first email to Carl. In the meantime, however, Carl has sent them a withdrawal of his offer. The answer to whether there is a contract between Carl and OperaClassics depends, therefore, on whether Carl's revocation of his offer is effective; if it is not, then OperaClassics' acceptance will be effective to create a contract. Carl's only possibility of escaping this obligation will then lie under the Consumer Protection (Distance Selling) Regulations 2000.

The case law on revocation of offers establishes that offers can be withdrawn at any time prior to acceptance (*Payne v Cave* (1789)), provided that the withdrawal is communicated to the offeree. The latter point was confirmed by the decision in *Byrne v van Tienhoven* (1880), which concerned the revocation of an offer by telegram. Applying this to the dealings between Carl and OperaClassics, if OperaClassics received Carl's email before they sent their email confirming his order, then his revocation will be effective, and there will be no contract. This assumes, however, that the email is deemed to be communicated to OperaClassics as soon as it is received on their email system, and available to be read. They might wish to argue, on the other hand, that Carl's email was not communicated, and therefore not effective, until it was read by someone at OperaClassics. There is no case law which settles this issue. In *Entores v Miles Far East Corp* (1955), it was held that, in relation to 'instantaneous' communications, they take effect at the place where they are received. In *The Brimnes* (1974), it was held that a telexed withdrawal was effective when it was printed on the recipient's telex machine, not when it was actually read. In *Brinkibon Ltd v Stahag Stahl* (1982), however, the House of Lords refused to confirm any hard and fast rule, taking the view that the intentions of the parties and 'business practice' must be taken into account in deciding when such a communication is effective. If it is sent out of normal office hours, for example, it might not be treated as being communicated until the point when the office would be expected to re-open. These cases were concerned with telexes. Should the same approach apply to email? There seems no good reason why not, unless it is felt that emails are not in practice read as quickly as telex communications. In the absence of other authority, the test should probably be that the email communication should be taken to be read at the point when the sender would reasonably expect this to occur. When sending an email to a business in normal office hours, it would generally be reasonable to expect that it will be read almost as soon as it arrives.

If this approach is applied to the problem, then, in the absence of any more precise information about when the emails were sent, received and read, it would favour Carl, since OperaClassics' acceptance of his offer is not received by him until after the point when his withdrawal would have been received by OperaClassics. There is one other issue, however, which needs brief consideration. That is whether the 'postal rule' derived from *Adams v Lindsell* (1818) applies to emails. This states that an acceptance sent by post, where post is a reasonable means of communication, will take effect on posting rather than receipt. If this applied here it would require even further investigation as to the precise timings of the various communications. Fortunately, it was made clear in *Entores v Miles Far East Corp* that the postal rule does not apply to instantaneous communications. It is generally agreed that this will cover email, and so the time of communication, rather than the time of sending, is the relevant time. This will not therefore help OperaClassics.

Overall, then, as regards Carl's dealings with OperaClassics, he can be advised that on the facts as stated he has effectively withdrawn his offer before it was accepted by OperaClassics. He is not bound to the contract with them, and is entitled to instruct his credit card company not to make the payment to OperaClassics.

However, even if the analysis of Carl's dealings with OperaClassics leads to the conclusion that there is a contract, he will probably be able to escape from this by virtue of the Consumer Protection (Distance Selling) Regulations 2000. These apply to contracts made by a 'consumer' (this will cover Carl) when there is no face to face contact with the seller of goods or supplier of services. They will therefore apply to most internet transactions. Where they do apply, the consumer is given the right to cancel the contract by giving written notice. The right lasts until seven days after goods have been received. Carl will therefore be able to escape from any contract with OperaClassics by exercising his rights under these Regulations.

Turning to Carl's dealings with DirectOpera, in this case Carl is trying to argue that there is a contract, based on the originally quoted price of £75. As has been established above, the advertisement on the website is an invitation to treat. Carl responds to this by filling in and submitting a form detailing his order and the method of payment. This may be regarded as an offer to buy the goods at the stated price. At this stage, DirectOpera would be free to accept or reject Carl's offer. If, for example, they were unhappy with his credit card details, or had at this stage realised that a mistake had been made with regard to the price quoted, they could have withdrawn from the transaction. What happens, however, is that they display a page setting out the details of Carl's order and asking if he wishes to continue. This is not an acceptance of Carl's offer, since it is allowing him the opportunity to back out. It must in its turn be regarded as a further offer to enter into a contract on the terms stated. Carl can be treated as accepting this offer by clicking on the 'confirm order' icon. DirectOpera will no doubt wish to argue that this was not an acceptance, but simply a restatement of Carl's offer, which DirectOpera were still free to accept or reject. On the basis of the general approach by the English courts to questions of offer and acceptance, there seems no reason why there should be this further stage. All the terms of the contract have been agreed, and the presentation of the page setting out Carl's order would surely be taken by a reasonable person as indicating that DirectOpera were prepared to contract on these terms. This would lead to the conclusion that Carl is entitled to enforce the contract against DirectOpera, on the basis that there is a binding agreement to supply the CDs for £75.

Before reaching a final conclusion, however, the possible effect of the European Directive on Electronic Commerce 2000 should be considered. This states that, where a contract is made over the internet, the 'service provider' should acknowledge a consumer's order without undue delay. This might indicate that where, as has been suggested is the case with Carl, the consumer accepts an offer made by the supplier, a further communication from the supplier to the consumer is needed before a contract comes into existence. If this were the case it would assist DirectOpera. In fact, however, the approach being adopted by the UK to the implementation of the Directive suggests that it will not be treated as affecting the rules as to the formation of contracts, but will simply lead to the consumer having a right to cancel the contract if the required acknowledgment has not been sent by the supplier.[1] If that is the case, then Carl will still be able to insist that he is entitled to be supplied with the CDs for £75 (or to receive compensation if he has to pay a higher price for them elsewhere).

Note

1   For further discussion of the Directive and its implementation, see Stone, *The Modern Law of Contract*, 5th edn, 2002, pp 55–56.

Question 5

Answer both parts.

(a) Jane's distinctive fibreglass racing bike is stolen. She puts an advertisement in the local paper advertising a reward of £100 to anyone who finds it. Peter, who has not seen the advertisement, discovers the bike abandoned on some wasteland, and takes it home. His wife, on seeing the bike, recognises it as the one for which the reward has been offered, and shows Peter the advertisement in the newspaper. Peter returns the bike to Jane, but she refuses to pay the £100, saying that the offer has been withdrawn.

Advise Peter.

(b) Brown knows that Wright has been keen to buy his car. On Monday, he tells Wright that he has decided to sell at a price of £2,000. Wright says that he is very interested, but would like to think about it. Brown says: 'I will assume that you want it, unless you tell me otherwise by Saturday.'

On Friday, Wright meets Green who tells him that Brown has just agreed to sell the car to Smith for £2,250. Wright, who has decided he wants the car, immediately puts a letter in the post accepting Brown's offer. Later that day, however, he has a change of mind, and calls on Brown to tell him to ignore the letter. Brown tells him that his deal with Smith has fallen through, and that he is still keen to sell to Wright.

Advise Brown and Wright.

Answer plan

Two part questions can be difficult in terms of deciding how much space to give to each part. Your assumption should generally be that, unless the question indicates otherwise, both parts carry the same marks. Here, as is usual with this type of question, the two parts deal with related issues. They need to be considered separately, however, in terms of planning your answer.

Part (a): the main issue here relates to the question of whether you can accept an offer which you do not know about. The cases of *Gibbons v Proctor* (1891) and *R v Clarke* (1927) will need to be considered. Subsidiary issues are the status of offers in advertisements and the possibility of the revocation of an offer in a unilateral contract.

Part (b): here, the issues are the question of acceptance by silence, communication of acceptance, communication of the revocation of an offer, particularly where it has been indicated that it will remain open until a particular date, and recall of a posted acceptance.

Answer

Part (a)

In order to advise Peter, it is necessary to consider the status of the advertisement placed by Jane, that is, whether it is an offer or an invitation to treat, and, if it is an offer, whether it matters that Peter was ignorant of it at the time he found the bike. Jane's power to withdraw her offer will also need to be considered.

The advertisement placed in the newspaper by Jane will almost certainly be regarded as an offer, capable of leading to a contract. Although in some situations newspaper adverts are regarded as being merely invitations to treat, the position is different here. In *Partridge v Crittenden* (1968), for example, an advert offering wild birds for sale was said to be an invitation to treat, largely because the seller did not have an unlimited supply of the birds, and so could not be taken to be intending to enter into a binding contract with everyone who replied. In *Carlill v Carbolic Smoke Ball Co* (1893), on the other hand, the court was prepared to accept that an advertisement promising £100 to anyone who caught influenza after using the advertiser's smoke ball was an offer. The difference between the two situations is largely that, in *Partridge v Crittenden*, the purported contract was a bilateral one whereas, in *Carlill*, it was unilateral.[1] Jane's advertisement is clearly of the *Carlill* type, and there is no problem as regards a risk of making more contracts than she can fulfil, since only one person is going to be entitled to the reward.

If it is accepted, then, that Jane's advertisement is an offer, has Peter accepted? He has found the bike, so that at first sight it would appear that he has accepted. There is a problem, however, in that at the time he discovered the bike he did not know about Jane's advert. Can you accept an offer of which you are not aware? This question has been raised in a number of cases. The most relevant English authority is *Gibbons v Proctor* (1891). Here, information was given by a police officer to his superior. This was passed on to someone who had offered a reward for the information. At the time the officer gave the information, he was unaware of the reward, but he knew about it by the time it reached the offeror. The officer was held to be entitled to claim the reward. By contrast, in the Australian case of *R v Clarke* (1927), a suspect who gave information leading to the conviction of a murderer was held unable to claim a reward. This was because he had acted solely to clear his name, and without any thought of the reward. On the other hand, in *Williams v Carwardine* (1833), the court treated the motive of the plaintiff as irrelevant, as long as she was aware that a reward had been offered for the information she was giving.

On balance, the facts of the problem would seem to be closer to *Gibbons v Proctor* than to *R v Clarke*. Peter does not know of Jane's offer when he finds the bike, but does by the time he returns it to her. The wording of the advert raises a difficulty, however, in that it refers to the 'finding' as the action which leads to the reward. If this is looked at strictly, then Peter did not know about the reward when he did the required act. It would surely be argued, however, that what Jane really wanted was not the simple finding of the bike, but also its return to her. Since, by the time Peter brought the bike to her, he knew of the reward, and was acting in response to her advertisement, he ought to be able to claim the £100.

A final point which needs to be considered is whether Jane could argue that her offer has been withdrawn before Peter has accepted. Although, in theory, it seems that in a unilateral contract such as this the offeror is entitled to withdraw at any time before performance is complete, in practice, the courts have tended to the view that withdrawal after performance has begun should not be allowed: *Errington v Errington* (1952); *Daulia Ltd v Four Millbank Nominees* (1978). Moreover, there is no indication that Jane has made any attempt to communicate the withdrawal of the offer. Her attempt to back out when Peter has arrived on her doorstep with the bike would seem to come much too late, even if the required act is the return of the bike, rather than finding it.

In conclusion, Peter can be advised that he is fully entitled to the £100.

Part (b)

There are three main issues to consider here: silence as acceptance; revocation of an offer via a third party; and recall of a posted acceptance.

Looking first at the question of silence as acceptance, can Brown's statement 'I will assume that you want it, unless you tell me otherwise' lead to a contract without some response from Wright? If so, it could be argued that there is a contract as soon as Wright has definitely decided that he wants the car. There are two problems with this, however. The first is that it would be difficult to say that a contract had come into existence before Saturday, unless Wright takes some action to commit himself to it, since he has until then to change his mind. If Saturday had passed without anything else happening, then it might be arguable that there was a contract. There is a more general problem with this, however, which arises from the case of *Felthouse v Bindley* (1862). An uncle and nephew had been negotiating for the sale of a horse. The uncle made an offer, saying, in effect: 'If I do not hear from you, I shall assume that the horse is mine.' It was held that there was no contract, because it was not permissible for one side to impose an agreement on the other in this way. Although the House of Lords has suggested, in *Vitol SA v Norelf Ltd* (1996), that in certain circumstances silence might be treated as an acceptance, provided that it is 'clear and unequivocal', that does not seem to be the case here,[2] so we must look for some positive acceptance by Wright, if there is to be a contract between him and Brown.

There is the possibility of such an acceptance in Wright's letter. Again, however, there are difficulties with this. We must first look at the effect of Wright's conversation with Green. Green tells Wright that Brown has agreed to sell the car to someone else. It might be argued that this amounts to a revocation of Brown's offer. In *Dickinson v Dodds* (1876), the defendant had offered to sell a house to the plaintiff, and to leave the offer open for three days. In the meantime, however, the plaintiff learnt from a reliable third party that the defendant was selling the property to someone else. It was held that this amounted to a communication of the revocation of the defendant's offer, so that the plaintiff could no longer accept it. The only difference between the situation in the problem and *Dickinson v Dodds* is that there, the sale to the other party went through,[3] whereas here it does not. Therefore, it may well be the case that Wright is unable to accept Brown's offer. If this is so, then his letter itself becomes an offer to buy, which will only be effective on communication to Brown. Before Brown receives it, Wright arrives in person to say that he does not want to buy. This amounts to an effective revocation of his offer, so the conclusion will be that there is no contract.

There is, however, the possibility that *Dickinson v Dodds* will not be applied, either because Smith was not someone who could be relied on as a reliable intermediary, or because the decision in that case depended on the other contract having been completed at the time the information was given. What then would be the status of Wright's letter? As a posted acceptance it might well be the case that it would take effect on posting under the *Adams v Lindsell* (1818) rule. This would be the case provided that post was a reasonable means of communication: *Henthorn v Fraser* (1892). The question that then arises is whether Wright is irrevocably bound by this acceptance, or whether he can, by his visit to Brown before the letter arrives, recall it, and escape from the contract he no longer wishes to make.

There is no English authority on this issue. The Scottish case of *Dunmore v Alexander* (1830) is sometimes cited for the proposition that recall of a posted acceptance is possible, but it is not a clear decision.[4] There are cases from other jurisdictions which suggest that no recall is possible.[5] This would be the result of applying the normal rule about acceptances, which is that once they are made they cannot be recalled. On the other hand, there does not seem to be any particular harm in allowing recall by a speedier means. By definition, the offeror does not know about the acceptance, and so cannot have acted on it, and it might seem a little odd to apply a rule which was devised for the benefit of acceptors[6] in a way which acts to their disadvantage.[7]

If the *Adams v Lindsell* rule does not apply to Wright's letter, then of course he has no problem. His acceptance will not take effect until his letter arrives, and there is then no reason at all for stopping him telling Brown to ignore the letter.

In conclusion, then, it seems that whatever analysis is applied, the most likely result is that there is no contract between Brown and Wright for the sale of the car. Brown can of course make a fresh offer, but Wright will again be free to accept or reject this in the same way as Brown's initial offer.

Notes

1   In other words, if the advert in *Partridge v Crittenden* had been in the form 'if you are one of the first 100 people to send me 25 shillings, I will send you a bramblefinch', then the court might well have been prepared to regard it as an offer.

2   In an earlier case, *The Leonidas D* (1985), Goff J had suggested that acceptance could only be inferred from silence 'in the most exceptional circumstances'.

3   And, indeed, the purported acceptance was not received until after the sale had been completed.

4   Apart from anything else, it is not clear that the relevant communication was an acceptance rather than an offer.

5   For instance, *Wenckheim v Arndt* (1873) (New Zealand) and *A to Z Bazaars (Pty) Ltd v Minister of Agriculture* (1974) (South Africa).

6   That is, so that they can carry on their business on the basis that they have a contract, without having to wait to hear if the acceptance has arrived.

7   Others argue, however, that this gives the acceptor the best of both worlds. An offer to buy shares, for example, could be accepted by a letter, but then withdrawn if, while the letter is in transit, the share price falls: see, for instance, Stone, *The Modern Law of Contract*, 5th edn, 2002, pp 63–66 and Treitel, *The Law of Contract*, 10th edn, 1999, p 28.

CHAPTER 2

INTENTION AND CONSIDERATION

Introduction

The two other elements, apart from offer and acceptance, which the courts look for in relation to the formation of contracts are intention and consideration, and the questions in this chapter deal with these.

The issue of intention to create legal relations is very straightforward. There are two basic rules:

- if the contract is a 'domestic' agreement, then there is a presumption that there is no intention to create legal relations (*Balfour v Balfour*); and
- if the contract is 'commercial' in nature, then there is a presumption that it is intended to be legally binding (*Edwards v Skyways*).

All that needs to be done is to apply these to the facts of any problem asked, and consider whether there is any reason why the presumption should be rebutted.

Because it is such a simple issue, questions about intention will rarely, if ever, stand alone, but will be contained within some other topic. Here, intention is linked with consideration, which is quite common in contract questions.

The topic of consideration, by way of contrast, is definitely difficult. Some aspects are, however, reasonably straightforward. It is not too difficult to learn the rules and the cases relating to:

- the difference between 'adequate' and 'sufficient' consideration – what kinds of actions or promises can or cannot amount to consideration – the general irrelevance of the value of consideration (for example, *Chappell v Nestlé*);
- past consideration – the reformulation of the rules relating to this in *Pao On v Lau Yiu Long* needs to be learnt and understood; and
- existing obligations as consideration – whether owed to the public, a third party, or the other contracting party. Here, the case of *Williams v Roffey*, and its effect on *Stilk v Myrick*, will need to be considered.

Where things start to become more difficult, however, is in relation to the variation of contracts, and how the doctrine of consideration applies to this. Once again, the implications of *Williams v Roffey* need to be considered, but more generally the whole topic of 'promissory estoppel' must be faced.

Promissory estoppel is a topic which students do not like. If you are going to prepare yourself to deal with questions on consideration, however, it is something you will have to get to grips with. Four out of the five questions in this chapter raise promissory estoppel issues in one way or another. The points that need to be understood are:

- the basic elements of the doctrine as laid down by Lord Denning in *Central London Property Trust v High Trees House*;
- the origins of the doctrine in the 19th century 'waiver' cases, like *Hughes v Metropolitan Rly*;
- the limitations on promissory estoppel derived from post-*High Trees* cases, such as *Combe v Combe* ('shield not a sword') and *D & C Builders v Rees* (must be equitable to use it);
- the relationship between *High Trees* and the cases on part payment of debts, such as *Pinnel's Case* and *Foakes v Beer*; and
- the unresolved problem of whether the doctrine is only suspensory of rights, or whether it can have an extinctive effect.

None of these points is easy. In relation to some of them, it has to be accepted that there is no clear answer from the case law, and you must therefore argue from general principles. You should not be afraid to do this. Whatever the conclusion arrived at, if the argument is presented carefully, logically and consistently with the cases, it will be likely to obtain high marks.

Checklist

You should be familiar with the following areas:

- Intention to create legal relations: the presumptions applying to domestic and commercial agreements.
- The meaning of 'consideration'.
- The difference between 'adequate' and 'sufficient' consideration.
- Past consideration, and when it can be effective.
- Existing duties, and when they can amount to good consideration for a fresh promise. The rules relating to public duties, contractual duties owed to a third party, and contractual duties owed to the promisor, all need to be understood.
- Promissory estoppel: its origins, development and limitations.

Question 6

Arthur's daughter, Belinda, aged 21, was studying for some accountancy examinations at Ademup College. It was a contractual requirement that students in residence at the College were non-smokers, and Belinda therefore gave up smoking. Arthur, however, was worried that under the pressure of preparing for the examinations Belinda would start smoking again, and so he promised to pay her £100 if she did not smoke at all until she had completed the course. He also promised to buy her a car if she passed the examinations.

Arthur runs a small business, and asked Belinda to prepare a short report on the taxation of companies. He was pleased with the result, and said he would give her £50 'for all her hard work'.

Belinda passed her examinations, and has not started smoking again.

Arthur has not made either of the promised payments, or bought the car. He seeks your advice as to whether he is legally obliged to do so.

Advise Arthur.

Answer plan

There are three possible contracts to be discussed here, relating to the smoking, the promise of a car, and the work on company taxation. The question is primarily concerned with various aspects of consideration:

- the need for benefit or detriment;
- past consideration; and
- validity of contractual obligations to a third party as consideration.

In addition, however, it is important not to overlook the fact that the situation, being one of father and daughter, may well involve the issue of whether any of Arthur's promises were intended to create legal relations. It is probably best to deal with this issue generally, either at the beginning or at the end of the answer, rather than in relation to each promise separately.

Answer

The elements which make a contract binding under English law are offer and acceptance, consideration, and intention to create legal relations. There is no problem with the existence of offer and acceptance here, but there may be difficulties with both intention and consideration which may enable Arthur to avoid fulfilling his promises to his daughter.

There are three possible contracts to consider:

(1) the promise of £100 if Belinda refrained from smoking;

(2) the promise to buy a car if Belinda passed all the examinations; and

(3) the promise of £50 for the work on company taxation.[1]

In relation to all of them, Arthur may wish to raise the defence that he did not intend to create a legal relationship. The attitude of the English courts to this issue can be illustrated by two cases, *Balfour v Balfour* (1919) and *Edwards v Skyways* (1964).

In *Balfour*, a husband and wife had to separate because the wife was not well enough to travel back to the husband's place of work (Ceylon). The husband promised to pay her £30 per month. When he failed to keep up the payments, she sued. The court held that she could not succeed because there had been no intention to create legal relations.[2] Lord Atkin said that, in the case of social and domestic arrangements, there was a presumption against there being an intention to create legal relations. This presumption could be rebutted but in this case there was no evidence to suggest that it should be, and the wife's action therefore failed.[3]

In *Edwards v Skyways*, however, the presumption operated in the opposite way. An airline pilot who was made redundant was offered what was described as an *ex gratia* payment by way of compensation. When this was not paid, the pilot sued. It was held that in commercial relationships there was a strong presumption that there was an intention to create legal relations, which it would be difficult to overturn. In this case, the mere use of the phrase *ex gratia* was not sufficient to rebut the presumption, and the pilot's action succeeded.

Applying this to Arthur and Belinda, the first question is whether we are dealing with commercial arrangements, or social and domestic arrangements. This should not depend solely on the relationship between the parties. There is no reason why members of the same family cannot make perfectly binding commercial contracts between themselves. It depends also on the nature or subject matter of the contract. Here, the promises about the smoking and the passing of the examinations may be argued to be 'domestic'; the promise in relation to the work done on company taxes is more obviously 'commercial'. There is no evidence provided in the problem from which either of the presumptions which would arise from these categorisations can clearly be rebutted. It is quite likely, therefore, that a court would find promises (1) and (2) unenforceable for lack of intention to create legal relations. Promise (3), however, would be likely to be held to have been intended to be legally binding.

Leaving this issue aside for the moment, let us now turn to the question of consideration.

The doctrine of consideration is fundamental to English contract law. It requires that, for a promise to be binding, something must be given or done in exchange by the promisee. In this case, the things which might constitute consideration on Belinda's part are: (a) refraining from smoking (in respect of the promise to pay £100); (b) passing her examinations (in respect of the promise to buy a car); and (c) doing the work on company taxes (in respect of the promise to pay £50). There are, however, problems with all three as regards their acceptance as valid consideration.

One of the requirements of consideration is sometimes said to be that it must be of some economic value. For example, in the case of *White v Bluett* (1853), it was held that a son who promised to stop complaining provided no consideration for a promise by his father not to enforce a promissory note. This might cast doubt on the validity of both the abstention from smoking and the passing of the exams. The requirement of value is not, however, applied very strictly. In *Chappell v Nestlé* (1960), for example, worthless chocolate wrappers sent in return for a 'special offer' were nevertheless regarded as part of the consideration. Similarly, in *Edmonds v Lawson* (2000), the Court of Appeal was prepared to accept the general benefits to chambers in the operation of a pupillage system as being sufficient to amount to consideration in relation to contracts with individual pupils, without defining with any precision the economic value of such benefits.

The requirement of economic value can also be overshadowed by the rule that consideration need not provide a benefit to the promisor if it is a detriment to the promisee. Belinda could say that her promises to her father are to her detriment. Here again, however, she has problems in that it can be argued that giving up smoking and passing her examinations are in fact both to her benefit. The only counter to this is the argument that many, if not most, contracts are entered into on the basis that they are at least perceived to be to the benefit of both parties, so that the requirement of detriment does not match the reality of the relationship.

There is one more issue that must be looked at as regards the abstention from smoking. Belinda is already obliged in her contract with Ademup College not to smoke. Can doing something which you are already contractually obliged to do in an agreement with a third party still amount to consideration? Here, the answer is clearly in Belinda's favour. In *Shadwell v Shadwell* (1860), it was held that a marriage to which the plaintiff was (under the law at the time) legally bound was good consideration for a promise of an annual payment from his uncle. The principle has been accepted without question by the Privy Council in both *The Eurymedon* (1974) and *Pao On v Lau Yiu Long* (1979). So, if Belinda's giving up smoking satisfies the other requirements of valid consideration (which is doubtful), it will not be struck down because of her agreement with the College.

The third suggested contract, that is, the promise of £50 for the taxation work, does not raise the same problems. The work done by Belinda is clearly of economic value, and a detriment to her, as well as a benefit to Arthur. The way in which Arthur may escape legal liability in this case is from the doctrine of so called 'past' consideration. This states that if a promise is made after work has been done, or some other benefit conferred, that work or benefit is not consideration for the promise, which is therefore unenforceable. This is a result of the idea of contract involving a mutual exchange. How can work be given in return for a promise, if the promise is not made until after the work is completed? An example of the application of this rule is *Re McArdle* (1951). Two members of a family, who were living in a house which had been left jointly to them and other members of the family, did some improvements on it, and then sought promises to contribute to the costs of the work from their relatives. It was held that they could not enforce the relatives' promises to pay, since they were given after the work was completed. The work was therefore past consideration and could not be relied on.

The courts have recognised, however, that this rule can operate harshly in certain circumstances and have therefore formulated an exception to it. The principles derived from the earlier case law have now been restated in *Pao On v Lau Yiu Long* in the following way:

(a) the act must have been done at the promisor's request; this derives from *Lampleigh v Braithwait* (1615);

(b) the parties must have anticipated at the time the work was done that it was to be paid for; this derives from *Re Casey's Patents* (1892); and

(c) the promise must have been legally enforceable if it had been made in advance.

Applying these requirements to the problem, it is clear that the first and third are satisfied. We are told that Arthur asked Belinda to do the work, and the arrangement is clearly one which could have been enforced had the promise been made before the work was done (subject, of course, to the issue of intention). As to the second requirement, it is difficult to answer without more facts. Was there any earlier mention of payment? Had Belinda been paid for any similar work in the past? The answers to these questions will help to determine whether there is valid consideration for Arthur's promise.

In conclusion, Arthur seems to be on strong ground legally as regards the promises to pay £100 and to buy the car. In both cases there are doubts about the intention to create legal relations and the validity of the consideration supplied by Belinda. The morality or wisdom of thwarting his daughter's expectations in this way is another matter! As regards the £50, Arthur is in a much weaker legal position. Provided Belinda can establish that there was a prior expectation that the work on company taxation was to be paid for, she has good grounds for claiming a binding contract for the payment of £50 from her father.

Notes

1   Note that the first two are unilateral contracts, the third is bilateral.

2   The decision was also based on the lack of consideration provided by the wife for her husband's promise.

3   In subsequent cases, the presumption has been rebutted where the marriage is breaking down, for example, *Merritt v Merritt* (1970).

Question 7

Charles contracts to supply Peter with 10,000 widgets per month for 24 months, for a fixed sum of £20,000, payable in advance. After six months the market price of widgets unexpectedly doubles, due to the outbreak of war in Ruritania (the main widget-producing country). Peter, hearing that as a result of this Charles has started to cancel similar contracts, suggests to Charles that he will be prepared to take 7,000 widgets per month in satisfaction of their contract. Charles agrees, and delivers 7,000 widgets per month for the next five months. The war in Ruritania then ends and the market price of widgets collapses. Peter now demands: (a) the 15,000 shortfall in deliveries in relation to the past five months; and (b) 10,000 widgets per month for the rest of the contract.

Advise Charles.

Answer plan

This question raises in a fairly straightforward way the issue of equitable waiver, or promissory estoppel. Note that the problem does not involve part payment of a debt. The dispute is about the number of widgets to be supplied, not the amount to be paid for them. There is thus no need to discuss *Pinnel's Case* (1602) or *Foakes v Beer* (1884), or their relationship to promissory estoppel.

In this and similar questions, however, it is important to consider whether there is a binding variation of contract supported by consideration, as well as discussing the promissory estoppel issue.

The topics to be covered are therefore:

- the possibility of a binding variation;
- the requirements for promissory estoppel;
- the limitations of promissory estoppel – in particular, whether it is suspensory or extinctive in effect; and
- if promissory estoppel is suspensory, how its effect is terminated.

Answer

The dispute between Charles and Peter raises the issue of how a contract can be varied once it has been agreed. To explain this, and how it affects this situation, it will be necessary to consider the related issues of the doctrine of consideration and the concept of promissory estoppel.

The standard approach of English contract law is to say that a variation of an existing contract will only be binding if there is consideration to support it. In other words, the change in obligations must not be one-sided. If the reduction of the number of the widgets delivered had been accompanied by a drop in the purchase price, there would be no argument that the new arrangements were enforceable by both sides. Both Peter and Charles would have changed their position, and there would in effect be a new binding contract on the new terms.[1]

Turning to the facts of the problem, can we find any consideration for Charles' agreement to supply a smaller quantity of widgets? At first sight, the answer would seem to be no. Charles has not agreed to a reduction in price, or any other change of the agreement with Peter, which would be a benefit to Peter, or a detriment to Charles. On the contrary, the change appears to be made for Charles' benefit. On closer examination, however, the position is not so straightforward. The reason why Peter suggests the reduction is that he hears that Charles is cancelling similar contracts, and he presumably wishes to avoid this happening to his contract. Two possibilities exist here. The first is that the contract between Charles and Peter contains a provision which would allow Charles to cancel it without being in breach. If this is the case, then there is a strong argument for there being a binding variation. The benefit to Peter would be keeping the contract alive in some form, rather than being in a situation where he might have had to look elsewhere for his entire supply of widgets. There is also detriment to Charles in that he is still getting a lower price for his widgets than he might get on the open market. The second possibility is that if Charles cancels the agreement, it would be a breach of contract. Here, the argument for the change amounting to consideration is weaker. It is not, however, ruled out altogether. In *Williams v Roffey* (1990), the Court of Appeal was prepared to accept that the benefit to a contracting party (the defendant) of preventing the other side from failing to complete the contract could be good consideration for a promise by the defendant of extra payments on completion. If this line of reasoning is accepted, then there is an argument for saying that there is a binding variation here.

Two further points need to be noted. First, it is important for the argument for a binding variation that the initiative for changing the contract came from Peter. If Charles had come to Peter and said, 'if you don't agree to a change, I am going to cancel our agreement', this would have amounted almost to duress, and the courts would be unlikely to look sympathetically on Charles' claim for a binding change. This point was regarded as important in *Williams v Roffey*. Secondly, if there is a binding variation, this means that Charles can reject both of Peter's claims. The contract will have been varied with permanent effect, and if Peter wishes to return to the previous terms he will have to negotiate another mutually acceptable variation.

Let us now turn to the situation if it is decided that there is no consideration and, therefore, no binding variation. Here, Charles will only have a basis for resisting Peter's claim if he can invoke the doctrine of promissory estoppel.

It has been recognised by the courts for over 100 years that in certain circumstances an indication by a contracting party, by words or actions, that he is not going to insist on his strict contractual rights can be binding on him, at least to some extent. In *Hughes v Metropolitan Rly* (1877), the actions of the plaintiff had led the defendant reasonably to believe that a period of notice to quit which had been issued had been waived. The defendant had relied on this, and the House of Lords took the view that the plaintiff could not simply bring the waiver to an end and impose the notice to quit without more ado. This idea of 'equitable waiver' has developed into the modern doctrine of 'promissory estoppel' following the decision of Lord Denning[2] in *Central London Property Trust v High Trees House* (1947). As stated there by Denning, the doctrine is that 'a promise intended to be binding, intended to be acted upon, and in fact acted upon, is binding insofar as its terms properly apply'. The promise which Denning was considering here was to reduce the rent on a block of flats during part of the Second World War, which had led to many of the flats being unoccupied. Denning felt that this promise was binding, in that the landlord should not, at the end of the war, be able to go back on it, and claim the full rent for the war years.

As stated above, Denning's definition is too wide. Taken at face value, it would destroy the whole doctrine of consideration.[3] Various limitations to the doctrine have now been recognised.

First, there must be an existing legal relationship between the parties – probably, but not inevitably, a contract. In other words, the doctrine is concerned with the variation of legal obligations, rather than their creation. This links in with the second limitation, that promissory estoppel can only be used 'as a shield, and not as a sword'. This famous phrase comes from *Combe v Combe* (1951). A husband, who was divorcing his wife, made a promise to pay her £100 per annum. When he failed to do so, she sued. The judge at first instance allowed her to succeed, although she had provided no consideration for the promise, on the basis of promissory estoppel. The Court of Appeal held that this was a misuse of the doctrine, which could not create new legal rights.

The third limitation is that the doctrine will only be applied where it would be inequitable to allow the promisor to go back on the promise. Two cases are relevant here. In *D & C Builders v Rees* (1966), Lord Denning said that the doctrine should not be used where the promise had been extracted by improper pressure. The defendants had persuaded the plaintiffs to accept less than they were owed by a threat that if they did not accept they would get nothing. In *The Post Chaser* (1981), there was no impropriety on the part of the promisee, but Lord Goff thought that there was such a short period between the making of the promise and its withdrawal (a matter of days) that it was not inequitable to allow the promisor to escape from it.

The final possible limitation is that the doctrine only suspends rights, rather than extinguishing them. This is certainly what happened in *Hughes* and in *High Trees*. It is not clear whether this is a general rule, however, or something that depends on the individual circumstances of each case. One other point needs to be clarified. The promise itself may be expressed to be only applicable for a limited period. This was what Lord Denning meant by referring to the promise being binding 'as far as its terms properly apply'. In *High Trees*, the promise was taken to have been stated to be applicable only while the Second World War continued and the flats were not fully occupied. Once these conditions ceased to exist, the original terms automatically revived. If no limit is placed on the promise when it was made, it may still be terminable by notice. This was the case in *Tool Metal Manufacturing Co v Tungsten Electric Co* (1955). The House of Lords held that the initiation of a previous action amounted to notice that the promise (to accept a reduced royalty) was being withdrawn. For continuing contracts which involve periodic obligations, it seems then that rights which would have otherwise accrued during the currency of the promise will be lost; for the future, the previous position may be revived, either by the automatic termination of the promise or by giving notice.[4]

Applying this to the problem, we find a promise intended to be binding, intended to be acted upon, and in fact acted upon. It is a variation of an existing legal relationship, and Charles wishes to use it as a shield not a sword. The two remaining issues are related to the suspensory nature of the doctrine, and whether it would be inequitable to allow Peter to go back on it.

Dealing with the second issue first, it is significant here, as it was in relation to the argument about consideration, that the request for the change came from Peter. Had Charles in any sense been holding Peter to ransom, then Lord Denning's comments in *D & C Builders v Rees* might well have applied. This is not the case, however, and there seems no reason on the facts why equity should allow Peter to escape from his promise.

This leaves the issue of the duration of the promise. Peter may well wish to argue that the promise was only intended to last as long as the war in Ruritania continued. If that is right, he can insist on a return to 10,000 widgets per month for the future. There is no suggestion on the facts as given, however, that the promise was made in this form. This will mean, therefore, that Peter will have to give reasonable notice of his intention to return to the original terms, as in *Tool Metal v Tungsten*. What constitutes 'reasonable notice' must be a question of fact in each case. Looking at the overall duration of this contract, it is suggested that notice of two months would be perfectly reasonable.

In conclusion, the advice to Charles is that he does not have to provide the 15,000 shortfall in deliveries. This is because there has either been a binding variation, or Peter is estopped from going back on this part of his promise. As regards the future, there are three possibilities:

(a) there has been a binding variation, and so Charles can continue to supply 7,000 widgets a month for the rest of the contract;
(b) there is a promissory estoppel, which will come to an end at the end of the war in Ruritania – Charles will in this case have to return to 10,000 widgets a month immediately; and
(c) there is a promissory estoppel, determinable on Peter's giving reasonable notice – which would probably be two months.

It is submitted that, on the basis of the facts given, there is no clear evidence of consideration to support a binding variation, or that the promise was expressed to last only for the duration of the war. As a result, (c) above would seem to be the most likely outcome to this dispute, and Charles should be advised accordingly.

Notes

1   The alteration of one term can be binding if it potentially benefits either party – for example, altering the date on which either party can terminate a lease: *Fenner v Blake* (1900). If the change is entirely one-sided, however, and there is no consideration, the variation will be unenforceable, unless the equitable doctrine of promissory estoppel applies.

2   Or 'Denning J', as he was at that time.

3   This may have been Denning's intention – see his comments on the case in *The Discipline of Law*, 1979, Pt 5 – but he backed away from going this far in later cases.

4   The position is more complicated in respect of single obligation contracts. If promissory estoppel has any effect, it must surely be to extinguish the obligation completely.

Question 8

'The doctrine of promissory estoppel cannot be regarded as casting doubt on the decision in *Foakes v Beer* (1884). If that case were to occur today, the House of Lords would decide it in exactly the same way.'

Discuss.

Answer plan

This is a fairly straightforward essay question, in which the main topic is the doctrine of 'promissory estoppel'. The particular issue on which your answer should focus, however, is the relationship between that doctrine and the part payment of debts, and in particular the extent to which the principles applied in *Foakes v Beer* would still be used if similar facts arose today.

To answer the question properly, it is of course necessary to have a reasonable understanding of the facts of *Foakes v Beer*, and the reasons which the House of Lords gave for deciding it in the creditor's favour. The extent to which promissory estoppel has developed into a concept which might now provide a direct challenge to this decision must then be discussed.

The following order of treatment is suggested:

• description of *Foakes v Beer*;

• outline of the development of promissory estoppel;

• particular significance of promissory estoppel for part payment of debts;

- relationship between promissory estoppel and *Foakes v Beer*; and
- likely attitude of the House of Lords to *Foakes v Beer* today.

Answer

Foakes v Beer (1884) concerned an action to recover interest on a judgment debt. Mrs Beer had obtained judgment against Dr Foakes. They made an arrangement under which Dr Foakes was to pay off the debt by instalments. When he had completed the instalments, Mrs Beer sued to recover interest on the debt. In holding that she was entitled to recover,[1] the House of Lords confirmed a rule that had originally been stated in *Pinnel's Case* (1602). This was that part payment of a debt on the due date can never be satisfaction for the full amount owed. If, however, the creditor agrees to early payment or payment by means of goods (even though worth less than the full amount), or even payment on the day at a different place, then the debt will be discharged. The reason for this is that payment in a different form will provide consideration for the promise to accept less than was owed.

The confirmation given to this principle by the House of Lords in *Foakes v Beer* ensured its acceptance[2] until the intervention of Lord Denning in 1947 in *Central London Property Trust v High Trees House* (1947). The owners of a block of flats in London agreed that the lessees could pay a reduced rent during the Second World War because of the difficulty in sub-letting the flats. When, after the war, they brought an action to enforce the contract on its original terms, Denning J indicated that they would not be able to recover for the 'war years', although they could subsequently revert to the original agreement. Denning's statement on this issue was clearly *obiter*, since the action brought only applied to the period after the end of the war, but it was regarded as a challenge to the decision in *Foakes v Beer*. According to the original contract, the defendants in *High Trees* owed money to the plaintiffs for the war years. There was no consideration for the promise to accept less. Under *Foakes v Beer*, therefore, the plaintiffs appeared to have an unanswerable case.

Lord Denning, however, felt that the effect of *Foakes v Beer* could be circumvented by using an equitable doctrine which he traced back to the case of *Hughes v Metropolitan Rly* (1877). Here, the owners of some houses gave notice to the tenants to carry out repairs within six months. If the repairs were not done within that period, the landlord was entitled to forfeit the lease. Shortly after the notice was given, however, the parties entered into negotiations for the sale of the property to the tenants. These negotiations collapsed, and the landlord sought to forfeit the lease in accordance with the terms of his original notice. The House of Lords said that he could not. His actions in entering into the negotiations had to be taken as indicating that he was 'waiving' the notice while the negotiations continued. The courts of equity would not allow him to go back on this indication of waiver, on which the defendant had relied. In effect, the notice to repair was suspended while the negotiations were going on, and time only began to run again when they ceased.

In *High Trees*, Lord Denning took this principle from *Hughes v Metropolitan Rly*, which has since come to be known as 'promissory estoppel',[3] and applied it to the case before him. He said that in both cases there had been a promise made which was intended to be binding, intended to be acted on, and in fact acted on. Such a promise should be binding, insofar as its terms properly apply. The novelty of this approach was that it extended the notion of equitable waiver into the area of part payment of debts, where it had previously been assumed to be inapplicable because of the authority of *Foakes v Beer*. Lord Denning met this objection by arguing that *Foakes v Beer* was decided on common law principles, ignoring the role of equity. In the light of the fact that *Foakes v Beer* was decided after the 'fusion' of law and equity in the 1870s,[4] and that some of their Lordships expressed regret at the outcome, it seems hard to accept that they would have overlooked what Lord Denning seems to regard as an obvious escape route from the harshness of the common law rule.

There is, however, no doubt that promissory estoppel has been accepted as being applicable to variations of contract which involve the payment of money. In *Tool Metal Manufacturing Co v Tungsten Electric Co* (1955), it was accepted that the variation of the amount payable on a royalty was enforceable under the doctrine. It may be significant, however, that, as in *High Trees*, *Tool Metal v Tungsten* was concerned with a continuing contract involving periodic payments. It is possible to argue in such cases that promissory estoppel has only a suspensory effect and is, therefore, less directly in conflict with *Foakes v Beer*. This is true in the sense that the parties could at the end of the war (in *High Trees*), or upon giving notice (*Tool Metal v Tungsten*) revert to the original terms of their agreement. On the other hand, the shortfall in the money which under the original agreement would have been payable during the variation is clearly regarded as being irrecoverable. In that sense, therefore, a debt is being satisfied by part payment.

A more direct challenge to *Foakes v Beer* would arise if promissory estoppel were found to be applicable to a debt comprising a single sum of money. There is no reported case where this has happened. The nearest to it is *D & C Builders v Rees* (1965). The plaintiffs had done work for the defendants. After pressing for payment, they were told by the defendants that if they did not accept a lesser sum in settlement of the account they would get nothing. The plaintiffs agreed to take this smaller sum, but then sued for the balance. It was argued that their action should fail on the basis of promissory estoppel. Having promised to accept a lesser sum, the plaintiffs should not be allowed to renege on that promise. The Court of Appeal decided in favour of the plaintiffs. Only Lord Denning considered the promissory estoppel issue in any detail. He was clearly of the view that promissory estoppel could operate in this situation. It is, however, an equitable doctrine, and the defendants had acted inequitably in pressurising the plaintiffs into accepting the lesser sum, so Lord Denning refused to allow them to rely on promissory estoppel. The rest of the Court of Appeal were content simply to apply the principles from *Pinnel's Case* and *Foakes v Beer*, and hold the defendants liable because they had provided no consideration for the promise to accept the lower amount. Moreover, the Court of Appeal has more recently confirmed, in *Re Selectmove* (1995), that it remains bound by the principle in *Foakes v Beer*.

Is the statement in the question correct? Would *Foakes v Beer* be decided in the same way today? It is clear that the strict rule about part payment of debts has been weakened by *High Trees* and decisions which have followed it. As we have seen, however, the doctrine of promissory estoppel has been found most useful in relation to continuing, rather than one off, contracts. Given the approach taken by the majority in *D & C Builders v Rees*, it seems likely that Mrs Beer would still be successful in recovering the interest on her debt.

Notes

1 It was not in fact clear that Mrs Beer had ever intended to promise to forgo the interest.

2 At times, the acceptance was reluctant: in *Foakes v Beer* itself, for example, Lord Blackburn expressed the view that part payment may in fact be more beneficial to the creditor than relying on his or her strict legal rights.

3 It is also sometimes referred to as 'quasi-estoppel' or 'equitable estoppel'.

4 That is, the provision of the Judicature Acts 1873–75 that, henceforth, all courts could apply the principles of law and equity, and that where there was a conflict equity was to prevail.

Question 9

Armadillo plc make a contract with Movit Ltd, under which Movit agree to transport 3,000 rolls of material from Armadillo's warehouse in London to Armadillo's factory in Leicester. The contract specifies that the material is to be delivered at a rate of 150 rolls per week for 20 weeks. The contract price is £20,000. Just before deliveries are to start, Movit realise that it is only possible to carry 100 rolls at a time on their lorry. They ask Armadillo to agree to deliveries being made over 30 weeks. Armadillo, who are suffering from a fall in business, agree. After five weeks, Armadillo sign a very valuable contract for the production of T-shirts which will require their factory to operate at full capacity. They ask Movit to return to delivering 150 rolls per week, and say that they will pay an extra £5,000 on completion of the contract. Movit hire an additional small lorry and complete the contract at 150 rolls per week. Armadillo, who are now in financial difficulties, refuse to pay more than £20,000. Movit accept and are paid this, but now want to bring an action to recover the additional £5,000 which they say they are owed.

Advise Movit.

Answer plan

At first reading, some problems, like this one, look more complicated than they actually are. There are really only two points of dispute here, although they are interlinked. They are: (a) was the first variation of the contract (that is, regarding the number of rolls to be delivered) either a binding variation or enforceable under the doctrine of promissory estoppel?; and (b) was there any consideration for the promise to pay the additional £5,000? The answer to the second question will depend to some extent on the answer to the first. It will also involve consideration of the effect on the case of *Stilk v Myrick* (1809) of the decision in *Williams v Roffey* (1990).

Note that, although the facts of this case are in some respects similar to *Atlas Express v Kafco* (1989), which is a duress case, no issue of duress really arises here.

Answer

Movit Ltd are seeking to recover the £5,000 additional payment which they were promised by Armadillo. The difficulty which Movit face is in arguing that there was consideration for this promise. Armadillo may well claim that, in delivering 150 rolls per week, Movit were doing no more than they were already contractually obliged to do, and so, on the basis of the rule in *Stilk v Myrick* (1809), cannot enforce the promise of extra payment. To discover if Movit have any answer to this argument, it is necessary to examine in detail what happened between the parties during the course of this contract.

The first problem arises when Movit discover the difficulty with the capacity of their lorry, and ask for a variation of the agreement. It is clear that at this point Armadillo would be entitled to refuse to entertain any change, and to insist that deliveries follow the pattern agreed in the contract. Movit could have had no cause for complaint had this been the line taken. Instead, however, Armadillo agree to the change. Is this a binding variation of the contract? It is quite clear that if the parties to a contract agree to a variation which is mutually beneficial, this will be binding on both of them. In other words, consideration would exist to support the change in terms. Was there any consideration given here for Armadillo's agreement to accept delivery at a slower rate over a longer period? The answer would seem to be 'no'. Armadillo did not vary their side of the bargain in any way – there is, for example, no reduction in the amount to be paid to Movit. The only possibility would be if it could be said that, because of the fall in their business, it is to Armadillo's benefit that the contract is varied in this way. It is likely that something more than indifference on the part of Armadillo will need to be shown. If, for example, the continuation of deliveries at 150 rolls per week would mean that Armadillo would have to find storage space for some of them in Leicester, then avoiding this could be said to be consideration. It might still be objected that this benefit would be incidental, and would not move from the promisee, as is normally required. The Court of Appeal, in *Williams v Roffey* (1990) (which will be discussed in more detail later), appear to have relaxed this requirement somewhat. Even so, it is submitted that the odds are against Movit being able to establish a contractually binding variation.

If the change does not operate in this way, then it is necessary to consider whether it takes effect as a promissory estoppel.

The modern form of the doctrine of promissory estoppel is derived from the judgment of Denning J (as he then was) in *Central London Property Trust v High Trees House* (1947). It states that where a promise is made which varies existing contractual obligations between the parties, and that promise is intended to be binding, intended to be acted upon, and is in fact acted upon, then it will be binding insofar as its terms properly apply. There are two principal limitations on this. First, the promissory estoppel cannot be used to found a cause of action (it can only be used as a shield not a sword: *Combe v Combe* (1951)). Secondly, it must be inequitable to allow the promisor to go back on the promise (*D & C Builders v Rees* (1965); *The Post Chaser* (1981)).

There seems to be no reason here why Armadillo's promise to take the smaller deliveries should not be regarded as giving rise to a promissory estoppel.

We now need to turn to the second change in the contract. After five weeks, Armadillo ask Movit to revert to 150 rolls a week, and agree to pay £5,000 extra. This is the promise which Movit now wish to enforce. To do so, they will need to show some consideration for Armadillo's promise of the extra money. Armadillo will no doubt claim that, far from providing consideration, Movit were only doing what they were contractually obliged to do. Three possibilities need to be considered.

First, if the original change was a binding contractual variation, Armadillo will have no defence to Movit's claim. Movit would then have a contractual right to continue to deliver 100 rolls per week. Their surrender of that right would clearly be good consideration for the promise to pay the extra £5,000.

Secondly, if the first change was not a binding variation but a promise enforceable under the doctrine of promissory estoppel, Movit might argue that in not relying on the promissory estoppel they were again providing good consideration for the promise to pay £5,000. The problem with this is that promissory estoppel is often only suspensory in its effect (*High Trees* (1947), *Tool Metal Manufacturing Co Ltd v Tungsten Electric Co Ltd* (1955)). In other words, Armadillo might well be entitled to bring the promissory estoppel to an end by giving notice (as in *Tool Metal v Tungsten*). What is appropriate and reasonable notice will be a question of fact in each case. Here, given the relatively short length of the entire contract, very little notice might be required. This would make it more difficult for Movit to argue that the consideration for the promise of £5,000 was the waiver of their right to insist on notice of the termination of the promise to accept 100 rolls per week.

A further difficulty with Movit's reliance on promissory estoppel might appear to arise from the fact that they would be the claimants in the action to recover the £5,000. As we have seen, promissory estoppel can only be used as a shield and not a sword. But in fact Movit's claim would not be based on the promissory estoppel. The basis of the *claim* would be Armadillo's promise, and promissory estoppel would only be used to resist Armadillo's *defence* that the terms of the original contract were still binding.[1]

The third possibility arises if neither of the first two arguments succeeds. Is there any possibility for Movit still to be able to succeed in an argument that the promise of £5,000 is enforceable? There are two cases which must be considered here – *Stilk v Myrick* (1809) and *Williams v Roffey* (1990).

In *Stilk v Myrick*, some members of the crew of a ship deserted part way through a voyage. The captain promised the remaining crew extra money if they got the ship home safely. When they arrived back, however, the shipowners refused to pay. The crew's action to recover the additional payment failed, because it was said that they provided no consideration. They were already contractually bound to get the ship home safely, and performing this existing contract could not amount to consideration for a new promise from the same promisor.[2] This was taken to establish the general rule that existing contractual obligations owed to the promisor could not be good consideration. This would clearly be fatal to any claim by Movit outside the first two possibilities noted above. In *Williams v Roffey*, however, the Court of Appeal seemed to weaken, if not destroy, the *Stilk v Myrick* principle. The main contractors on a contract for the refurbishment of a block of flats promised one of the sub-contractors, who were on the point of abandoning the contract through financial pressures, extra money if they continued with the contract. When the sub-contractors sued to recover some of these promised payments, the defendants, the main contractors, resisted on the basis that no consideration had been provided. The Court of Appeal, however, said that there was consideration in that it was to the benefit of the defendants that the contract should continue. They would not then have the trouble and expense of finding others to complete the work. They would also avoid having to make payments under the main contract in relation to delay in completion.

The case shows a much wider approach to consideration than that in *Stilk v Myrick*. Movit might well be able to argue on similar lines that it was to Armadillo's benefit that Movit should go back to 150 rolls per week, and that if they had not done so Armadillo might have had to try to obtain additional transport from elsewhere. Since, in this case, as in *Williams v Roffey*, the initiative for the increased payment came from the promisor, and was not in any way the result of pressure from the promisee, there would be no reason not to hold the promisor to it.

In conclusion, then, Movit's possibility of recovering the £5,000 will depend on their being able to show consideration for the promise to pay it. This they might do by arguing: (a) that the initial change was a binding variation; or (b) that their relinquishing of promissory estoppel rights provided consideration; or (c) that the benefits to Armadillo in continuing the contract at 150 rolls per week provided consideration, on the basis of the approach taken in *Williams v Roffey*. Of these three, it is submitted that (b) and (c) are the arguments most likely to succeed.[3]

Notes

1   The point that promissory estoppel may be available to a claimant in some situations is discussed further in Treitel, *The Law of Contract*, 10th edn, 1999, p 107; see also Stone, *The Modern Law of Contract*, 5th edn, 2002, p 100.

2   The true basis for the decision in *Stilk v Myrick* is unclear. One of the reports of the case suggests that it was public policy (that is, the need to avoid crews holding their captain to ransom) rather than the doctrine of consideration which decided the case. Nevertheless, it has long been taken as authority for the proposition stated here.

3   Note that Movit may need to rely on *Foakes v Beer* (1884) as regards their action for the £5,000, having accepted the £20,000. Armadillo might resist on the basis of promissory estoppel, but it is submitted that the case is analogous to *D & C Builders v Rees*, and so they would be unlikely to succeed with this argument.

Question 10

Sarah is going abroad for three months. She asks Laura, who is a police officer and who lives in the same street, to keep an eye on her house for her while she is away. Sarah says that she will pay Laura £100 for doing this when she returns.

Sarah has an expensive art magazine delivered fortnightly. She arranges with the paperboy, Kevin, that while she is away he will post this through the letter box in the back door, rather than leaving it in the front porch which lets in the rain. She pays him £10 to do this.

On her return from abroad, Sarah finds that Kevin has left the magazines in the front porch, and that half the copies have been badly damaged by rain. It will cost Sarah £25 to replace them.

Laura asks Sarah for her £100. Sarah explains that she is overdrawn at the bank and is short of money. She does, however, have £80 in traveller's cheques. She offers these to Laura, saying 'I'm afraid you are not going to get any more out of me'. Laura accepts the traveller's cheques, but on discovering the following week that Sarah has just taken a very well paid job, now wishes to recover the additional £20.

Advise Sarah.

Answer plan

This problem focuses on the issue of the circumstances in which the promise to perform, or the performance of, an existing obligation can amount to good consideration. The question of intention to create legal relations should also receive at least brief discussion. The three potential contracts, or variations of contract, must be considered in turn.

Laura – the initial arrangement with Laura is in the form of a contract – 'you look after my house, and I will pay you £100'. The only problem is that Laura, as a police officer, may be said to be under a public duty to do this already. The case of *Glasbrook v Glamorgan CC* (1925) will need consideration, and the extent to which Laura can be said to be doing more than her obligations as a police officer require of her.

Traveller's cheques – the answer to this part of the problem will depend in part on whether the initial arrangement with Laura is contractual. Assuming that it is, then the question is whether it can be discharged by the payment of £80 in traveller's cheques in place of £100 cash. *Pinnel's Case* (1602), *Foakes v Beer* (1884) and *D & C Builders v Rees* (1966) will all need discussion. The questions will be whether the cheques can be considered as something different from cash, and whether the doctrine of promissory estoppel affects this type of situation.

Kevin – the agreement with Kevin is also potentially contractual. It may be argued, however, that Kevin provides no consideration, because he is doing no more than he is already bound to do under his contract with the newsagent. *Shadwell v Shadwell* (1860), *The Eurymedon* (1975) and *Pao On v Lau Yiu Long* (1979) are the relevant authorities here.

Answer

The arrangements which Sarah has made with Laura and Kevin raise the issue of what amounts to good consideration, so as to create a contractual obligation. There is also the question of whether there is an intention to create legal relations. Finally, the offer of the traveller's cheques in payment of a debt requires investigation of the rules relating to part payment of debts.

Looking first at the question of intention to create legal relations, the rules are that in a 'domestic' agreement there is a presumption against such an intention (*Balfour v Balfour* (1919)), whereas in 'commercial' agreements there is a strong presumption the other way (*Edwards v Skyways* (1964)). The problem is identifying the category into which the arrangements in this problem should fall. As regards Laura, the fact that Sarah is promising to pay as much as £100 suggests that this is something more than an informal social transaction. Similarly, as regards Kevin, he is already engaged in paid work connected with the delivery of papers and magazines to Sarah. It is submitted, therefore, that both arrangements should be regarded as 'commercial' and therefore presumed to be intended to be legally binding. There is nothing in the facts which would suggest that this presumption should be rebutted, and so the advice to Sarah should be that she has made binding contracts with Laura and Kevin, unless they fail on the issue of consideration.

It should also be noted that we are not told Kevin's age. If he is under 18, and therefore a minor, it is likely that any contract will be unenforceable against him. As no mention is made of his age, however, it will be assumed that he is over 18 and, therefore, has full contractual capacity.

We now turn to the issue of consideration. Sarah has made an arrangement for Laura to keep an eye on her house while she is away. In return, Sarah has promised £100. The question is whether Laura's promise to keep an eye on the house is good consideration for Sarah's promise of payment. There would be no doubt that it is, were it not for the fact that Laura is a police officer. It may be argued that, as such, she already has a public duty to 'keep an eye on' other people's property, and that in doing this for Sarah she is therefore not providing consideration. In *Collins v Godefroy* (1831), it was held that a promise to pay a witness for attending a trial was unenforceable because the witness provided no consideration. Attending to give evidence was a public duty, and could not form consideration for a private contract. In *Glasbrook v Glamorgan CC* (1925), however, an exception to this was noted. The owners of a mine, where there was a strike taking place, sought police presence to guard the mine. The police were prepared to send a mobile force, but the owners insisted that the police should be billeted on the premises. They promised to pay for this, but later reneged on this promise, arguing that it was unenforceable. They claimed that the police provided no consideration, because it was their public duty to keep the peace. The court rejected this. The police, by providing the protection beyond what they thought was necessary, had exceeded their public duty. By doing more than was required, they had provided good consideration.[1]

As between Laura and Sarah, therefore, the question is whether Laura has exceeded her public duty. The answer would almost certainly be 'yes'. Although police officers do have a general duty to prevent crime, this does not extend to keeping an eye on particular properties. Laura, by agreeing to do this for Sarah, has gone beyond her normal public duty, and has therefore made a binding contract. The only doubt about this would arise if it was felt that it was contrary to public policy to allow police officers to make private contracts of this kind. It could be argued that this, rather than the strict requirements of consideration, is the true reason why agreements to perform a public duty are unenforceable.[2] On the authority of the *Glasbrook* case, however, and the fact that Laura is going beyond her normal duties, it is suggested that the courts would regard this as an enforceable contract.

This answer affects the position as regards Sarah's offer of the traveller's cheques. Clearly, if the original arrangement with Laura was not a binding contract, any payment by Sarah is *ex gratia* rather than contractual, and so Laura would have no legal claim to the extra £20. If, however, as we have concluded, there was a contract, we must consider the effect of Sarah's part payment. The starting point is *Pinnel's Case* (1602). This suggested that payment of less than the amount owed on the due date could not be good consideration, although the acceptance by the creditor of early payment of a lesser amount, or a chattel (no matter what the value) instead of cash, would be sufficient. This was confirmed by the House of Lords in *Foakes v Beer* (1884). The question then is whether the traveller's cheques, which have a cash value less than the debt, can be regarded as something different from cash, and thus sufficient to discharge the debt.

A case that is relevant in this context is *D & C Builders v Rees* (1966). The plaintiffs were owed money for building work. Being desperate for cash, they accepted a cheque for less than was owed from the defendants, agreeing that this was in satisfaction of the debt. They later sued for the balance and were allowed to recover. The Court of Appeal had to consider whether payment by cheque was different from cash payment. There were old authorities that suggested that this was so.[3] The Court of Appeal were unable to see that there was any such distinction, and overruled the earlier cases. They could not, however, overrule *Sibree v Tripp* (1846), a case that said that a promissory note was sufficiently different from cash to amount to good consideration, because it was a decision of a court of equivalent authority.[4] They therefore ruled that a cheque was distinguishable in law from a promissory note. This was because a cheque was only conditional payment, in that the debt was not discharged until the cheque was honoured, whereas the promissory note was unconditional, and discharged the debt immediately. The question here, then, is whether the traveller's cheques should be regarded as more like cash, or a promissory note, or indeed goods. There is no direct authority, but it is submitted that since the traveller's cheques are only exchangeable for their face value in cash, or the equivalent in goods or services, there are no grounds for treating them as anything other than cash. They will not, therefore, provide good consideration for Laura's promise to accept them as discharging Sarah's debt.

Can Sarah argue that she is nevertheless protected by promissory estoppel, as derived from the case of *Central London Property Trust v High Trees House* (1947)? In other words, can she claim that, whether or not there was consideration, Laura should not be allowed to go back on her promise to accept the lesser amount? The relevant authority is again *D & C Builders v Rees*. It was accepted by Lord Denning in this case that promissory estoppel could apply to single debts, as well as to ongoing payments, as in *High Trees*.[5] He emphasised, however, that promissory estoppel is an equitable doctrine, and on the facts the promisees had not acted equitably. Here, it may well be the case that, since Sarah now has a good job, and it is only a week since the £80 was paid, there is nothing inequitable in allowing Laura to go back on her promise and claim the additional £20 that she is owed.[6]

Finally, it should be noted that, in *Re Selectmove* (1995), the Court of Appeal refused to apply the more flexible approach to variation of contracts taken in *Williams v Roffey* (1990) to the situation of the remission of a debt, and re-affirmed *Foakes v Beer*.

As far as her relationship with Laura is concerned, therefore, the advice to Sarah is that she is probably obliged to pay the additional £20.

Turning to the agreement with Kevin, Sarah will presumably wish to recover the £10 which she paid him, plus £25 to cover the cost of replacing her magazines. To do this she will need to show that there was a binding contract between them as to the arrangement for putting the magazines through the back door. Kevin may object that he was under an existing contractual obligation with the newsagent for which he works to deliver the magazines to Sarah, and that therefore there is no consideration for her promise of payment. Sarah has two possible answers to this. The first is to say that, in the same way as in the agreement with Laura, Kevin did in fact promise to do more than his existing duty. The agreement was not simply to deliver the magazines; her arrangement with him required them to be delivered to a particular place, and so went beyond his normal obligation. Even if this was not the case, however, Sarah would probably still be able to succeed. The question of existing contractual duties owed to a third party was considered in *Shadwell v Shadwell* (1860), where getting married was held to be good consideration for a promise of an allowance from the plaintiff's uncle, despite the fact that the plaintiff was already legally bound to go through with the marriage ceremony.[7] This, therefore, established the principle that the same promise or act could be good consideration for more than one contract. More recently, and in a commercial context, the Privy Council in *Pao On v Lau Yiu Long* (1979) accepted the point as not being in dispute, relying on the earlier decision of the same court in *The Eurymedon* (1975).[8]

It seems, then, that Sarah will be able to establish a binding contract with Kevin (providing he is over 18) and, therefore, will be able to recover damages from him for his breach of their agreement.

Notes

1   See also, as regards the obligation to pay for policing, s 25(1) of the Police Act 1996 and *Harris v Sheffield United FC Ltd* (1987).

2   See, for example, Stone, *The Modern Law of Contract*, 5th edn, 2002, pp 83–84.

3   That is, *Goddard v O'Brien* (1882).

4   That is, the Exchequer Chamber.

5   There is, however, no reported place where it has been so applied.

6   Cf also *The Post Chaser* (1981), where the short space of time between a promise and its withdrawal contributed to a decision that it was not inequitable to refuse to apply promissory estoppel.

7   Note that, at the time, a promise of marriage was a legally binding contract.

8   The court here relied in turn on *Scotson v Pegg* (1861).

CHAPTER 3

PRIVITY

Introduction

The doctrine of privity of contract is related to the issues of the creation of contractual obligations looked at in Chapters 1 and 2, in that it is concerned with the question of who has rights and liabilities under a contract. It is sometimes argued that some aspects of the doctrine are just another way of stating the rule that consideration must move from the promisee, and so questions may sometimes involve looking at both consideration and privity issues. More commonly, in the past, questions have tended to relate to the two sides of the basic privity doctrine, that is:

• that a person cannot sue on a contract made for their benefit if they were not a party to it; and

• that a person cannot have obligations imposed on them by a contract to which they are not a party.

The first part of the doctrine, relating to the conferring of benefits, was the subject of major reform in the Contracts (Rights of Third Parties) Act 1999. This Act was based on the recommendations of the Law Commission Report No 242, *Privity of Contract: Contracts for the Benefit of Third Parties* (Cmnd 3329), and applies to contracts made on or after 11 May 2000. Although the old law may still be applicable to some contracts, most questions on privity will now require you to show an understanding of the new legislation. You may well be asked, however, whether the reform is satisfactory, and this will also require knowledge of the previous law. All the questions and answers in this chapter touch on one or more aspects of the new legislation.

It is relatively unusual to find a question which deals solely with the second aspect of the privity doctrine – the imposition of obligations. Generally, questions on this area will be linked with one on the conferring of benefits, very often in the form of a two part question. It is important, therefore, to have a good grasp of the whole privity area if attempting questions on this topic.

Two privity related issues which are not dealt with in detail in this chapter, but which you may need to take account of, depending on the details of the syllabus for your course, are:

• exemption clauses and privity (see Question 22 in Chapter 6 for some discussion of this); and

- privity and the tort of negligence (for example, the implications of the case of *Junior Books v Veitchi*).

The reasons for not looking at the second issue in this book are first that, although the area is discussed in some of the textbooks (for example, Treitel, *The Law of Contract*, 10th edn, pp 560–70), it is not an issue that appears with any frequency on exam papers; and, secondly, that the recent trend of House of Lords decisions on negligence has meant that the *Junior Books* line of argument is of much less significance than at one time it appeared likely to be.

Checklist

You should be familiar with the following areas:

- The basic doctrine of privity, derived from *Tweddle v Atkinson*, *Dunlop v Selfridge* and *Beswick v Beswick*.
- The two aspects of the doctrine, relating to the conferring of benefits, and the imposition of obligations, on a third party.
- The major reform to the first part of the doctrine contained in the Contracts (Rights of Third Parties) Act 1999.
- The devices previously used to avoid the first part of the doctrine: for example, trusts, agency and collateral contracts.
- The more limited exceptions to the second part of the doctrine: for example, restrictive covenants (*Tulk v Moxhay*), and their application in the shipping cases, and the use of tortious remedies, as in *Lumley v Gye*.
- The Law Commission's proposals in Report No 242, *Privity of Contract: Contracts for the Benefit of Third Parties*.

Question 11

Answer both parts.

(a) Outline the effects of the Contracts (Rights of Third Parties) Act 1999. To what extent does this Act mean that the devices previously used to confer benefits on a third party are no longer needed?

(b) In January, Peter sells his Rolls Royce to David for £30,000. One of the terms of the contract is that Peter will have the use of the car for the first week of August, when it will be used for his daughter's wedding and subsequent honeymoon.

In March, David sells the car to Jane. When Peter hears of this, he seeks your advice as to whether he will be entitled to the use of the car in August, as originally planned.

Advise Peter.

Answer plan

As is common with questions on privity, the two parts of this question relate to the two aspects of the doctrine. Part (a) is concerned with the situations where a third party can sue to obtain the benefit of a contract, whereas in Part (b) the focus is on the extent to which a person can be bound by the terms of a contract to which he or she is not a party.

In Part (a), the main body of the answer will be concerned with the provisions of the 1999 Act. As to the second part of (a), there is no need to go into detail on the 'devices previously used'. Some indication of them will be needed, but attention should be concentrated on the issue of the extent to which they will still be available or necessary now that the 1999 Act is in force.

In Part (b), the issues will be:

• whether the approach in *Tulk v Moxhay* (1848) can apply to this type of situation; and

• if not, whether a tortious remedy may be available.

Answer

Part (a)

The doctrine of privity of contract says that only a party to the contract can sue on it. This principle was recognised in *Tweddle v Atkinson* (1861), and confirmed by the House of Lords in *Dunlop v Selfridge* (1915), and again in *Beswick v Beswick* (1968).

The fact that as a result of this doctrine a third party who was intended to benefit from it could not sue to recover the benefit was the subject of much criticism. The Law Commission recommended in 1996 that the law should be reformed,[1] and this was put into effect by the Contracts (Rights of Third Parties) Act 1999.

As recommended by the Law Commission, the Act gives a third party the right to enforce a benefit where the parties to the contract intended to give him an enforceable legal obligation. The mere fact that a contract may incidentally benefit a third party is not enough; there must have been an intention to create a legal right. This objective is achieved by s 1 of the Act. It identifies two situations where a third party will be held to have an enforceable right. The first, and most straightforward, is where the contract expressly states that such a right is given. The second arises where a term in the contract purports to confer a benefit on the third party, but does not explicitly say that this is to be legally enforceable. The effect of s 1 is to say that such a benefit *will* be legally enforceable unless 'on a proper construction of the contract' it appears that it was not the parties' intention that the benefit should be enforceable by the third party.[2] In other words, wherever the contract purports to confer a benefit there is a rebuttable presumption of enforceability. If the parties do not wish such a presumption to be given effect, then the easiest way is to say so in the contract. In the absence of such a statement, the courts will presumably apply a test based on what reasonable contracting parties would be taken to have intended by the term in question. Where it is found that there is an intention to give a legally enforceable right, the third party will be able to enforce the beneficial term of the contract in exactly the same way as a party to the contract.

There is no need for the third party beneficiary to be in existence at the time of the contract, provided that there is adequate identification in it. Unborn children, future spouses and unincorporated companies can all be given enforceable rights in this way.

In general, the parties to a contract can negotiate changes at any time. How does this apply to a situation where a contract gives a third party a legally enforceable right? Does the third party have to agree to any change? The Act deals with this situation in s 2. This allows the contracting parties to override any third party rights by including a clause saying that any consent to a change is not required, or setting out its own procedures for such consent. In the absence of such a clause, however, s 2 provides that the parties to the contract will lose the right to withdraw the benefit promised to the third party if one of three conditions is satisfied. The first is that the third party has communicated to the promisor his or her assent to the term. The second is where the third party has relied on the term and the promisor is aware of this. The third is where the third party has relied on the term and the promisor could reasonably be expected to have foreseen this. Reliance does not have to be *detrimental* reliance, as long as the third party has acted on the promise. Relying on the promise of a sum of money by buying goods which have subsequently doubled in value would be sufficient for these purposes.

Section 3 of the Act deals with the availability of defences. Subject to any specific provisions to the contrary in the contract, the promisor will be able to raise against the third party any defences which would have been available against the other party to the contract (the 'promisee'). So, if the promisee has induced the contract by undue influence or misrepresentation, the promisor will be able to use that as a defence to any action by the third party. Equally, if the third party has acted wrongly, or owes money to the promisor from previous dealings, these matters can be used by the promisor in response to any action by the third party.

The right of the promisee, as opposed to the third party, to enforce the promise (as happened, for example, in *Beswick v Beswick* (1968))[3] is preserved by s 4. If the promisee has succeeded in an action against the promisor, however, this must be taken into account in any subsequent action by the third party, so that the promisor is not faced with double liability.

To what extent does the 1999 Act mean that devices previously used to avoid the doctrine will no longer be needed? The courts have in the past used, for example, trusts (*Re Flavell* (1883)), agency (*The Eurymedon* (1975)) and collateral contracts (*Shanklin Pier v Detel Products* (1951)) as ways of giving third parties rights. They have also recognised a limited scope for the promisee to recover damages on behalf of a third party (*Jackson v Horizon Holidays* (1975); *Linden Gardens v Lenesta Sludge Disposals* (1993)).[4] Section 7 of the Act says that all rights or remedies existing apart from the Act are preserved, so these approaches could still be used if necessary. Moreover, there are certain contracts which are not covered by the Act. These include contracts on a bill of exchange or other negotiable instrument, contracts of employment (as against the employee) and certain contracts of international carriage. In relation to the last category, the exception does not apply to exclusion clauses. Otherwise, where the Act does not, by virtue of s 7, apply, then there is still scope for using other means of giving rights to third parties.

In general, however, it is clear that the 1999 Act now constitutes the most important exception to the traditional doctrine of privity insofar as the conferring of benefits on third parties is concerned.

Part (b)

This part of the question is concerned with the situation where a person disposes of property, but wishes to maintain some control over it. It is a well established principle in land law that this can be done by means of restrictive covenants: *Tulk v Moxhay* (1848). The question arises as to whether a similar principle can be applied to property other than land. The answer appeared to be 'yes' in certain shipping cases, such as *Lord Strathcona SS Co Ltd v Dominion Coal* (1926).[5] The Privy Council held in this case that a person who had a time charter of a ship could enforce it against a new purchaser who had notice of it. The decision was, however, strongly criticised in *Port Line v Ben Line* (1958), and it seems that this line of argument will not now be followed. This does not mean, however, that Peter is necessarily without any remedy.

In certain situations, tortious remedies can be used to impose contractual obligations indirectly on third parties. The case of *Lumley v Gye* (1853) is one of the leading authorities. Here, the defendant, who encouraged an opera singer to break an exclusive contract to sing for the plaintiff, was held liable for the tort of wrongful interference with contractual rights.[6] This remedy has also been held to be available where goods are sold subject to a restriction on their disposal. In *BMTA v Salvadori* (1949), the purchaser of a new car agreed not to sell it for a year without first offering it to the plaintiff. The defendant bought the car with knowledge of this restriction, and was again held liable in tort.

Will this tortious remedy be of any use to Peter? The situation is not identical to those we have considered so far, but it is clear that there is a continuing contractual obligation as between Peter and David as to the use of the car in August. If it is unavailable, David will be in breach of contract. A remedy in damages is, however, unlikely to be satisfactory to Peter. He presumably wishes to have this particular car available for his daughter's wedding. What he will wish to do is to be able to obtain an injunction to restrain Jane from acting in a way which will infringe his contractual rights against David. On the basis of the cases noted above, he may be able to do this if he can show that when Jane bought the car from David she was aware of Peter's contractual claim to its use in August. If she was, then to act in a way which prevents Peter having access to the car will amount to the tort of wrongful interference with Peter's contractual rights, and he may well be able to obtain an injunction to prevent her from so doing.

A final possibility, suggested by the case of *Swiss Bank Corp v Lloyds Bank* (1979), is that Peter may have a remedy in equity if, as is quite likely, his contract with David is specifically enforceable. It was suggested in this case that in such a situation there was an equitable interest in the property which was the subject of the contract, as a result of the specifically enforceable obligation relating to it. This interest would operate against third parties who acquired the property, unless they did so in good faith, and without notice of the restriction on its use.[7] Again, to have a remedy, Peter would have to show notice on the part of Jane, although here it could be constructive notice, whereas for the tortious remedy it has to be actual notice.

It seems, then, that Peter has some chance of successfully gaining access to the car, but he will need to establish that Jane had notice, possibly constructive, preferably actual, of the restriction on its use.

Notes

1   Law Commission Report No 242, *Privity of Contract: Contracts for the Benefit of Third Parties* (Cmnd 3329).

2   See s 1(2).

3   See, for example, Stone, *The Modern Law of Contract*, 5th edn, 2002, p 132.

4   All these areas are discussed fully in Stone, *The Modern Law of Contract*, 5th edn, 2002, pp 139–49.

5   See also *De Mattos v Gibson* (1858).

6   The plaintiff was unable to get an order for specific performance against the singer herself: *Lumley v Wagner* (1852). See further on this, Chapter 12 below.

7   The principle which had been relied on by the judge at first instance in the *Swiss Bank* case was approved on appeal by the House of Lords, although they ruled that on the facts it did not apply, because there was no specifically enforceable obligation.

Question 12

In *Lloyd's v Harper* (1880), Lush LJ said: 'I consider it to be an established law that where a contract is made with A for the benefit of B, A can sue on the contract for the benefit of B, and recover all that B could have recovered if the contract had been made with B himself.'

To what extent does English law now allow a claimant suing on a contract to recover for losses suffered by a third party?

Answer plan

This essay is concerned with an issue which has been of considerable controversy, at least since 1975. To answer it, you will need to deal with:

- the attempt by Lord Denning in *Jackson v Horizon Holidays* (1975) to use the quote from Lush LJ as establishing a general right to recover damages for a third party;
- the disapproval of this approach by the House of Lords in *Woodar Investment Development Ltd v Wimpey Construction (UK) Ltd* (1980), and the consequent limitation of the scope of the *Jackson* decision;
- the renewed life given to recovering damages for a third party in a commercial context by *Linden Gardens Ltd v Lenesta Sludge Disposals Ltd* (1993);
- the review of the concept by the House of Lords in *Alfred McAlpine Construction Ltd v Panatown Ltd* (2000).

Note that the issue being dealt with here – A, the contracting party, recovering damages for the loss of B, a third party – is not directly dealt with by the Contracts (Rights of Third Parties) Act 1999; but its enactment may mean that there is less need to seek to rely on such an action in the future.

Answer

Generally speaking, a party to a contract who sues the other party can only recover for his or her own losses. The doctrine of privity has operated to discourage the award of damages for losses suffered by anyone other than a party to the contract. Nevertheless, the law has since at least 1975 recognised some exceptions to this general principle. The exact scope of those exceptions is still a matter of some uncertainty, despite recent reconsideration of the area by the House of Lords.

The starting point for the discussion of the modern law on this area is the case of *Jackson v Horizon Holidays* (1975). In this case, there had been a disastrous family holiday, and the father, who booked it, was suing the travel company. The Court of Appeal allowed the father to recover damages in respect of the losses suffered by the rest of the family. In doing so, Lord Denning relied heavily on the above quote from Lush LJ in *Lloyd's v Harper* (1880). He felt that where one person made a contract which was clearly intended to benefit others – as with a holiday, or a meal in a restaurant – the contracting party should be able to recover damages reflecting the loss of the other intended beneficiaries. The successful claimant would then be in a position to compensate the others from the damages recovered. Other members of the Court of Appeal, in particular James LJ, were more circumspect. He accepted that the father in *Jackson* was entitled to the enhanced level of damages awarded at first instance. He felt, however, that this could be justified on the basis that the discomfort suffered by the rest of the Jackson family was part of the father's loss. On this analysis, the loss was Mr Jackson's, and he would be under no obligation to compensate the rest of the family from the damages which he received.

The decision in *Jackson* was reconsidered by the House of Lords in *Woodar Investment Development Ltd v Wimpey Construction (UK) Ltd* (1980). This was a different type of contract to that in *Jackson*, in that it was a commercial construction transaction. Under it, Wimpey had agreed to pay £150,000 to a third party, Transworld, on completion of the contract with Woodar. The question before the court was whether Woodar, in an action against Wimpey for breach of contract, could recover the £150,000 promised to Transworld.[1] Reliance was placed on the statement by Lord Denning in *Jackson v Horizon Holidays* as supporting the possibility of such recovery. The House of Lords, however, held that Woodar should not be able to succeed in such an action.[2] In coming to this conclusion, the Lords made it clear that in their view Lord Denning had made improper use of the quotation from Lush LJ, in that he had taken it out of context. As Lord Russell pointed out, Lush LJ's statement was clearly made in the context of a fiduciary relationship between A and B, such as principal and agent. Where A (as agent) contracts with C for the benefit of B (A's principal), there is no particular difficulty in recognising that A may sue on behalf of B.[3] This falls far short, however, of recognising a general right to recover losses suffered by a third party to the contract.

Despite these criticisms of Lord Denning, the House of Lords in *Woodar v Wimpey* did not go so far as to say that *Jackson v Horizon* was wrongly decided. They felt that the decision could be upheld, either on the basis suggested by James LJ, that the discomfort of the rest of the family was part of the father's loss, or that there were some special situations which called for special treatment. These cases were situations where one person acts on behalf of a group by, for example, ordering a meal in a restaurant, or hiring a taxi for the group. In such situations it was obvious that a breach of contract would affect all members of the group adversely. An issue which was left open, however, was whether a claimant who successfully obtained damages on this basis would be obliged to pass on the compensation to the other members of the group. Lord Denning clearly thought that he or she would, but the award of damages in *Jackson* did not impose any obligation of this kind. The position was therefore unclear, and remained so after *Woodar v Wimpey*.

There the matter rested for the next 13 years, until the House of Lords again returned to the issue in *Linden Gardens Ltd v Lenesta Sludge Disposals Ltd* (1993). This concerned a building contract where the original employer had assigned its interests to a third party, but in such a way that the third party gained no legal right to sue on the contract. The original employer therefore sued the contractor for defects in the work. It was argued that, since these defects had occurred after the assignment of the employer's interests, it had suffered no loss. It would have appeared that the application of *Woodar v Wimpey* would support the defendant's arguments. The House of Lords, however, drew an analogy with cases in shipping law, where it is clearly established that the shipper of goods can sue on the shipping contract in relation to the loss of goods, even if at the time the ownership of the goods has been transferred to a third party. They felt that this principle could be applied to the case before them. The contractor knew that the employer was not going to occupy the premises itself and could therefore foresee that defects in the work would be likely to adversely affect whoever acquired the premises. On that basis, the case fell within one of the exceptions to the general rule that recovery of losses suffered by a third party is not possible.

There have been two subsequent cases in which this issue has been further discussed. The first was *Darlington BC v Wiltshire Northern Ltd* (1995), another building contract case, where the Court of Appeal held that the fact that there was no transfer of the property concerned did not prevent the application of the approach taken in *Linden Gardens*. It was necessary to provide a remedy to prevent an otherwise meritorious claim for defective work falling down the 'black hole', with neither the employer nor the third party being able to recover from the contractor.

The second case is *Alfred McAlpine Construction Ltd v Panatown Ltd* (2000). Once again, this concerned a major construction contract. The employer, P, had engaged the contractor, AM, to build premises on land owned by a third party, U. In addition to the contract between P and AM, there was at the same time executed between AM and U a 'Duty of Care Deed' (DCD). This gave U an action against AM for negligent performance of the construction contract, but was not identical to the obligations under the main contract (for example, it contained no provision for arbitration). When defective performance took place, P sued AM. AM's defence was that P had suffered no loss, and so could not recover. The case was different from the situations in *Linden Gardens v Lenesta* and *Darlington v Wiltshire* in that the third party, U, here had an independent cause of action under the DCD. There was therefore no question of defective performance falling down the 'black hole' referred to in the *Darlington* case.

P's response to this was to rely on a broader ground for recovery put forward by Lord Griffiths in *Linden Gardens*. This was based on the view that in this type of situation the employer suffers a loss, for which substantial damages can be recovered, simply because proper performance has not been supplied. The question of ownership of the property concerned is irrelevant. An analogy was drawn with a husband who contracts for work to be done repairing the roof of a house which, in fact, belongs to his wife. There should be no doubt that, in the event of defective performance, the husband can sue the contractor and recover substantial damages.

The majority of the House of Lords in *Alfred McAlpine Construction Ltd v Panatown Ltd* was not, however, prepared to follow Lord Griffiths' lead. Accepting the argument put forward by AM, they held that the existence of the DCD was fatal to P's claim. Thus, an employer in this type of situation is only able to recover substantial damages where the property in question belongs to a third party, if that third party has no independent right of action against the contractor. The existence of the Contracts (Rights of Third Parties) Act 1999, of course, means that such an independent action is now far more likely to arise.

One issue which is left unresolved is the question of whether, if damages are recovered for losses in relation to property owned by a third party, the successful claimant is obliged to pass this on to the third party. There are comments in all the cases which point in one direction or the other, but no clear statement of the position. This may well fall to be the subject of further litigation.

Overall then, the position remains that in general a contracting party cannot sue to recover damages in relation to losses suffered by a third party. There are, however, some very important exceptions to this. First, as in *Jackson v Horizon Holidays*, it may be possible to recover where a person is contracting for a group, and it is clear that all members of the group will suffer if there is defective performance. Secondly, there is the situation involving carriage of goods, where the shipper of the goods may recover even though the goods have been transferred to a third party. Finally, there are the situations recognised in the three recent cases concerned with construction contracts. Here, the employer of a contractor can sue and recover substantial damages for defective performance, even if that performance relates to property which is not owned by the contractor. This is subject to the limitation that the possibility of such recovery will disappear if the third party has an independent cause of action.

Notes

1   Note that, under the Contracts (Rights of Third Parties) Act 1999, it might well be possible for the third party in a situation like this to sue directly for the recovery of the promised benefit.

2   In fact, the House of Lords held that there was no breach of contract, so the comments on the privity issue relating to damages are strictly *obiter*.

3   For further consideration of the rules relating to agency, see Chapter 14 and Stone, *The Modern Law of Contract*, 5th edn, 2002, Chapter 6.

Question 13

The Seven Dwarves live in a row of cottages in Dingley Dell. Snow White lives next door. Because the cottages are in a valley, they have very poor television reception. This could be improved if a television aerial could be sited at the top of the hill, on land owned by Cruella, and then linked to the cottages. Snow White visits Cruella, and persuades her to erect an aerial at the top of the hill. Cruella demands an immediate payment of £1,000 to cover the cost of this, and as the price of her agreement. Snow White and Cruella enter into a written contract to this effect, and Snow White pays the £1,000. Snow White then collects £125 from each of the Dwarves. Unfortunately, before work can begin on the construction of the aerial, Snow White dies as a result of choking on a piece of apple. Her will names Cruella as her executrix. Cruella is now refusing to construct the aerial.

Advise the Seven Dwarves.

Would your answer be any different if Snow White had named the Seven Dwarves as her executors?

Answer plan

The issue here is whether the Seven Dwarves have any rights in relation to the contract made between Snow White and Cruella. They do not appear to be parties to this contract, even though its effect is to provide a benefit for them. The first part of the answer will need to consider whether the Dwarves can take advantage of the reform of the law of privity contained in the Contracts (Rights of Third Parties) Act 1999. The difficulty here may be in establishing that the contract identified the Dwarves as beneficiaries of the contract, and that it was intended to give them a right of action. Cruella is likely to dispute this unless the contract is clearly worded so as to favour the Dwarves.

If the 1999 Act does not apply, then other methods of avoiding the doctrine of privity should be considered (for example, trusts or agency), but none seems likely to be very helpful.

The alternative facts, placing the Dwarves in the role of executors, require consideration of the decision in *Beswick v Beswick* (1968), on the basis of which the Dwarves may be able to achieve a remedy of specific performance against Cruella.

Answer

The untimely death of Snow White has left the Seven Dwarves with a problem. She had negotiated a contract with Cruella which had the potential of benefiting them, in terms of improved television reception. Although they had paid a contribution towards this to Snow White, they were not parties to the contract, and so may have difficulty enforcing it against Cruella.

The traditional English doctrine of privity meant that only those who were parties to a contract could take action on it. Even if the agreement was clearly intended to benefit a third party, that person would not be able to enforce it. In *Tweddle v Atkinson* (1861), the plaintiff was not able to enforce an agreement made between his father and father-in-law to make a payment to him on the occasion of his marriage. The basic principle was confirmed in *Dunlop v Selfridge* (1915) and *Beswick v Beswick* (1968).

The traditional position has, however, been radically affected by the Contracts (Rights of Third Parties) Act 1999, which allows third parties in certain circumstances to enforce benefits due to them under a contract to which they are not a party. It is necessary to consider whether this will assist the Seven Dwarves in enforcing the contract against Cruella.

The main reforming provision of the 1999 Act is s 1. This allows a third party to enforce a contract in two main circumstances. First, such enforcement will be possible where the contract states that the third party is to have a legally enforceable right under it.[1] Secondly, a right of enforcement may also arise where the contract purports to confer a benefit on a third party, but without stating specifically that the third party is to be able to enforce it.[2] In this situation, it will be necessary to look at the agreement closely to determine its effect. Section 1(2) of the Act provides that a clause purporting to confer a benefit on a third party will not be enforceable by that party if it appears on a 'proper construction' of the contract that that was not the intention of the parties. In other words, where the contract purports to confer a benefit, there is a presumption that it is to be enforceable, unless a contrary intention appears from the contract. In assessing this, it is assumed that the courts will adopt an objective test, considering what intentions can reasonably be identified from considering the wording of the contract.

How does this apply to the dispute between Cruella and the Seven Dwarves? One problem is that we do not have details of the wording of the written contract entered into by Cruella and Snow White. If that contract names the Seven Dwarves and states that they are to have an enforceable right under the agreement, then there is no problem. Although under the common law the Dwarves would have had difficulty enforcing such a right, even when stated explicitly, the 1999 Act means that they will be able to take action against Cruella just as if they were parties to the original agreement.

The second possibility is that the contract is stated to be for the benefit of, for example, all the residents of Dingley Dell, but does not make it clear that such residents are to be given a right to enforce the agreement. It does not matter that the Dwarves are not mentioned by name; as long as the intended beneficiaries are sufficiently identified as, for example, the members of a particular class, then that satisfies the requirements of s 1(3) of the 1999 Act. The question will then become whether the presumption that such third parties will be able to enforce is rebutted by the rest of the contract. Again, it is not possible to answer this question without having the details of the wording of the agreement. It seems unlikely, however, that Snow White, who clearly entered into the contract intending it to be for the benefit of the Seven Dwarves, would have included wording which prevented them from being able to enforce it. The likelihood, therefore, is that in this situation, as in the first, the Dwarves will be able to take legal action to require Cruella to perform her part of the contract, or at least to pay damages for non-performance.

The third possibility is that the contract makes no mention of the Seven Dwarves, or the residents of Dingley Dell. This will make the Dwarves' position much more difficult. The Act follows the recommendation of the Law Commission that the simple fact that a third party will benefit from the performance of a contract should not in itself give a right of action under it. The example used by the Law Commission was an agreement between a highway authority and a construction company for the building of a new road. This may well benefit all those whose journeys are made easier by the existence of the new road, but it would not be correct to give them all a right of action against the construction company should the road prove to be defective, or the project delayed.[3] If, then, the contract between Cruella and Snow White makes no reference, direct or indirect, to the Seven Dwarves, then they will not be able to use the 1999 Act to take action against Cruella.

If that is the situation, are there any other ways in which the Dwarves can avoid the doctrine of privity? Of those used in the past, it does not seem likely that on the facts a trust (as in *Les Affréteurs Réunis v Walford* (1919)) or a collateral contract (as in *Shanklin Pier v Detel Products* (1951)) could be constructed so as to give a remedy. If the contract had given continuing rights over Cruella's land, then it is possible that s 56 of the Law of Property Act 1925 could be brought into play. But in *Beswick v Beswick* (1968), the House of Lords made it clear that s 56 was not relevant to contracts which were not concerned with interests in land. Here, the contract is simply for the erection of the aerial by Cruella, and does not involve any land law rights.

Another possibility might be to argue that Snow White was acting as agent for the Dwarves in making the contract with Cruella. It would not matter that she had not made this explicit to Cruella, since it is quite possible for an agent to act on behalf of an undisclosed principal (that is, the Seven Dwarves) so as to bring that person into a contractual relationship with the other party (that is, Cruella). The difficulty here is that there is no evidence that the Dwarves had delegated Snow White to negotiate with Cruella. Snow White appears to have been acting entirely independently in going to Cruella, and it is only subsequently that she seeks a contribution towards the contract from the Dwarves. The Dwarves may well have a difficulty, therefore, in basing a claim on agency.

Overall, it seems unlikely if the Dwarves do not come within the scope of the 1999 Act that they will be able to use any of the other devices to take action against Cruella. They are probably even more unlikely to succeed given that, with the passing of the 1999 Act, the courts may well be more reluctant than they have been in the past to use what have often been rather artificial devices to avoid the perceived injustice of the strict application of the doctrine of privity. Given that the parties to a contract can now avoid the doctrine by wording their agreement appropriately, there is much less incentive for the courts themselves to try to find ways around it.

Turning now to the alternative scenario, where Snow White has named the Dwarves as her executors, their position will be considerably stronger. First, of course, they may still be able to use the 1999 Act if the contract between Cruella and Snow White allows this. If this is not the case, however, they may still be able to require Cruella to go through with the agreement on the basis of the approach adopted in *Beswick v Beswick* (1968). In this case, a nephew had promised his uncle, on acquiring the uncle's business, that he would, after his uncle's death, pay an annuity to his aunt. The nephew failed to make the payments. His aunt had, however, been appointed administratrix of her late husband's estate. In that capacity, the House of Lords held that she was entitled to step into her husband's shoes, and seek an order of specific performance from her nephew. Can the same argument apply here? One of the conditions for the courts' being prepared to grant an order of specific performance is that damages would be an inadequate remedy. In *Beswick v Beswick*, this was felt to be the case because the uncle's estate would only have been entitled to nominal damages, since it had suffered no financial loss. The position is slightly different in the problem, in that Snow White was herself going to benefit from the contract with Cruella. This might suggest that her estate could recover more than nominal damages from Cruella for the breach. It might even be arguable that this is a contract of the special type recognised in *Woodar v Wimpey* (1980), where a party may be able to claim damages on behalf of others who were intended to benefit from the performance of the contract. It was suggested that this category of contracts could include holiday contracts (*Jackson v Horizon Holidays* (1975)), meals in restaurants, and hiring a taxi for a group. Could it also include a contract which has the effect of providing improved television reception for a group of people? This is possible, but, on the other hand, the benefits are not easily quantifiable in monetary terms. There is no indication of a way in which the Dwarves, by spending money in some other way, could achieve the improved reception. It is a strong possibility, then, that on applying the basic test of 'are damages an adequate remedy?', the answer would be 'no'. This would then allow the Dwarves, as executors of Snow White's estate, to obtain an order of specific performance requiring Cruella to construct the aerial, thus achieving the benefit they are seeking.

Finally, if all else fails, the Dwarves should be able to recover from Snow White's estate the £125 they each paid, on the basis of a restitutionary action.

Notes

1   Section 1(1)(a) of the Contracts (Rights of Third Parties) Act 1999.

2   Section 1(1)(b) of the Contracts (Rights of Third Parties) Act 1999.

3   This example is contained in the Law Commission Consultation Paper No 121, which preceded Report No 242 on which the 1999 Act was based.

CHAPTER 4

CAPACITY

Introduction

Capacity is considered at this point as one of the factors which is needed before an enforceable contract can be made. Alternatively, of course, the issue can be looked at from the opposite point of view, that is, incapacity can be regarded as a 'vitiating factor', which prevents a contract being enforced. Whichever approach is taken (and it really does not much matter which), the rules relating to capacity are a reflection of the fact that the law of contract recognises that in some situations people need protection from themselves, in that they may enter into agreements which are not to their benefit, because they are not capable of properly understanding the implications of what they are doing. The argument may seem a little dubious where the 'incapable' individual is an intelligent 17 year old, but the law can only operate practically by the use of broad categories and fixed borderlines.

Three principal types of incapacity are recognised in English law:

- being under 18 (a 'minor');
- being mentally incapacitated; and
- being intoxicated.

Most of the law relates to the first category, and this is the one about which questions are most commonly asked.

Checklist

You should be familiar with the following areas:

- Presumption of unenforceability against a minor.
- Meaning of 'necessaries' in the context of both goods and services: as regards goods, the provisions of the Sale of Goods Act 1979 should be noted.
- Meaning of a 'beneficial contract of service'.
- Provisions of the Minors' Contracts Act 1987.
- Principles applying to the intoxicated or mentally incapacitated: in particular, the issue of awareness of the other party as to the incapacity at the time of the contract.

Question 14

McKendrick comments that, despite the enactment of the Minors' Contracts Act 1987, 'the rules of law remain in need of further rationalisation in an effort to provide a better balance between, on the one hand, the protection of minors and, on the other hand, the interests of those who deal in all good faith with them' (*Contract Law*, 14th edn, 2000).

Do you agree?

Answer plan

The focus of the answer to this problem must of course be the changes made by the Minors' Contracts Act 1987. You should not attempt this question unless you have at least a reasonable idea of the position prior to 1987, and the reforms that the Act introduced. Simply describing the provisions of the 1987 Act will not be enough to fill a whole essay. You will need, in addition, to look more generally at the rules which protect minors, and those which protect people who deal with minors. McKendrick is clearly of the view that there is currently an 'imbalance'. You are specifically asked whether or not you agree with this. Whichever conclusion you come to (and you will not be marked down simply on the basis of the line you take) must be supported by argument.

The following approach is suggested:

- outline of rules protecting minors;
- outline of rules protecting those dealing with minors;
- outline of changes made by the Minors' Contracts Act 1987;
- discussion of possible remaining areas of 'imbalance'; and
- conclusion.

Answer

English law adopts a paternalistic approach to the question of minors' contracts (a 'minor' being any person under the age of 18). Those under the age of 18 are thought to need protection from exploitation by unscrupulous traders, so the presumption is that all contracts made by minors are unenforceable against them.[1] There are, however, a number of exceptions to this general rule. Some of these, as we shall see, however, are themselves designed for the benefit of the minor. The Minors' Contracts Act 1987 altered the rules applying to minors' contracts, with the aim and effect of improving the position of those who deal with minors. The changes were not extensive, however, and many of the rules which applied before 1987 continue to operate in the minor's favour.

The first major exception to the general rule of unenforceability relates to contracts for 'necessaries'. The reasoning here is that a total rule of unenforceability would act to the minor's disadvantage. If traders knew that any contract with a minor would involve the risk of the minor deciding not to honour it, they would be reluctant to enter into such contracts at all. As a consequence, the minor would have difficulty acquiring the basic requirements of everyday life, such as food or clothing.[2] The concept of necessaries, both goods and services, was explained in some detail in *Chapple v Cooper* (1844). It means not only things which are absolutely necessary for survival, but those which are required for a reasonable existence. Food and clothing are obviously covered, but medical assistance and education also fall into this category. Once the goods or services are of a kind which can be put in the general category of 'necessaries', there is then a further question as to whether they are appropriate to the particular minor. Whether a silk dress can count as a necessary will depend on the minor's normal standard of living. It will also depend on whether the minor is already adequately supplied with goods or services of this kind: *Nash v Inman* (1908).[3] It should be noted that this case made it clear that the trader who is ignorant of the minor's situation will not be protected. The decision is made by looking at matters entirely from the minor's point of view.

The second major category of enforceable contracts is that of 'beneficial contracts of service': in other words, employment contracts. It is recognised that the minor should be able to earn a living, but if such contracts were void or voidable, he or she might have great difficulty in finding anyone prepared to offer employment. The contract as a whole must be beneficial, however. In *De Francesco v Barnum* (1889), a very restrictive apprenticeship was held not to be binding on a girl dancer.

There are also certain contracts which are voidable, in the sense that they will be enforceable unless repudiated by the minor before attaining the age of 18, or within a reasonable time thereafter: *Edwards v Carter* (1893). The main ones are: contracts relating to an interest in land, for example, a lease; obligations of shareholding, for example, to pay the 'calls';[4] partnership agreements;[5] and marriage settlements.

From this, it can be seen that there are considerable risks in contracting with minors. The provisions of the Minors' Contracts Act 1987 (MCA) now need to be considered.

The main effect of s 1 of the MCA is to repeal the provision of the Infants Relief Act 1874, which prohibited the minor from ratifying an unenforceable contract after attaining majority. The reason for this was the wish to prevent minors from being pressurised into making enforceable an agreement which was previously unenforceable. There was an anomaly, however, in that the minor could be bound if a fresh agreement, supported by consideration, was made after majority. The change in the MCA means that once the minor has attained majority, the law recognises that the need for protection disappears, and the individual must be allowed to decide whether to accept a particular obligation or not.

The Infants Relief Act 1874 had also caused some conceptual problems by its statement that certain contracts, including contracts for goods other than necessaries,[6] should be 'absolutely void'. This clearly did not correspond to reality, in that a contract for the sale of non-necessary goods, if carried out, was regarded as effective to transfer the ownership of the goods and the money. If it had truly been 'absolutely void', then this would not have happened. Section 1 of the MCA repeals the relevant provision, so that such contracts can now have limited legal effect.[7]

Perhaps the most important provision of the MCA for the person contracting with a minor is s 3. Under the law prior to the MCA, the person who supplied non-necessary goods to a minor ran a great risk. It should be remembered that the contract is unenforceable whether the supplier knows that the other party is a minor or not. Moreover, even if the supplier knows the minor's age, ignorance of the fact that the minor is already adequately supplied with the relevant goods will not prevent the contract being unenforceable: *Nash v Inman* (1908). Under the pre-MCA law, the supplier who had supplied non-necessary goods on credit could recover nothing unless the minor had fraudulently induced the contract. In other words, the minor could retain the goods, and was not obliged to pay anything for them. Now, s 3 of the MCA allows a restitutionary remedy. It states that, where a contract is unenforceable against a defendant, or has been repudiated because the defendant is a minor, the court can order the defendant to return any property received under the contract, or other property representing it, to the claimant.[8] Thus, non-necessary goods can no longer be retained, and the minor cannot be unjustly enriched. If, however, the goods have been consumed or otherwise disposed of without being exchanged for other property, the supplier will still have no remedy.

The final provision of the MCA which should be noted is s 2. This deals with the situation where a contractor is aware that the other party is a minor, and so seeks a guarantee from an adult third party. Prior to the MCA, such contracts were thought to be void. Section 2 now makes it clear that they are enforceable against the guarantor.

From the above, it can be seen that the MCA has improved in various ways the position of a person dealing with a minor. Are there still areas where there is, as McKendrick suggests, a need for a better balance between the parties?

There are two areas where the law might be thought still to operate harshly on those who contract with minors. First, s 3 of the Sale of Goods Act 1979 provides that, even where goods supplied fall into the category of necessaries, the supplier can still only recover a 'reasonable' price rather than the contract price. Once the enforceability of a contract is recognised, there seems to be no strong reason for not allowing it to have full effect. Moreover, no equivalent rule seems to apply in relation to services or contracts of employment – there is no obligation, for example, to pay reasonable wages.[9]

Secondly, the law still operates strictly against those who act without knowing that the other party is a minor, or who are unaware of the fact that goods supplied are either inappropriate to the minor's lifestyle or surplus to the minor's reasonable requirements. In such a situation (unlike the equivalent position in relation to other types of incapacity, such as mental incapacity or intoxication), the ignorance of the contractor provides no basis for compensation.

Although the MCA 1987 has removed a number of anomalies, and to some extent improved the position for those who contract with minors, McKendrick is probably right, for the reasons noted above, in asserting that there is still room for improvement and 'further rationalisation'.

Notes

1   Note that the minor may, nevertheless, be able to enforce.

2   Note, however, that many basic transactions involve an instantaneous exchange of goods for cash, where there is little risk for the trader.

3   These tests are given statutory form, as far as goods are concerned, by s 3 of the Sale of Goods Act 1979.

4   That is, a demand to pay money due in relation to a share price payable by instalments – not an uncommon procedure in relation to new issues of shares.

5   The minor is partially bound, in that he or she is not personally liable for partnership debts, but cannot prevent their discharge. On reaching majority, the former minor will become fully bound unless he or she repudiates.

6   The other contracts were contracts of loan and contracts for accounts stated.

7   The MCA also repeals s 5 of the Betting and Loans (Infants) Act 1892, which invalidated contracts (made after reaching majority) to repay loans advanced during minority.

8   The power is to be used where it is 'just and equitable to do so'.

9   Though, of course, if the wages are totally derisory, the contract may well not be regarded as being 'beneficial'.

Question 15

Sue Smasher was a promising young tennis player. In July 2000, when she was 16, she entered into two separate agreements, both of which were to run until July 2003:

(1) with Lew Lobb, a noted tennis coach, whereby he undertook to organise her training and decide which tournaments she should play in. In return, Sue agreed to act on Lew's advice and to pay him 20% of her winnings from tournaments; and

(2) with Drivepowa Ltd, whereby Sue promised to use their sports equipment in all tournaments, in return for Drivepowa's paying all her travelling expenses.

In July 2001, Sue disobeyed Lew's instruction to play in the Tournament of the Century in the USA, where the total prize money was £1.5 million, and returned to England to defend her title at the Eastmouth Championships, where the total prize money was only £20,000. Because these championships would receive far less publicity than the Tournament of the Century, Drivepowa refused to pay her air fare from the USA. Sue therefore decided not to use their rackets any more, and ordered ten 'Diamond' rackets from Hitfirm plc. These rackets had a genuine diamond fixed into the handle, and cost £1,000 each. After five rackets had been delivered, but before any had been paid for, Sue decided to retire from professional tennis.

What is the position as to the enforceability of Sue's contracts with Lew Lobb, Drivepowa Ltd and Hitfirm plc?

Answer plan

Since Sue is under 18 when she makes the contracts, she has limited capacity. The three contracts raise different issues related to contracts with minors:

• Lew Lobb's contract concerns the enforceability of a contract for services, which will depend on whether those services are 'necessary';

- Drivepowa have broken their contract. Here, the issue is whether such a contract is enforceable by a minor; and

- the contract with Hitfirm is for goods. Are these goods necessaries? If so, what are Hitfirm's rights? If not, can they recover the rackets already delivered?

The best way to deal with problem questions of this type is to give a short introduction dealing with the general issues arising in the area, and then to take each contract in turn.

Answer

Under English law, minors, that is, people under the age of 18, have limited capacity to make contracts. Sue Smasher has made three contracts, two when she was 16, one when she was 17. Two of these have been broken, one by Sue and one by the other contracting party. One of them is still partially executory. Each of them needs to be considered individually as to the rights and remedies that may be available.

The basic approach of the law is to say that contracts are not enforceable against minors, but then to allow some exceptions to this. The two main exceptions are:

- contracts for 'necessary' goods and services; and
- 'beneficial' contracts of employment.

The issues that then arise are: (a) what is meant by 'necessary'?; (b) what is meant by 'beneficial'?; and (c) what are the consequences if the contract falls within one of the exceptions, that is, is it then fully enforceable against the minor, or is the remedy more quasi-contractual or restitutionary? (a) and (c) will need to be considered here, but probably not (b), as we will see.

The first contract to consider is that with Lew Lobb. At first sight, this might seem to come within the category of an employment contract, since it relates closely to Sue's career as a professional tennis player. On closer inspection, however, it is clear that Sue is not employed by Lew. He is simply providing her with the benefit of his advice and experience, in return for a share of her winnings. In other words, he is providing her with 'services'. The question, then, is whether these are 'necessary' services.

The approach to the definition of 'necessaries' in English law has two elements, one objective, the other subjective. The objective element asks whether what has been supplied comes into the general category of something which is necessary. As Alderson B said in *Chapple v Cooper* (1844), 'things necessary are those without which an individual cannot reasonably exist', such as food, clothing, lodging and education. The subjective element asks whether the particular thing supplied is appropriate to the particular minor who has received it. Just because food is a necessary, it does not mean that a contract to buy caviar is a contract for necessaries. This issue is considered further below, in relation to the contract with Hitfirm plc.

As regards the contract with Lew Lobb, this might well be regarded as a contract for necessaries on the basis that it is analogous to a contract for education. The relevant authority is *Roberts v Gray* (1913). In this case, the defendant was an aspiring billiards player, who made a contract to go on a world tour with the plaintiff, who was an experienced player. The Court of Appeal had no difficulty in regarding this as a quasi-educational contract, and therefore within the scope of a contract for necessaries. If that is the case here, then Sue's contract with Lew Lobb should also be enforceable.[1] The issue then arises as to what the consequences are of Sue's failure to follow Lew's instructions, thus breaking the contract. In *Roberts v Gray*, it was argued by the defendant that the plaintiff should only recover on a *quantum meruit* basis, rather than full contractual damages.[2] The court refused to accept this, and allowed the plaintiff to recover his full losses, even though the contract in this case was almost entirely executory.[3] It seems, then, that Lew will be able to recover, for example, for the lost opportunity of taking a 20% share of the much higher prize money available at the Tournament of the Century.

Turning now to the contract with Drivepowa, the position appears to be much more straightforward. There is no indication that Drivepowa have specified in their contract with Sue that she should play in any particular tournaments. That being so, their failure to pay Sue's air fare from the USA would be a breach of contract. Sue has treated this as a repudiatory breach,[4] and has ordered tennis rackets from another firm. Whether or not the contract with Drivepowa is a contract for necessaries (which is arguable) is thus probably irrelevant, since it is Sue that is likely to be suing Drivepowa rather than vice versa. It is accepted that even in relation to contracts that are unenforceable against the minor, the minor can enforce against the other party. Sue should be able to recover the cost of her air fare from Drivepowa, and should face no further action from them.

The third contract to consider is that with Hitfirm plc. Here, the issue is whether the tennis rackets are 'necessaries'. The leading authority is *Nash v Inman* (1908). A university student placed an order for 11 fancy waistcoats with a tailor. These were supplied, but the student refused to pay. The tailor sued, but the student claimed that, as he was a minor,[5] the contract could not be enforced against him. The Court of Appeal held that, although clothing was clearly something which came within the category of necessary goods, the trial judge had been justified in ruling that the waistcoats were not necessaries. This was because the student was already adequately supplied with waistcoats, and there was no evidence that they were appropriate to the lifestyle of the student.[6] Section 3 of the Sale of Goods Act 1979 similarly states that necessary goods are those 'suitable to the condition in life of the minor ... and to his actual requirements at the time of sale and delivery'.[7]

How does this apply to the case of Sue and Hitfirm plc? Tennis rackets would not normally be considered 'necessaries'. But presumably, since Sue uses them to earn her living, in this situation they may come under the heading of 'tools of the trade'. The issue then becomes whether the 'Diamond' rackets are appropriate to Sue's 'condition in life'. If she were a very successful tennis player, then probably rackets of this kind, costing such a large sum each, would be appropriate. Since she is only 'promising', they may not be. Moreover, it may well be the case that Sue is still adequately supplied with Drivepowa's rackets, so that this element of the test would not be satisfied either.

If the rackets are not necessaries, s 3(1) of the Minors' Contracts Act 1987 gives the court power to order her to return to Hitfirm the five that have been delivered, if it is just and equitable to do so. There seems no reason why she should not be so ordered here. She will have no other obligation under the contract however. If, on the other hand, the rackets were regarded as necessaries, which it is suggested is unlikely, s 3 of the Sale of Goods Act says that the minor must pay a reasonable price for goods 'sold and delivered'. This would mean that she would have to pay a reasonable price, which might be less than £5,000, for the five rackets she has received, but would not be obliged to take delivery of, or pay for, the remaining five.[8]

In summary, therefore, it looks as though Sue will have to pay some compensation to Lew Lobb for her breach of the contract with him. She, in her turn, will be able to recover damages from Drivepowa for their refusal to pay her air fare. The most tricky issue relates to the 'Diamond' tennis rackets. She may be obliged to return them, or she may have to pay a reasonable sum for the five which she has received. What is certain is that she will have no obligation as regards the five that she has ordered, but which have not yet been delivered.

Notes

1   Note that contracts for necessaries must be generally beneficial to the minor: *Fawcett v Smethurst* (1914). Lew Lobb's contract, and in particular the percentage he is taking, is probably acceptable. If, however, he had been taking say 75% of her winnings, there would have been a strong case for saying that, although

ostensibly for necessaries, it should be unenforceable because of harsh or onerous terms.

2   As will be seen below, this appears to be the position as regards necessary goods.

3   This approach is closer to that which the courts take in relation to beneficial employment contracts. This has led some commentators, for example, Furmston, Cheshire and Fifoot, *Contract Law*, 14th edn, 2001, p 481, to argue that contracts of the *Roberts v Gray* type would fit better in this category, as opposed to the category of 'necessaries'; cf Stone, *The Modern Law of Contract*, 5th edn, 2002, p 184.

4   The issue of repudiatory and other breaches, and their consequences, is discussed in Chapter 11.

5   At that time, the age of majority was 21, and those under that age were generally referred to by the law as 'infants'.

6   The court considered that the burden of proof on both these issues was on the plaintiff, that is, the tailor.

7   The court in *Nash v Inman* considered the equivalent provision under the Sale of Goods Act 1893.

8   Note the contrast with the position regarding necessary services as stated in *Roberts v Gray*.

Question 16

To what extent does the law provide sufficient protection for those who enter into a contract with a person who, through age, mental illness or intoxication, may be said to lack the capacity to make a binding agreement?

Answer plan

This is a straightforward essay question dealing with capacity. Note, however, that it is not limited to the position in relation to minors, but brings in mental illness and intoxication as well. There is no point in attempting this question unless you are aware of the basic principles of these areas. Inevitably, because of the fact that there is more law to be discussed, much of the essay will be devoted to minors' contracts, but an essay which ignored the other two aspects altogether would be likely to be heavily marked down.

The law relating to all three areas needs to be outlined. The question then asks you to say whether there is sufficient protection for the other contracting party in this situation. In other words, you are asked to look at the position not through the eyes of the minor or other 'incapacitated' individual, but through the eyes of the person contracting with them. One issue which will certainly need to be considered here is the extent to which knowledge of the incapacity is necessary before it affects the other party's ability to enforce an agreement. The rules as to recovery of property transferred under an unenforceable agreement will also need to be discussed.

Answer

In order to answer this question, it is necessary to outline the basic rules which apply to each of the three situations, that is, minors, mental illness and intoxication. The greater part of the law in this area is concerned with minors' contracts, but we shall start with the other two.

As regards mental incapacity, persons whose mental state is such that their affairs are under the control of the court by virtue of the Mental Health Act 1983 cannot contract on their own behalf at all, and any purported contract will be void. Those who are not subject to the control of the court, but are, as a result of mental incapacity, shown to be unable to appreciate the nature of the transaction, may also not be bound by the contract. Here, however, this will only be the case if the person can show that the other contracting party was aware of the incapacity: *Imperial Loan Co v Stone* (1892). If that is so, then the contract will be voidable at the option of the mentally disordered person. However, even if there was such an awareness on the part of the other party, the mentally disordered person may still have some liability if what was to be supplied comes into the category of 'necessaries'. This issue is considered in more detail in relation to minors' contracts, below.

The approach to the intoxicated contractor is very similar. In other words, the drunken individual will be bound to the contract unless it is shown that the other party was, at the time of the contract, aware that they were contracting with someone incapable, through inebriation, of understanding the nature of the transaction: *Gore v Gibson* (1843).[1] Once again, however, if 'necessaries' have been supplied, there may still be some liability.

The most detailed set of rules, however, are those applying to minors' contracts. A minor is a person under the age of 18. The basic rule is that contracts made by such a person are unenforceable against the minor. A person contracting with a minor is, therefore, in a risky position.[2] Some contracts are, however, enforceable. There are two main categories:

- contracts for 'necessaries'; and
- beneficial contracts of employment.

Contracts for necessaries include contracts for goods or services. Necessary goods are defined in s 3 of the Sale of Goods Act 1979 as goods suitable to the condition in life of the minor, and to the minor's actual requirements at the time of sale and delivery.[3] The approach of the courts to this definition[4] has been to say that there are certain categories of goods that come within the scope of necessaries, that is, food, clothing, etc. Once it is determined that the goods are of this type, then the two tests from the Sale of Goods Act must be applied, that is, are they suitable to this particular minor, and does the minor have enough of them already? The first part of the approach (that is, are the goods *capable* of being necessaries?) is clearly objective, and will not vary from case to case. The Sale of Goods Act tests are subjective, and will vary depending on the minor concerned. As was stated in *Chapple v Cooper* (1844), which contains one of the fullest statements of the courts' position on this issue,[5] articles of mere luxury will never be necessaries, but luxurious articles of utility may be in some circumstances. In *Peters v Fleming* (1840), it was accepted that an undergraduate student could claim that a watch was a necessary, but whether one which had a gold chain was appropriate to his lifestyle was a matter for the jury. In *Ryder v Wombwell* (1868), however, the court[6] held that a pair of diamond and ruby cufflinks and a silver goblet could not possibly be necessaries.

As to the issue of 'adequate supply' in *Nash v Inman* (1908), where the items concerned were 11 fancy waistcoats, it was held that the onus was on the supplier to show that the minor did not have an adequate supply of waistcoats.

In applying both tests, it seems that the knowledge, or lack of knowledge, of the supplier as to the minor's position as regards lifestyle, or supply of the goods in question is irrelevant.

The above approach to necessary goods has been applied in much the same way to services. In other words, certain types of service, such as provision of lodging, education, or medical treatment, are regarded as within the category of 'necessaries'. Whether they are such in a particular case again involves looking at the needs and reasonable expectations of the minor concerned.

The second main category of enforceable contracts is beneficial contracts of employment. A minor needs to be able to earn a living,[7] but must be protected from exploitation. Contracts of employment are valid, therefore, but they must, judged overall, be beneficial. So, in *De Francesco v Barnum* (1889), a very restrictive contract for apprentice dancers was held invalid. The girls concerned were bound for seven years, were required not to marry, and had no guarantee that they would be provided with work during the contract. On the other hand, the contract must be looked at as a whole. In *Clements v London & NW Rly* (1894), a railway porter was employed under a contract which contained an accident compensation scheme that provided lower rates of compensation than the statutory scheme which would otherwise have applied. However, the contractual scheme covered a wider range of accidents, so the court was not prepared to say that it was not overall a beneficial contract.

What then is the position of the person who contracts to supply goods and services to someone who may lack capacity? The first thing to note is that there is a distinction between contracting with minors and contracting with those suffering from mental incapacity and drunkards. In relation to the latter two categories, the contractor will only be unable to enforce the contract if he or she was aware of the lack of capacity on the other side. If the contract is made in ignorance of the disability, it will be fully enforceable. Such ignorance on the part of the other contracting party will not, however, prevent a minor escaping from the contract. The balance here is more in favour of the minor.

Secondly, where goods which are necessaries are supplied to a person lacking capacity, the supplier will not necessarily recover the full price. The Sale of Goods Act 1979 only requires that a 'reasonable' price should be paid: s 3(2). Here, again, the supplier is in the worse position. Moreover, the Sale of Goods Act makes it clear that this only applies to goods actually delivered. If the contract is wholly or partly executory, then, even if the goods are necessaries, the supplier can claim no damages for failure to take delivery.[8]

The position seems to be different as regards necessary services. In *Roberts v Gray* (1913), the court allowed recovery of damages for what was largely still an executory contract for the supply of services. The same is true of a beneficial contract of service, which is regarded as being fully binding.

What of the person who supplies non-necessary goods or services? As far as goods are concerned, s 3 of the Minors' Contracts Act 1987 allows the court to order the return of such goods, or other property representing the goods.[9] This will not apply, however, where the incapacity is mental or caused by intoxication. Here, the supplier seems to have no remedy. The same would appear to be the case in relation to all types of incapacity where it is services rather than goods that have been supplied.

Finally, it should be noted that a trader who knows that the other party is a minor can achieve some protection by requiring an adult to give a guarantee. Such guarantees are made enforceable against the adult, by virtue of s 2 of the Minors' Contracts Act 1987, even if the contract with the minor is unenforceable.

The conclusion in answering the question posed as to the sufficiency of protection for those who contract with those lacking capacity must be that there are some imbalances. In relation to mental incapacity and intoxication, the contracting party is probably sufficiently protected, because of the requirement of knowledge. In relation to minors, however, the supplier of goods or services may not know that the other party is under 18. Moreover, in relation to all types of incapacity, it seems hard that goods or services can lose their status as necessaries simply because, without the knowledge of the supplier, the other party is already adequately supplied with goods of that type. In these respects, the law seems to be stretching perhaps too far in the way of protecting the incompetent contractor.

The provisions of the Minors' Contracts Act 1987 have helped to make things a little less risky for the person who contracts with those under 18, but the advice must still be that a person should be very wary of contracting with someone who does not appear to know what they are doing, or appears to be under 18. Where goods or services are to be supplied in such a situation, it will always be the safest course to insist on payment in advance. If credit is given, it may be that the contract will be avoided, and there will then be no means of redress.

Notes

1   See also *Matthews v Baxter* (1873). As with mental incapacity, the contract is voidable, not void.

2   In practice, of course, the majority of contracts made by children will involve straightforward simultaneous exchanges of money for goods. Questions of enforceability will rarely arise in this context.

3   This definition appears in s 3(3), and applies to goods supplied to those incompetent to contract by reason of mental incapacity or drunkenness, as well as age.

4   Virtually the same definition was used in the Sale of Goods Act 1893.

5   In the judgment of Alderson B.

6   It was an appeal to the Court of Exchequer Chamber, the equivalent of the modern Court of Appeal.

7   But note the reluctance of the courts to give effect to trading contracts, for example, *Cowern v Nield* (1912), which makes things difficult for the underage business person.

8   Nor can specific performance be ordered.

9   It is not clear whether this includes money received where the minor has sold the goods to a third party.

CHAPTER 5

CONTENTS OF THE CONTRACT

Introduction

In this chapter, we turn from looking at the question of whether there are any contractual obligations between the parties to the content of any such obligations. In other words, where there is a contract, how do the courts determine what the terms are?

There are two main issues to be considered here:

- the status of pre-contractual statements; and
- the question of 'implied terms' under statute and, more particularly, at common law.

The first of these requires a knowledge of the rules by which the courts decide whether a particular statement made during negotiations is to be regarded as part of any subsequent contract, and the use of the collateral contract. If a statement is not part of the main contract or a collateral contract, then the possibility of an action for misrepresentation should be considered. This requires looking at:

- the requirements for a statement to be regarded as a 'misrepresentation'; and
- possible remedies under the common law and the Misrepresentation Act 1967.

Sometimes, a contract question will call for discussion of liability for negligent misstatements under *Hedley Byrne v Heller*. This complicated topic, however, is more appropriately dealt with in tort, and there is no detailed discussion of it in any of the suggested answers in this chapter.

Note also that there is further discussion of the law relating to misrepresentations in Chapter 7.

In relation to implied terms, the most commonly used examples of statutory implied terms are ss 12–15 of the Sale of Goods Act 1979. Detailed knowledge of these sections will not, however, generally be required in answering questions in a basic contract course. They are, however, discussed further in Chapter 15. Under the common law, the following issues need to be understood:

- the *Moorcock* test;
- the 'officious bystander' test; and

- the approach of the House of Lords in *Liverpool City Council v Irwin*.

Two issues related to the contents of the contract are not dealt with here:

- incorporation of terms. This is covered in Chapter 6, in relation to exemption clauses, but remember that the rules of incorporation potentially apply to all clauses, as shown by the decision in *Interfoto Picture Library v Stiletto Visual Programmes*; and
- the distinction between 'conditions', 'warranties' and 'innominate terms'. This is dealt with in Chapter 11, in connection with performance and breach.

Checklist

You should be familiar with the following areas:

- The distinction between 'representations' and 'terms', and its importance.
- Remedies for misrepresentations under the common law.
- Remedies under the Misrepresentation Act 1967.
- The concept of the collateral contract.
- Statutory implied terms.
- Terms implied at common law: the *Moorcock* test, the 'officious bystander' test and *Liverpool City Council v Irwin* (1976).

Question 17

'... in business transactions what the law desires to effect by the implication [of a term] is to give such business efficacy to the transaction as must have been intended by the parties.' (Bowen LJ in *The Moorcock* (1886–90).)

Does this still accurately represent the courts' approach to the implication of terms? Does Parliament, as, for example, in the Sale of Goods Act 1979, take a different approach?

Answer plan

There are two main aspects to this question: (1) the consideration of the approach of the courts to implied terms; and (2) the comparison with the approach of the legislature. There is no reason why these two aspects should not be dealt with separately, almost as if you were writing two short essays rather than one long one. The issues you will need to consider are:

First part:

- the meaning of the *Moorcock* test at the time it was first used;
- the development of rules regarding implication of terms – the 'officious bystander' test, etc; and
- the effect of the decision in *Liverpool City Council v Irwin* (1976).

Second part:

- the types of terms implied in the Sale of Goods Act 1979;
- the reason for implying them; and
- comparison with the reasons for common law implication.

Answer

From time to time, the parties to a contract may find that, for some reason, their agreement will not in practice work as they intended. One reason for this may be that there is a gap in the contractual terms which they have expressly agreed. One or other of the parties may then wish to argue that a term should be implied to fill that gap. Sometimes, the custom of a particular trade or place of business may indicate what term is to be implied (for example, *Hutton v Warren* (1836)), but that is not what we are primarily concerned with here. *The Moorcock* (1886–90) was concerned with the extent to which terms could be implied in the absence of any external source for such a term. The case concerned a contract which involved the plaintiff's ship mooring at the defendant's wharf on the Thames. The Thames being a tidal river, at low tide the ship, as both parties knew would be the case, settled on the river bed. Unfortunately, the ship was damaged, because of the nature of the river bed at that point. There was no express term as to the suitability of the river bed for mooring the ship there. It was held that a term could be implied to that effect. It was assumed that this must have been the intention of the parties; without such a term the contract was effectively unworkable.

This type of implication is often referred to as implication in fact. This indicates that what the courts are trying to do is decide, as a matter of fact, what the parties' unstated intentions were as to that particular aspect of the contract. The difficulty arises in trying to pin down that intention. In *The Moorcock*, it was based on the idea of 'business efficacy', in other words, what is necessary for the contract to work. The courts will not generally imply a term simply because it appears to be 'reasonable'. It cannot be assumed that the parties would have agreed to something reasonable, rather than necessary.

Later cases have looked for other ways of determining the intention of the parties. The most famous of these alternative approaches is the 'officious bystander' test. This was first stated in *Shirlaw v Southern Foundries Ltd* (1939). It operates by imagining what would have happened if, at the time of the contract, an 'officious bystander' had suggested the particular term which it is proposed should now be implied. If the likely reaction of the parties would have been a testy 'of course', because what was being put forward by the bystander was so obvious that it should go without saying, then the courts should be prepared to imply the term. As can be seen, this is simply another way of trying to determine what the parties must have intended at the time of contracting.

A different approach was taken by the House of Lords in *Liverpool City Council v Irwin* (1976). They were faced there with tenancy contracts relating to a block of flats, in which nothing was said about who was responsible for maintenance of the common parts of the block and, in particular, the lifts and rubbish chutes. The House of Lords implied a term that the landlord should take reasonable steps to keep the common parts in good repair. It cannot be said that such a term was necessary to make the contract work, in the *Moorcock* sense. It would have been quite possible to have a tenancy agreement in which responsibility for the common parts was shared among all the tenants of the block. Nor would the officious bystander test be likely to provide an agreed answer. What the House of Lords was doing here was in effect to say that: (a) the agreement was incomplete (it contained very little at all about the obligations of the landlord); (b) it was an agreement of a type that was sufficiently common that the court could decide that certain terms would normally be expected to be found in such an agreement; and (c) the term implied was the one which the House thought was reasonable in relation to the normal expectations of the obligations as between landlord and tenant.[1] This is sometimes referred to as a term implied in law, rather than in fact. It is imposed on the parties by the courts, rather than reflecting what they would have agreed on if they had thought about the matter at the time of the contract.

The distinction between the two approaches has been very clearly analysed by Lord Denning in *Shell v Lostock Garages Ltd* (1977). In contracts which are of such a common type (for example, sale of goods, landlord and tenant, employment) that the courts are able to identify typical obligations,[2] the *Liverpool City Council v Irwin* approach may be used to fill in gaps. If the agreement is not of this type (as was the case in *Shell v Lostock Garages*), then the test of necessity derived from *The Moorcock* would have to be used.

How do these two approaches relate to the approach of the legislature in the Sale of Goods Act 1979? This Act contains a number of implied terms in ss 12–15. Most of them relate to the quality of goods sold. For example, s 13 implies a term that goods should match their description, and s 14 that they should be of satisfactory quality.[3] We are clearly dealing here with terms implied in law, rather than in fact. The terms will be implied whatever the intentions of the parties at the time of the contract. They are not there for business efficacy, but because these are regarded as the normal obligations of a contract for the sale of goods. To this extent, the implication of terms in the Sale of Goods Act would seem to have close links with the approach in *Liverpool City Council v Irwin*, particularly as interpreted by Lord Denning in *Shell v Lostock Garages*. Closer analysis, however, shows that the Sale of Goods Act goes further than this. It is not simply that the statute fills in the gaps with typical terms. If this was all, then, as is the case with the *Liverpool City Council v Irwin* type of implication, it could be avoided if the parties included a specific term to deal with the matter.[4] In contrast, the Sale of Goods Act terms are always implied, and only in very limited circumstances can the parties agree not to be bound by them. Only business contractors (as opposed to consumers) are allowed to agree to modification of these implied terms, and then only if the courts think that it is reasonable (see s 6 of the Unfair Contract Terms Act 1977).[5] The object of the implied term here is not to make the agreement work, but to protect purchasers and, in particular, consumer purchasers, from the harshness of the common law rule of *caveat emptor*.[6]

In conclusion, it can be said that the quotation from *The Moorcock* does still represent the courts' approach to implication of terms, but it does not give the whole picture. There is now the different approach taken in *Liverpool City Council v Irwin*, which is not based on business efficacy, nor on the intention of the parties. This newer approach is similar to that taken by Parliament in the Sale of Goods Act 1979, but the terms implied by that statute go further than the common law in imposing obligations on the parties, in the interests of protecting the weaker party in a sale of goods transaction.

Notes

1　Note that Lord Wilberforce, nevertheless, still insists on talking about a 'necessity' test.

2　It was made clear, in *Ashmore and Others v Corp of Lloyd's (No 2)* (1992), that the fact that a number of contracts all had identical terms did not constitute a contract of a 'type' which would enable the court to use the *Liverpool v Irwin* approach.

3　Section 12 deals with title, and s 15 with sales by sample. Note that s 14 in fact contains two implied conditions – 'satisfactory quality' (14(2)) and 'fitness for a particular purpose' (14(3)).

4   This was more or less the case with the original 1893 Sale of Goods Act, which allowed for exclusion of the implied terms.

5   Section 12 cannot be excluded by anyone. It would be possible to include a more favourable term as to quality – as, for example, is done in some 'money back' guarantees.

6   That is, 'let the buyer beware', as the courts will not protect him or her from the consequences of making a bad bargain.

Question 18

Peter wants a wall built in his back garden. He goes to Duff & Co, a local firm of builders, and is advised by Mr Duff that he should have the wall constructed of Nubrix, a new type of building material. Peter is dubious, but is assured by Mr Duff that all his builders have received training in working with Nubrix. Mr Duff also says that they have built several walls with Nubrix with very satisfactory results. Peter says that he would like to have time to think it over, and rings up Nubrix Ltd. Alison, Nubrix's sales manager, confirms that Duff & Co are 'authorised Nubrix builders'. She says that Nubrix Ltd can guarantee that a Nubrix wall will need no maintenance for at least 15 years. The next day Peter enters into a contract with Duff to build the wall with Nubrix. Two years after it is completed, however, the wall collapses. Peter has discovered that Mr Duff's builders had had no training in using Nubrix, and that at the time he entered into the contract at least one other wall built by Duff with Nubrix had collapsed within a year of its construction.

Advise Peter as to his remedies, if any, against Duff & Co and Nubrix Ltd.

Answer plan

There are no particular difficulties in this problem, which raises the issue of liability for statements made prior to a contract.

Statements made in pre-contractual negotiations can give rise to liability in four ways:

*   as terms incorporated into the contract;
*   as misrepresentations;
*   as part of a collateral contract; and
*   in the tort of negligence, under *Hedley Byrne v Heller*.

For the reasons given in the introduction to this chapter, the fourth possibility is not pursued here. The first three, however, need to be considered in relation to the statements by Mr Duff. Alison's remarks may give rise to liability under a collateral contract.

Answer

This problem is concerned with the effect of statements made during negotiations which lead to a contract. Such statements can sometimes be incorporated into the main contract, or they may take effect as part of a separate, collateral contract. They may also give rise to liability for misrepresentation.

Peter is seeking compensation for the fact that his wall has collapsed. We are not told of any written contract or any specific terms agreed, so it will be assumed that there is nothing relevant in these areas.[1] This means that Peter will have to rely on the statements made by Mr Duff and Alison as the basis for legal action.

Mr Duff made two statements prior to the contract. The first was that his builders had been trained in the use of Nubrix; the second, that other walls had been built by his firm successfully with Nubrix. Both of these statements were untrue, in that none of his builders had received training, and that at the time of the contract (and it is assumed at the time of Mr Duff's statement) at least one wall built with Nubrix had collapsed within a year. Does this give rise to any liability on the part of Duff & Co?

The first possibility to consider is that the statements might have become part of the contract. This can occur if the courts regard a pre-contractual statement as being sufficiently important that it must have been intended to be part of the contract. This was the case in *Bannerman v White* (1861), where a buyer of hops had been assured that sulphur had not been used in their production. He had made it clear that he would not be interested in buying them if it had. When it turned out that sulphur had been used, he was entitled to reject them for breach of contract. In considering whether the statement is of sufficient importance to be incorporated, the courts will also look at the lapse of time between the statement and the contract (*Routledge v McKay* (1954)) and whether the party making the statement has held himself out as having special knowledge. In *Oscar Chess v Williams* (1957), a private seller of a car was held to have no special knowledge as to its year of manufacture. In contrast, in *Dick Bentley v Harold Smith* (1965), a car dealer was taken to have special knowledge as regards the mileage of a second hand car, so that his statement became part of the contract.

Applying this approach to the negotiations between Peter and Duff, it does not seem as though the statements will be incorporated. Although Mr Duff can be regarded as having special knowledge, there is a clear gap between the statements and the contract, and they do not seem to be about matters which are central to the contract, in the way that the use of sulphur was in *Bannerman v White*, or the mileage of the car was in *Dick Bentley v Harold Smith*.

We turn then to the possibility of liability for misrepresentation. A misrepresentation is a false statement of existing fact, made by one contracting party to another, which induces the contract. Statements of opinion or intention are not actionable, as long as they are honestly made (*Bisset v Wilkinson* (1927)). The first statement by Mr Duff, about the training, is clearly a statement of fact, which was untrue at the time it was made. The second statement is more ambiguous. Whether results are 'satisfactory' or not could be said to be a matter of opinion. If, however, Mr Duff knows at the time that one of the walls which his firm had built had collapsed within a year, then he would have no reasonable basis for his opinion, and he could still be liable for misrepresentation. In *Smith v Land & House Property Corp* (1884), for example, the description of a tenant as 'most desirable', when he had in fact been in arrears with his rent for a long time, was regarded as a misrepresentation.[2]

The next requirement for misrepresentation is that the statement induces the contract. This means that it must relate to something which a reasonable person would regard as material to the contract, and it must actually have been relied on by the claimant in entering into the contract. In *JEB Fasteners v Bloom* (1983), a purchaser of a company had been shown inaccurate accounts. It was clear, however, that he would have bought the company even if he had known the truth, and so was unable to bring an action based on the misrepresentation.

It is clear that Peter did not place sole reliance on Mr Duff's statements, in that he checked with Nubrix Ltd before committing himself to the contract.[3] The comments by Alison, however, do not cover exactly the same ground as Duff, and Peter could argue that he did, at least in part, rely on Mr Duff's assurances. Partial reliance is enough to ground liability – *Edgington v Fitzmaurice* (1885).

If Peter can show reliance in this way, then he will be able to claim damages for either fraudulent or negligent misrepresentation. Since the damages for negligent misrepresentation are the same as for fraud,[4] he would be best advised to rely on s 2(1) of the Misrepresentation Act 1967. This in effect creates liability for negligent misrepresentation unless the defendant can show reasonable grounds for believing the statement to be true. In other words, the burden of proof is on the defendant.

The other possible line of action for Peter is to sue Nubrix Ltd on the basis of the statements made by Alison, their sales manager. There is no possibility of using misrepresentation here, because Nubrix Ltd are not a party to the contract for the construction of the wall. Peter could, however, try an action based on a collateral contract.

The device of the collateral contract is well illustrated by the case of *Shanklin Pier v Detel Products* (1951). The plaintiff pier owners wished to repaint their pier. The defendants, who were paint manufacturers, told them that their paint would last for seven years, and on this basis the plaintiffs specified the defendants' paint for use in the painting contract. It began to peel off after three months. The plaintiffs did not appear to have any remedy, since they had specified the paint to be used but had not themselves bought it. It was found, however, that the defendants could be liable on a 'collateral' contract. This took the form of a promise that, if the plaintiffs specified their paint for the main contract, the defendants would guarantee that it would last for seven years.[5]

The facts of the problem are very similar. It is unlikely that anything can be based on the statement that Duff & Co are 'authorised Nubrix builders', assuming this is true. But the guarantee of no maintenance for 15 years could clearly be an enforceable promise, if backed up by consideration. The possible consideration in this case would be the specification of Nubrix for the contract to build the wall, thus creating a collateral contract. It would have to be shown, however, that the statement by Alison was made in a situation where it was the expectation that a contract would follow. In other words, it would be important for Peter to show that Alison knew that he was considering making the contract with Duff, and that this was very likely to follow as a result of her reassurance.[6] From the facts, it seems that this may well be possible, since he has clearly told her that he is considering using Duff & Co to build a wall with Nubrix.

An action based on breach of this collateral contract would enable Peter to claim damages from Nubrix Ltd on the normal contractual measure. This would mean compensation to provide him with a maintenance-free wall for the remainder of the 15 years.

It might also be possible to use a collateral contract against Duff & Co, since it is available in two-party as well as three-party situations (*Esso v Mardon* (1976)). On the facts, however, Mr Duff's statements are more in the nature of assertions of fact, rather than promises for the future, and it is probably better to treat them as misrepresentations.

In conclusion, Peter has possible actions against both Duff & Co and Nubrix Ltd. Both would provide him with compensation for his losses. Given the current generous approach of the courts to damages under s 2(1) of the

Misrepresentation Act, that may be the best to pursue, since the burden of disproving negligence is on the defence. On the other hand, Nubrix Ltd, as a large firm, may be in a better position to meet a claim for compensation. The best advice is probably to initiate both actions, and then to pursue the one which seems most likely to lead to success.

Notes

1   It should perhaps also be assumed that there is no liability on the basis of the implied terms in the Supply of Goods and Services Act 1982.

2   Duff would also be liable if the wall collapses between statement and contract: *With v O'Flanagan* (1936).

3   Cf *Attwood v Small* (1838), where a plaintiff purchaser of a mine had sought to confirm the seller's statements of its potential by commissioning his own report. There was thus no reliance on the seller's misrepresentation.

4   See *Royscot Trust Ltd v Rogerson* (1991). But note that the House of Lords in *Smith New Court Securities Ltd v Scrimgeour Vickers (Asset Management) Ltd* (1994) expressed some scepticism as to whether this was the correct approach. It did not go so far as to overrule *Royscot v Rogerson*, however, so the case must still be regarded as good law.

5   From this, it will be seen that the collateral contract will generally also be a unilateral contract, of the form 'if you will enter into the main contract, I will promise you X'.

6   In *Wells v Buckland Sand and Silica* (1965), this was referred to as the need for an *animus contrahendi*.

Question 19

Anna wants to buy a Gorden car – a rare make of sports car, built during the 1960s. She answers an advert placed by Bill, asking for £3,000 for a Gorden car. Anna inspects the car on 6 October, and says that she wants to buy it. She agrees that it is worth £3,000, but does not have the money available. She asks Bill to keep the car for her until 20 October, in order to allow her to try to raise the cash. Bill agrees that he will not sell the car to anyone else in the meantime.

Two days later, Bill is visited by Carol, who is also keen to buy the car. She asks him about petrol consumption, and Bill says that the car will average 30 miles per gallon in everyday use. Carol says that if Bill pays for a full service of the car at a garage of her choice, she will give him £3,500 for it. Bill agrees. Carol telephones Fixit Garages, and asks them if they can service Gorden cars. They claim to be experts in this sort of work, and Carol therefore tells Bill to take the car to Fixit. He does so. A week later, when Carol has paid Bill and taken delivery of the car, she discovers that as a result of poor servicing the engine is misfiring badly. She has also learnt from a specialist magazine that Gordens never average more than 25 miles per gallon.

On 20 October, Anna contacts Bill and tells him that she now has the £3,000, only to be told that the car has been sold to Carol.

Advise Anna and Carol.

Answer plan

This question is mainly concerned with collateral contracts, though there is also the issue of whether Bill's statement concerning the petrol consumption is a misrepresentation, or part of the contract with Carol.

You are asked to advise Anna and Carol, and the two parts of the answer should be dealt with separately.

Anna

Generally, an offeror is not obliged to keep an offer open for a particular time. Nor can there be an 'agreement to agree': *Courtney and Fairbairn v Tolaini Bros (Hotels) Ltd* (1975). It has been recognised, however, in *Walford v Miles* (1992) and *Pitt v PHH Asset Management Ltd* (1993), that in certain circumstances there can be a binding, collateral, 'lock out' agreement, preventing a party from contracting with anyone else. This part of the answer will have to examine whether the arrangement between Anna and Bill meets the requirements of such an agreement, and, if so, what Anna's remedy will be.

Carol

Carol has two potential actions:

- against Bill in relation to his statement about the petrol consumption: is this part of the contract, a misrepresentation, or a collateral contract?; and

- against Fixit Garages in relation to their defective servicing work. Carol has no direct contract with Fixit: can she recover from them on the basis of a collateral contract, as in *Shanklin Pier v Detel Products* (1951)?

Note that, assuming that Bill is selling the car as a private individual rather than in the course of business, Carol will have no action against him in relation to the implied terms as to quality under s 14 of the Sale of Goods Act 1979. These terms only apply where the sale is in the course of business. Section 13, the implied term as to compliance with description, does apply to private sales, but Bill does not seem to be in breach of this term, since the car is a Gorden sports car.

Answer

This problem is largely concerned with pre-contractual statements, and the extent to which they can form the basis of legal liability. Anna and Carol both have potential actions against Bill. In addition, Carol may wish to pursue Fixit Garages for compensation in relation to their apparently defective servicing of the car.

The negotiations between Anna and Bill have effectively resulted in a situation where Bill has agreed to sell the car to Anna, provided that she can raise the £3,000 by 20 October. Generally, a promise to keep an offer open for a particular period of time is not binding on the offeror, as in *Routledge v Grant* (1828). Nor is it possible to make a binding 'agreement to agree', as in *Courtney and Fairbairn v Tolaini Bros (Hotels) Ltd* (1975). In two cases, however, it has been recognised that in certain circumstances there can be a binding 'lock out' agreement, collateral to a main contract, whereby one party agrees not to negotiate with anyone else. *Walford v Miles* (1992) concerned the sale of a business, and the prospective purchasers argued that the seller had agreed to negotiate with them, and not to negotiate with anyone else. The House of Lords rejected the idea that there could be a collateral contract imposing a positive obligation to negotiate. They held, however, that there could be a binding agreement not to negotiate – a 'lock out' agreement. For this to be enforceable, there would have to be consideration supplied, and the agreement could not be indefinite – it must be for a fixed period. On the facts, the House felt that no such binding agreement had been established. In *Pitt v*

PHH Asset Management (1993), the Court of Appeal applied the House of Lords' reasoning in *Walford v Miles* to find a binding collateral lock out agreement. The negotiations here concerned the sale of a property. The defendant received an offer from the plaintiff, and agreed not to consider any further offers on the basis that the plaintiff agreed to complete the transaction within two weeks of the receipt of a draft contract from the defendant. The defendant supplied a draft contract, but then proceeded to sell the property to a third party. It was held that there was a binding lock out agreement with the plaintiff. The agreement was for a fixed time (two weeks from the receipt of a draft), and consideration was provided by the plaintiff's commitment to complete within two weeks. The conditions laid down by the House of Lords in *Walford v Miles* were thus satisfied, and the plaintiff was entitled to damages for breach of this collateral contract.

How does this apply to Anna? She will wish to argue that she has a lock out agreement with Bill which should prevent him from selling the car to anyone else. Are the conditions laid down in *Walford v Miles* satisfied? There is no problem over the length of the arrangement, in that it is clearly for a fixed two week period, finishing on a specific date. There is more difficulty in identifying consideration supplied by Anna. It will be remembered that, in *Pitt*, this was found in the plaintiff's promise to complete within a specific period. Anna has not promised, however, to complete the contract by 20 October. The clear implication of the arrangement is that if she fails to raise the money by that date, neither of them will be under any obligation. Anna might argue that she has impliedly agreed that she will not seek another car, or withdraw her offer to buy, within this period. If that was accepted, then it might be enough to satisfy the consideration requirement. Her position would be much stronger, however, if she had specifically promised to act in this way. As it stands, a court might well feel that the arrangement was not sufficiently specific to be enforceable.

If Anna can persuade the court that there was a binding lock out agreement, she will be entitled to damages. These will presumably be assessed on the basis of the price she would now have to pay to purchase an equivalent car.[1]

Carol has two possible claims, one against Bill, relating to his statement about the likely petrol consumption, and the other against Fixit Garages, for their poor servicing work.

As far as Bill's comment is concerned, Carol has a number of possibilities. She might try to argue that the statement was part of the contract for the sale of the car. To succeed in this she will have to show that it was of considerable importance to her, as held in *Bannerman v White* (1861). In effect, she will have to prove that a reasonable person would have thought that this statement was intended to be part of the contract. The fact that she entered into the contract almost immediately after the statement was made would be in her favour (*Routledge v McKay* (1954)). She might also be able to argue that, although Bill is a private seller rather than a dealer, he can be said to have special knowledge on this issue. If so, then Carol could argue that she was relying on his skill and knowledge, as in *Dick Bentley Productions v Harold Smith (Motors)* (1965). If the statement is part of the contract, Carol will be able to claim damages.

The second possibility is that Carol could argue that the statement was a misrepresentation which induced the contract. For this to be available, there has to have been a statement of fact, not opinion or law. Bill says that the car 'will' do 30 miles per gallon. Can this be implied as meaning that it has, while being used by Bill, done this mileage? If so, then this is a statement of fact. If, however, the statement should be taken as applying only to the future (perhaps because Bill has modified the engine in a way which he expects to improve the petrol consumption), then it will not be a statement of fact, but an expression of opinion or a promise for the future.

On the basis of the information given in the problem, it is quite likely that this statement would be treated as a statement of fact. The next requirement for it to be actionable as a misrepresentation is that it is untrue. The figure given in the specialist magazine suggests that it is, but this will still have to be proved in relation to the particular car. Assuming that this can be done, Carol will then have to prove that the statement induced the contract, at least in part (*Edgington v Fitzmaurice* (1885)). Can Carol say that she would not have entered into the contract if Bill had told her that the petrol consumption was 20–25 miles per gallon? This is a question of fact which will largely depend on Carol's own evidence. In her favour, as with the argument for incorporation, is the fact that she entered into the contract immediately after the statement had been made. This may well indicate that it was a factor in her decision.

If an actionable misrepresentation has been made, then Carol will be able to rescind the contract, and probably claim damages for negligent misrepresentation under s 2(1) of the Misrepresentation Act 1967. These damages would be available if Bill is unable to prove that he had reasonable grounds to believe that his statement was true.

The final possibility in relation to Bill is that his statement can be construed as part of a collateral contract, that is: 'If you will buy the car, I will guarantee that it will do 30 miles per gallon.' Although such a collateral contract is possible between the parties to a main contract (*Esso v Mardon* (1976)), such an argument seems unlikely to succeed on these facts if the argument for the statement being part of the main contract fails. In both cases, Carol would have to establish that Bill was warranting the petrol consumption. The collateral contract argument thus has little advantage here, given that the remedies for breach of the main contract are liable to be more extensive (and may include the possibility of repudiation).

We now need to consider the possibility of Carol being able to take action against Fixit Garages because of their defective work. Her difficulty is that she does not, on the face of it, have a contract with them. She nominated them as the garage for Bill to use, but the actual servicing contract would have been between Bill and Fixit. Carol is not a party to this contract. Nor is it likely that the contract between Bill and Fixit will have stated that it is made for Carol's benefit, so as to bring it within the scope of s 1 of the Contracts (Rights of Third Parties) Act 1999. Carol may again, however, be able to use the collateral contract device.[2] The position is similar to that in *Shanklin Pier v Detel Products* (1951), where the owners of a pier nominated the paint to be used, on the recommendation of its manufacturers. When the paint turned out to be unsuitable, the pier owners were held to be able to recover damages from the manufacturers on the basis of a collateral contract. Likewise, in *Wells v Buckland Sand & Silica* (1965), wholesale suppliers of sand, who had promised that it had a low oxide content, were held liable on a collateral contract with the promisee who had ordered the sand from a third party. The collateral contract which Carol would be alleging would be in the form of: 'We promise to do a good job in servicing the car, if you nominate us to Bill.' In order to be successful in this, Carol would have to show, first, that there was an express or implied promise to 'do a good job'; the only specific statement we are told of is that Fixit Garages are 'experts', which may or may not be true. Secondly, Carol will have to prove that the statements (express and implied) made by Fixit Garages were made with the expectation that the contract with Bill would follow. As it was expressed in *Wells v Buckland*, there must be an *animus contrahendi* about the statements.

If Carol can satisfy these requirements, she will be able to recover damages from Fixit for their defective work.

Notes

1   An alternative measure would be any expenses incurred towards the contract – that is, the 'reliance' interest.

2   There is also some possibility of Carol basing an action on negligence, but that is not pursued here.

EXCLUSION CLAUSES

Introduction

The questions in this chapter, like those in Chapter 5, are concerned with the contents of the contract. In this chapter, however, the focus is on a particular type of clause – the exclusion or exemption clause.

To answer questions on this topic, it is necessary to have a good grasp of the common law rules, the provisions of the Unfair Contract Terms Act 1977 (UCTA) and the Unfair Terms in Consumer Contracts Regulations 1999 (UTCCR). Although the interrelation of common law and statute causes some complications, the rules themselves are relatively well established and clear. Provided a systematic approach is adopted, then writing a good answer should not prove too difficult.

In answering a problem question, for example, the following issues should normally be considered in the following order:

- Is the clause incorporated?
- Does it cover the breach?
- Does UCTA apply? For example: (a) is it business liability – s 1(3)? And (b) is it a clause of the type covered by UCTA? See s 13 and, for example, *Smith v Bush* (1989).
- Is it a negligence case? If so, look at s 2 of UCTA.
- Is it a consumer contract or a standard term contract? – if so, look at s 3 of UCTA.
- Does the test of reasonableness apply and, if so, is it satisfied? Section 11 of and Sched 2 to UCTA.
- Is the situation affected by the provisions of the UTCCR (see Question 21)?

Two other issues may need consideration:

- Is there a privity problem? That is, does the clause try to exclude the liability of someone who is not a party to the contract? (An example of this is to be found in Question 22.)
- Is it a sale of goods contract? If so, then look at s 6 of UCTA. (An example of this type of case is to be found in Question 23.)

Essay questions will frequently require you to compare the common law and the statutory approach to exclusion clauses. Much of the above material will still be relevant. In addition, however, you may need here to say something about the doctrine of 'fundamental breach'. This doctrine has for all practical purposes been abolished by a combination of the decision in *Photo Production v Securicor* and s 9 of UCTA, but it played a significant role in the development of the common law approach to the control of exclusion clauses, and so in this context may need to be considered.

Checklist

You should be familiar with the following areas:

- The rules of incorporation.
- The rules of construction.
- The doctrine of fundamental breach (at least in outline).
- General provisions of UCTA 1977: ss 1, 2, 3 and 11.
- Special provisions of UCTA relating to sale of goods contracts: s 6 and Sched 2.
- Meaning of 'reasonableness' under UCTA.
- The provisions of the UTCCR 1999.

Question 20

Pamina owns a washing machine which has needed regular repair over the past two years. On the latest occasion on which it breaks down, she phones David, who has mended the machine on previous occasions. He agrees to come out on the basis of an 'all inclusive' charge of £50. When he has repaired the machine, he asks Pamina to sign a form stating that all work has been completed satisfactorily, that David will replace any parts which break down within three months, but that otherwise David accepts no liability for loss or damage caused by his work. Pamina signs the form.

The next time that Pamina uses the washing machine, it floods, causing £500 worth of damage to Pamina's carpets. When Pamina tries to switch it off, she receives a powerful electric shock from the casing, which severely burns her arm.

Advise Pamina.

Answer plan

This is a straightforward exclusion clause problem. As with most such problems, the issues to be considered are:

- was the exclusion clause incorporated?;
- if so, does the clause cover the breach (rule of construction)?;
- if so, does UCTA apply?;
- if so, is the clause void? Or, if applicable, does it satisfy the requirement of reasonableness?; and
- what is the effect of the UTCCR?

An answer of 'no' to either of the first two questions strictly speaking concludes the answer. In practice, however, even if you think that the clause was not incorporated or does not cover the breach, you should go on to deal with the applicability of UCTA and the UTCCR.

Note that the issue of incorporation, which generally turns on the time and extent of notice, is here further complicated by the fact of previous dealings between the parties.

Answer

This question concerns the issue of whether David can rely on the exemption clause contained in the document that Pamina signed.

To start with, it is assumed that the problems of the flooding and the electric shock result from work that David has done. If he has done the work with reasonable care, and the subsequent problems arise from some other cause, then he will not be in breach of contract, nor liable in tort for negligence, and Pamina will have no remedy. If, on the other hand, the problems are a consequence of the work, then Pamina may have an action in contract or tort, or both.

If Pamina tries to sue David, and can establish causation and negligence on his part, he will no doubt try to rely on the exemption clause in the document which Pamina signed as protecting him from liability. For an exemption clause to be valid it must be incorporated, and must on its true construction cover the breach that has occurred. If it satisfies both these tests, then it will be necessary to consider whether it is affected by the Unfair Contract Terms Act 1977 (UCTA) or the Unfair Terms in Consumer Contracts Regulations 1999 (UTCCR).

To start with incorporation, the first rule is that the clause must have been put forward before, or at the time, the contract was made. If it is introduced later, then it cannot be part of the contract. This is illustrated by *Olley v Marlborough Court* (1949), where an exemption clause displayed in a hotel bedroom was held not to be incorporated, since the contract had been made at the reception desk. How does this apply here? Pamina might well argue that she made her contract with David over the phone. He agreed to do the work; she agreed to pay £50. All the essential elements of a contract seem to be present. If that is the case, then the document containing the exemption clause can be said to have come too late, and so not be part of the contract.[1] On the other hand, David might well be able to rely on the fact that he has dealt with Pamina in the past. Assuming that she has always had to sign a form of the kind used in this case, he might argue that she had sufficient notice of the clause from previous dealings. This was the approach taken by the court in *Spurling v Bradshaw* (1956), where the clause was in a document delivered several days after the contract was made. It was, nevertheless, held to be effective because a similar document had been supplied in previous contracts between the parties. The course of dealing must be consistent, however. If David has sometimes used this document in his dealings with Pamina, but has not always done so, he may not be able to rely on it: *McCutcheon v McBrayne* (1964).

Provided the point as to timing is satisfied, Pamina will have difficulty arguing against incorporation of the term on the basis of lack of reasonable notice, which was the test established by *Parker v South Eastern Rly* (1877). Since she signed the document containing it, she will be deemed to have notice of its terms: *L'Estrange v Graucob* (1934).

The next issue to consider, assuming that the clause is incorporated, is whether it covers the breach which occurred. The basic approach to construction is the *contra proferentem* rule, which means that any doubt or ambiguity will be interpreted against the person trying to rely on the clause. The particular issue that may be relevant here is liability for negligence. In *White v John Warwick* (1953), it was held that the phrase 'nothing shall render the owners liable' referred only to strict liability under the contract, not to liability for negligence. Pamina might argue here that David's clause only refers to his liability to supply materials of satisfactory quality,[2] and not to his negligent repairs. In recent cases, however, the appellate courts have emphasised the undesirability of seeking strained construction of clauses in order to strike them down: for example, *George Mitchell v Finney Lock Seeds* (1983). Parliamentary intervention in the area by means of UCTA to protect the claimant, and in particular the consumer claimant, means that the courts should simply give the words of the clause their natural meaning. It is by no means clear that the simple lack of an all-encompassing phrase such as 'howsoever caused' will prevent David claiming that the clause does cover the breach.

If he succeeds on the incorporation and construction arguments, David will then face the restrictions of UCTA. UCTA applies mainly to attempts to exclude liabilities arising in the course of a business: s 1(3).[3] The main provision which is relevant here is s 2, which deals with 'negligence'. This covers both tortious negligence and the negligent performance of a contract. It is assumed here that the cause of the problems with Pamina's washing machine is David's negligent workmanship. Section 2(1) says that in relation to personal injuries caused by negligence there can be no exclusion of liability. As far as Pamina's injury to her arm is concerned, therefore, David will not be able to rely on the clause at all. The same approach to exclusion of liability for personal injury is taken in the UTCCR.

In relation to other loss and damage caused by negligence, s 2(2) says that an exclusion clause will only be liable insofar as it satisfies the requirement of reasonableness. This is set out in s 11, and states that a clause must be a fair and reasonable one to have been included in the contract. The test relates to the time the contract was made, not the time when it was broken.[4] There is little guidance from the case law as to how exactly the test should be applied. The appeal courts clearly feel that it is a matter best decided by the trial judge, who has heard all the evidence, and they have indicated a reluctance to lay down guidelines: *Mitchell v Finney Lock Seeds* (1983).[5] The Act itself contains, in Sched 2, some guidelines to be applied in relation to sale of goods cases. The Court of Appeal has confirmed that it is appropriate to consider these guidelines whenever the test of reasonableness is in issue: *Overseas Medical Supplies Ltd v Orient Transport Services Ltd* (1999). They include strength of bargaining power as a matter to be considered.

The court may also be influenced by the practice in other parts of the industry: *Mitchell v Finney Lock* (1983). In the end, the court has simply to decide whether the level of exemption was reasonable in all the circumstances. In this case, was it fair and reasonable for David to exclude his entire liability for any property damage caused by his negligently defective workmanship? It might well have been reasonable for him to limit his liability to a specified sum, but it is submitted that the attempt to reduce liability to zero goes too far, and that the court ought to hold this clause unreasonable. Again, the application of the provisions of the UTCCR is likely to result in a similar conclusion.

In conclusion, then, it seems that Pamina has a good chance of success. David's strongest ground probably relates to the construction of the clause. It does seem to cover the situation that has arisen. But, even if David can show that the clause was a part of the contract with Pamina, and this is by no means certain, the effect of UCTA and the UTCCR will be that he will certainly be unable to avoid liability for Pamina's injury to her arm, and may well also be liable for the damage to her carpets.

Notes

1   There may be an argument that there is a separate contract, that is, the guarantee of the parts in exchange for the exemption of other liability, in which case the timing problem disappears.

2   That is, under the Supply of Goods and Services Act 1982.

3   It has a wider scope in relation to sale of goods contracts – see s 6.

4   This was confirmed by the Court of Appeal in *Stewart Gill Ltd v Horatio Myer & Co Ltd* (1992).

5   Note that this case was decided on the basis of the pre-UCTA 'reasonableness' test contained in the Supply of Goods (Implied Terms) Act 1973. A similar approach was taken in the more recent Court of Appeal decisions in *Schenkers Ltd v Overland Shoes Ltd* (1998) and *Overseas Medical Supplies Ltd v Orient Transport Services Ltd* (1999).

Question 21

To what extent do the statutory controls over exclusion clauses in English law provide better protection for the consumer as opposed to the business contractor? Are the differences in treatment justifiable?

Answer plan

This question requires you to demonstrate a good understanding of the Unfair Contract Terms Act 1977 (UCTA) and the Unfair Terms in Consumer Contracts Regulations 1999 (UTCCR). There are several ways in which it could be tackled, but it will always be important not to overlook the second part of the question. A simple exposition of the law, without any attempt to discuss the justification for the differences between the treatment of consumers and businesses, will be unlikely to receive high marks.

The following approach is suggested:

•   introduction, indicating that the common law did not distinguish between consumers and business contractors;

•   discussion of the definition of 'consumer' in UCTA and the UTCCR, and the differences between them;

- the effect of the decision in *R & B Customs Brokers v UDT* (1988) on who is a 'consumer' for the purposes of UCTA;
- consideration of the ways in which UCTA distinguishes the treatment of consumers and businesses (that is, principally, ss 3, 6 and 7); and
- discussion of whether the differences in the treatment of businesses and consumers are justifiable.

Answer

There are two sets of statutory provisions which control the use of exclusion clauses in English contract law – the Unfair Contract Terms Act 1977 (UCTA) and the Unfair Terms in Consumer Contracts Regulations 1999 (UTCCR). Prior to this, the English common law made no formal distinction in the way in which it treated consumers and businesses. Some of the common law rules relating to exclusion clauses were, however, developed in ways which assisted consumers. The rules of incorporation and construction, for example, could in some instances be seen to be applied more strictly to the business contracting with a consumer as opposed to the situation where two businesses contract with each other. The statutory controls have made this explicit, and in various ways provide greater protection to the consumer than to the business contractor.

The first issue which must be considered is: 'What is the definition of a consumer?' This differs between UCTA and the UTCCR and so the two must be considered separately. Looking first at the UTCCR, reg 2 states that a consumer is a 'natural person' contracting for purposes outside his business. Thus, under these Regulations it is impossible for a limited company to be a consumer. The corresponding provision in UCTA is s 12. This does not define the word 'consumer' itself, but rather the phrase 'dealing as a consumer', which is used at various points in the Act. Under s 12, a person deals as a consumer when he does not contract 'in the course of a business' and does not 'hold himself out as doing so', where the other party *does* make the contract in the course of a business. Where the contract is for the sale or supply of goods, there is an additional requirement that the goods in question are of a type 'ordinarily supplied for private use or consumption'.[1] If they are not, then the person will not be dealing as a consumer. Finally, a person buying at an auction or by competitive tender is never to be regarded as dealing as a consumer.[2]

It will be seen that the definitions in both UCTA and the UTCCR are linked to the concept of 'business'. This is defined in both sets of provisions as including a profession and the activities of central or local government or other 'public authority'. Neither attempts a full definition, however, and so there are some grey areas. What, for example, is the position of a church which holds a sale to raise funds – is it contracting as a business? If it is not, then people who buy from it will not be dealing as consumers, and so will not be able to rely on the relevant protective provisions in UCTA and the UTCCR.

The phrase 'dealing as a consumer' under UCTA received judicial consideration in the case of *R & B Customs Brokers v UDT* (1988). The plaintiff in this case was a private company which had bought a car for the business and personal use of one of the directors. The company was in the export business, and had no connection with the motor trade. The Court of Appeal held that the company, in buying the car, was not buying in the course of business for the purposes of s 12 of UCTA. This meant that the company could be treated as dealing as a consumer, and therefore gain the stronger protection against exemption clauses provided by s 6 of UCTA, which is discussed below.

This was regarded as a somewhat surprising decision, but it has stood for 14 years. It was regarded with some scepticism by the Court of Appeal in *Stevenson v Rogers* (1999), which was concerned with the phrase 'in the course of business' as used in s 14 of the Sale of Goods Act 1979. This had no direct effect on the *R & B Customs Brokers* decision, however, and that case must still be regarded as good law as regards the definition of 'dealing as a consumer' under UCTA. Potentially, it could also apply to the UTCCR. Although, as we have seen, a company cannot be a consumer for the purposes of these Regulations, a sole trader who bought goods partly for private use might be able to argue that this meant that he or she was purchasing as a consumer. Given the generally hostile reaction to the *R & B Customs Brokers* decision, however, it is unlikely that the courts would look to extend its scope.

Turning to the way in which UCTA and the UTCCR distinguish between businesses and consumers in the protection provided, the position with the UTCCR is straightforward. The Regulations adopt an all or nothing approach. If you contract as a consumer, you have the full protection of the UTCCR; if you contract as a business, they do not protect you at all. As a consumer you are entitled to expect the contract to be in 'plain, intelligible language' (reg 7). Moreover, you will not be bound by any provision which offends against the requirement of 'good faith' and causes a 'significant imbalance' to your rights vis à vis the other contracting party (regs 5 and 8). Schedule 2 gives a list of terms which may be considered unfair. This includes terms restricting liability for personal injury, or allowing a supplier to provide goods or services other than those contracted for. In general, this Schedule is concerned with terms which impose unexpected and unduly onerous obligations on the consumer.

The position under UCTA is different. Some provisions of the Act apply to all contractors, whether they are consumers or not.[3] Examples of this type of control are the prohibition in s 2 of any clause restricting liability for causing death or personal injury through negligence,[4] and the prohibition of any exclusion of the implied term as to title under s 12 of the Sale of Goods Act 1979 (s 6).

In other respects, differences are drawn between the consumer and the business contractor. In s 3, for example, which deals with the exclusion of liability arising in contract, one of the tests for the section to apply is where a person contracts as a consumer. Such a person will always have the protection of the section, which subjects most clauses limiting contractual liability to the test of reasonableness in s 11. The other test for the applicability of s 3 is where the party contracts on the other's written standard terms of business. Many business contractors will, therefore, come within the protection provided by the section. The consumer does not need to show, however, that the contract was made on written standard terms.

Section 5 deals with manufacturers' guarantees. These may not be used to exclude negligence liability where loss or damage results from the goods proving defective while in consumer use. 'Consumer use' is further defined as where the goods are being used, or held for use, other than 'exclusively' for a business. The goods must be of a type ordinarily supplied for private use. The section is therefore most likely to operate to protect the consumer, but there is the possibility of a business using it where 'consumer' goods are bought for use partly for the business and partly for private use.[5]

Contracts for the sale or supply of goods are dealt with by ss 6 and 7 of UCTA. These deal with the exclusion of the implied terms contained in the Sale of Goods Act 1979, or the equivalent under other legislation. In relation to the implied terms as to quality (covering correspondence with description, satisfactory quality and fitness for a specified purpose), the approach is that there can be no exclusion at all against a person contracting as a consumer. As regards the business purchaser or hirer, the position is that there may be exclusion, but the clause must satisfy the requirement of reasonableness under s 11 of UCTA.

From the above, it will be seen that under UCTA there is greater protection for the consumer than for the business. The business contractor, however, is by no means left without any redress as regards exclusion clauses; moreover, the *R & B Brokers* decision means that there are more situations than might have been expected where a 'business' can claim to be dealing 'as a consumer'. Under the UTCCR, only consumers are protected. Is the difference in treatment justifiable? It is no doubt acceptable that consumers should have greater protection than businesses. They are more vulnerable to having unfair terms imposed upon them – through ignorance or inequality of bargaining power. Most consumers dealing with a business are faced with a 'take it or leave it' contract, the terms of which are not negotiable. Strong protection is therefore required. Business contractors, on the other hand, should be able to stand up for themselves and so avoid being pushed into making contracts on unfair and unreasonable terms. But does this accord with reality? In practice, even between businesses there is often considerable inequality of bargaining power, and scope for the imposition of unfair terms. It is right, then, that UCTA should not ignore the business contractor, and should extend some protection where exclusion clauses cover negligence liability, are contained in written standard terms, or purport to limit liability for breach of the implied terms under the Sale of Goods Act 1979. In this respect, and subject to the doubts about whether the *R & B Brokers* decision should stand, UCTA probably gets the balance between the consumer and business contractor about right: both have some protection, but that available to the consumer is considerably greater. The approach of the UTCCR is different and more limited as regards the contractual relationships which it covers. It does nothing to protect the business contractor from unfair terms. There is an argument that the Regulations' 'good faith' approach should be given wider application, and operate between businesses as well, at least where it is clear that there is significant inequality of bargaining power.

Overall, the conclusion is that the current provisions are very much on the right lines as far as balancing the protection between consumers and businesses, though there may be some scope for tightening the definition of a consumer under UCTA, and, at the same time, expanding the scope of the principles contained in the UTCCR to cover some business contractors.

Notes

1   This is contained in s 12(1)(c).

2   See s 12(2).

3   The other party must be contracting in the course of business – s 1(3).

4   'Negligence' including both the tort of negligence and negligent performance of a contract. The exclusion of liability for other loss or damage caused by negligence is subject to the 'requirement of reasonableness': this applies to both consumer and business contractors.

5   Cf the situation in *R & B Customs Brokers v UDT* (1988).

Question 22

Alan's car breaks down on his way to work. He telephones his local garage, Cedar Motors, who agree to send out Bert, a mechanic, to repair the car. Bert tells Alan that the car cannot be repaired at the roadside but will have to be towed to the garage. Alan agrees to this. Bert winches up Alan's car in order to tow it to the garage, but a worn clip on the towing gear being used by Bert slips open, allowing the car to fall. The car runs backwards over Alan's foot, breaking several toes. The car's suspension is severely damaged in the fall. Displayed on the back of the towing vehicle is a notice: 'All towing takes place at the customer's risk. Cedar Motors and their employees accept no liability for any damage, injury, or consequential loss, howsoever caused, while a car is being towed.'

Alan wishes to sue Cedar Motors and Bert, both of whom claim to be protected by the notice.

Answer plan

This question, like Question 20, involves a discussion of the effectiveness of exemption clauses. The issues outlined for discussion in the answer plan to that question, relating to the common law, the Unfair Contract Terms Act 1977 (UCTA) and the Unfair Terms in Consumer Contracts Regulations 1999 (UTCCR), need to be looked at here as well.

There is an additional problem, however, in that in this case Alan is said to wish to sue Bert, the employee. The exemption clause purports to exclude Bert's liability. This calls for a discussion of the application of the doctrine of privity to exclusion clauses. The possibility of Bert being able to claim the benefit of the exemption clause, by virtue of the Contracts (Rights of Third Parties) Act 1999, must be considered. If, for some reason, the Act does not apply, then common law ways around the doctrine of privity, as used in *The Eurymedon* (1975) and *Southern Water Authority v Carey* (1985), will need to be discussed.

Answer

For Alan to have a cause of action on these facts, he will have to establish one of three things:

(a) breach of a strict liability under the contract with Cedar Motors;[1] or

(b) negligent performance of the contract by Cedar Motors (or their authorised employee); or

(c) tortious negligence on the part of Bert.

It is assumed that there was no breach of a specific contractual obligation here, giving rise to strict liability. The facts suggest, rather, that the injury and damage arise from negligent performance of the contract. This kind of issue can become very complicated.[2] For the purposes of answering this question, it is assumed that either Bert or one of Cedar Motors' other employees should have noticed that the clip was worn, and that therefore there was negligence which caused the injury and damage.

If this is the case, can either Cedar Motors or Bert, or both, escape liability by relying on the notice on the back of Bert's van, which attempts to operate as an exclusion clause? The position of Cedar Motors will be considered first.

The notice will only be effective to prevent Alan suing Cedar Motors if it can be said to have been incorporated into their contract. A clause can become incorporated by being contained in a document which is signed by the contracting parties (*L'Estrange v Graucob* (1934)). Alternatively, reasonable notice of the clause must be given (*Parker v SE Rly* (1877)) before or at the time of the contract (*Thornton v Shoe Lane Parking* (1971)). Since Alan did not sign a document containing the clause, there are two issues here. First, when was the contract made? Secondly, was reasonable notice of the clause given before or at that time?

It might be argued that the contract is made when Alan first contacts the garage. At this stage, however, the discussion relates to repair, and not towing. It is only when Bert realises that a roadside repair is impossible that the question of towing Alan's car arises. It seems then that a separate contract for towing comes into existence when Alan agrees to this. Did he at that time have sufficient notice of the exclusion clause, which was contained in a notice on the back of the lorry? It has been accepted in many cases that the display of a notice may be sufficient to incorporate a clause into a contract. In *Thornton v Shoe Lane Parking*, for example, the court had no difficulty with the concept that a notice displayed outside a car park could potentially be used to exclude liability.[3] Whether the clause was in a document or on a notice, the test of incorporation is the same, that is, did the defendant give the claimant reasonable notice of the clause? The test is an objective one, and it is irrelevant if the claimant suffered from some unknown disability which prevented him from reading the clause: *Thompson v LM & S Rly* (1930). How will this apply to the facts of our problem? It will clearly be relevant to know how prominent the notice is on the back of the towing vehicle. The wider or more unexpected the clause, the clearer the notice expected. As Lord Denning said in *Spurling v Bradshaw* (1956), some clauses might need to be in red ink with a red hand pointing to them before the courts would accept that reasonable notice had been given. This approach to incorporation of unusual terms was confirmed in the non-exclusion clause case of *Interfoto Picture Library Ltd v Stiletto Visual Programmes* (1988). The clause here is wide, but probably not that unexpected, in that the towing firm might well try to place some limits on its liability for what is an inherently dangerous operation. Clearly, if Bert had drawn specific attention to it before Alan agreed to the towing, the clause would be incorporated. Otherwise, the question of incorporation will depend on the size of the writing, the opportunity that Alan had to read it, and even the time of day when the incident occurred. If it was at night, it is less likely that it will be reasonable for Alan to have seen the clause without his attention being drawn to it.

If the incorporation issue is decided in Alan's favour, then there is no need to consider the clause further. Assuming, however, that it is incorporated, does it cover the breach? This is where the rule of construction applies. The courts will interpret the clause strictly against the defendants: for example, *White v John Warwick* (1953).[4] In this case, wide words are used, including the phrase 'howsoever caused', which is likely to be interpreted as covering negligence as well as strict liability. It is possible, however, that Alan could argue that the events which caused the injury and damage were not within the scope of the clause. This is because the clause refers to losses 'while a car is being towed'. Alan might say that his car was not in fact being towed when the incident occurred, but was simply being lifted as a preliminary to being towed. If that is right, then the defendants will be unable to rely on the clause. There would be some logic to such an interpretation, as it is presumably during the actual process of towing that the greatest risk of injury or damage arises. On the other hand, the courts have in more recent cases discouraged the practice of nit-picking interpretation of exclusion clauses. In *Ailsa Craig Fishing Co v Malvern Fishing Co* (1983), for example, Lord Wilberforce said that words should normally be given their natural plain meaning. It is, nevertheless, a possibility that a court would view the accident in this case as falling outside the clause.

Assuming that this line is not taken, and the wording of the clause is regarded as being apt to cover the situation, a further hurdle exists for the defendant in the form of the Unfair Contract Terms Act 1977 (UCTA) and the Unfair Terms in Consumer Contracts Regulations 1999 (UTCCR). In particular, s 2 of UCTA, which deals with exclusion of liability for negligence, will be relevant. Where such liability arises in the course of a business,[5] s 2(1) states that no exclusion is possible as regards death or personal injury. The defendants will thus undoubtedly be liable for the injury to Alan's toes. The UTCCR take a similar line as regards personal injury, but are not as specific on this point as UCTA, which is therefore the better provision for Alan to rely on as regards this issue.

As far as the damage to the car is concerned, s 2(2) of UCTA says that exclusion for such liability is only permissible insofar as the clause satisfies the requirement of 'reasonableness'. This is partially defined by s 11, which says that the test of whether a clause satisfies the requirement is whether it was a fair and reasonable clause to include in the contract. This is a question of fact to be decided in each case, but it may be relevant that Alan here really had no option but to accept the contract subject to the exclusion clause. He was not in a position where he could 'shop around' for a better deal. A court may well feel disinclined to accept that a blanket exclusion of liability is fair and reasonable in such circumstances.[6] Similarly, the UTCCR emphasise the importance of the strength of the bargaining position of the parties as a factor in deciding whether a provision should be enforced. Application of the Regulations is likely to lead to the same conclusion as under ss 2(2) and 11 of UCTA.

A final issue which needs to be mentioned here is the position of Bert. If the clause falls at any of the hurdles set out above, then of course it cannot protect Bert. If, however, it was held, for example, that the part of the clause dealing with property damage did satisfy the requirement of reasonableness, could Bert take advantage of this? It is not uncommon for employers to try to protect employees in this way. The difficulty which arises is that to do so will almost certainly offend against the doctrine of privity. The contract in this case, for example, is clearly between Cedar Motors and Alan. Bert is not a party to the agreement. How then can he receive any benefit from it? This was the view taken in *Adler v Dickson* (1955), where a shipping company tried to provide protection from liability for its employees. It was held that the exclusion clause could only benefit the company. The common law position has, however, now been affected by the Contracts (Rights of Third Parties) Act 1999. This allows a third party to enforce a beneficial term in a contract if the term expressly provides that he or she may do so (s 1(1)(a)). It is possible that the clause in Cedar Motors' notice could be interpreted in this way, but the language might not be regarded as being sufficiently explicit. The clause undoubtedly 'purports to confer a benefit' on Bert, as an employee, however. This is sufficient to allow Bert to enforce the clause, unless the proper construction of it appears to be that the parties did not intend it to be enforceable (s 1(1)(b) and s 1(2)). There is no reason why this clause should be interpreted in such a way. Provided, therefore, that Bert could rely on the exclusion clause, if he were a party to the contract (s 3(6)), he will be able to enforce it against Alan. As indicated above, he will not be able to rely on it as regards Alan's personal injuries, but he may be able to do so in respect of the property damage.

If it was held that the 1999 Act did not apply to allow Bert to rely on the clause, there are two other methods of circumventing the doctrine of privity which might be considered. First, in *The Eurymedon* (1975), the doctrine of agency was used to construct a unilateral contract between plaintiffs (owners of goods) and defendants (stevedores) where at first sight the only contract appeared to be between the carriers and the stevedores. If applied here, it would mean treating Cedar Motors as agents for Bert in making a contract with Alan of the form 'I will tow your car, provided you give me the benefit of this exclusion clause'.

The second approach has been to say that, in relation to tortious liability, the existence of the exclusion clause can limit the duty of care: *Southern Water Authority v Carey* (1985). In theory, this could be relevant here, in that Bert's liability will be in the tort of negligence, but this argument, as with the agency argument outlined above, has only ever been successfully used against a 'business' claimant. It is submitted that it would be very unlikely that a court would allow either of them to be used against a consumer like Alan.

In conclusion, it appears that Alan has a good chance of success in actions against both Cedar Motors and Bert. Section 2 of UCTA makes it certain that he will be able to recover for his personal injuries; there is also a good chance that the clause will be held not to be incorporated, not to cover the breach, or not to be reasonable (s 2(2) of UCTA; the UTCCR). If any of these is the case, Alan will be able to recover for the damage to his car as well.

Notes

1   That is, breach of a specific contractual obligation which will give rise to liability irrespective of fault, such as the obligation to supply goods matching their description under s 13 of the Sale of Goods Act 1979.

2   See, for example, *Lambert v Lewis* (1982).

3   Other cases where this has been accepted include *Olley v Marlborough Court* (1949), *Chapelton v Barry* (1940) and, in a rather different context, *Ashdown v Samuel Williams* (1957).

4   That is, the *contra proferentem* rule.

5   See s 1(3).

6   Note also the 'guidelines' in Sched 2, which are not strictly relevant on the facts, but may well be referred to.

Question 23

Gull, the owner of a small business which manufactures furniture, decides to computerise his accounting system. He is visited by a salesman from Computacon Ltd, who advises him to buy a Computacon XLO 500. Gull asks about after sales service and is told: 'We have a team of service engineers on 24 hour call.' Gull immediately agrees to buy an XLO 500, with 128 megabytes of memory, for £2,500, and signs a contract for the supply of this. The contract states, in clause 7: 'We guarantee to deal with any problem with your XLO 500 within 24 hours of being notified of it.'

During the first three weeks of operation the computer breaks down several times and there are delays of up to three days in getting it repaired. Gull then discovers: (a) that the computer supplied has only 64 megabytes of memory, which explains why it is inadequate to handle his accounts; and (b) that Computacon employs only one service engineer.

Gull is suing Computacon for misrepresentation, breach of clause 7 of the contract, and breach of the implied terms under s 13 (description) and s 14(2) (satisfactory quality) of the Sale of Goods Act 1979. He is claiming damages of £7,500.

Computacon does not dispute liability, or the assessment of Gull's damages, but relies on the following clauses in the agreement which Gull signed:

8   This document contains all the terms of the agreement, other than implied terms under the Sale of Goods Act 1979, and no liability is accepted for any pre-contractual oral statements.

9   Liability for breach of any term of this agreement, or any implied term, is limited to the purchase price of the computer.

10 Any claim for breach of contract must be notified to Computacon within 14 days of delivery of the computer.

Advise Gull.

Answer plan

This question is long, but this is partly due to the fact that it sets out in detail a number of clauses of the contract. The number of issues raised is not, in fact, greater than normal. It is important to note that it is specifically stated that Computacon does not dispute liability, or the assessment of Gull's damages. Any student who spends time dealing with these issues will at best be wasting time, and at worst will lose marks for irrelevance. The question is concentrating on the exemption clause issues. There is little to be said either on incorporation (because it is a signed agreement) or construction (because the wording of the exclusion clauses seems unambiguous). The issues centre on the scope of UCTA, and are as follows:

- clause 8 – is the first part of this an exclusion clause? Is the second part caught by s 8 of UCTA?;
- clause 9 –
  - how does this affect the breaches of clause 7 of the contract, taking into account s 3 of UCTA?;
  - what is the position as regards excluding the Sale of Goods Act 1979 implied terms? Is Gull a 'consumer' or a 'business' for this purpose? Cf *R & B Customs Brokers v UDT* (1988); and
- clause 10 – is this an exclusion clause? If so, does it satisfy the requirement of reasonableness?

Each clause will need to be considered in turn.

Note that, because Gull is not a consumer, the provisions of the UTCCR will not need to be discussed in answering this problem.

Answer

We are told in this problem that Computacon has accepted liability, and the basis for the assessment of damages. The question is whether it can avoid paying more than £2,500 to Gull, by relying on the provisions of clauses 8, 9 and 10.

One of the common law controls over clauses attempting to restrict liability is the strict requirement of incorporation. This is unlikely to be an issue here, since Gull has signed the contract containing the clauses, and this is generally enough to deem them to be incorporated, whether Gull was aware of them or not: *L'Estrange v Graucob* (1934). The other main common law control is the rule of construction. Issues relating to this will be looked at in relation to each of the clauses as they arise. Much more important in this problem, however, are the statutory controls contained in the Unfair Contract Terms Act 1977 (UCTA). The contract here involves 'business liability' on the part of Computacon (see s 1(3) of UCTA), and so most of UCTA's provisions will apply. Because Gull is contracting in the course of his business, rather than as a consumer, however, the provisions of the Unfair Terms in Consumer Contracts Regulations 1999 (UTCCR) will not apply.

Clause 8 attempts to do two things: first, it attempts to prevent pre-contractual statements from being regarded as part of the contract; secondly, it attempts to restrict liability for misrepresentations. The effect of clauses of this kind has been considered by the courts in several cases, such as *Cremdean v Nash* (1977), *Thomas Witter Ltd v TBP Industries* (1996) and *Inntrepreneur Pub Co (GL) v East Crown Ltd* (2000). The result is that the first part of clause 8 is likely to be held to be effective to prevent an action based on a collateral contract, or on an argument that a pre-contractual statement has been incorporated into the main contract. It will not, however, be regarded as affecting the position as regards actions for misrepresentation. The second part of clause 8, on the other hand, will be treated as attempting to exclude liability for misrepresentation. From the facts, it does not seem that Gull is arguing for a collateral contract or the incorporation of a misrepresentation. His action will be based on the fact that the statement about the 'team of service engineers' was a false statement of fact which induced the contract. He is therefore likely to be arguing for liability for a negligent misrepresentation under s 2 of the Misrepresentation Act 1967. The second part of clause 8 attempts to exclude all liability for this. Section 3 of the Misrepresentation Act 1967, as substituted by s 8 of UCTA, says that it will only be able to do this to the extent that the clause satisfies the requirement of reasonableness under s 11 of UCTA. The burden of proof is on Computacon. The application of the requirement of reasonableness is considered further below.

Turning to clause 9, this again has two aspects. The first relates to the exclusion of liability for a term of the agreement. The relevant term here is clause 7, which gave a specific guarantee of the speed within which problems would be dealt with. This does not seem to be a question of negligent performance, so s 2 of UCTA will not apply.[1] The applicable provision will be s 3. This applies where one contracting party deals as a consumer or on the other's written standard terms of business. It is not necessary here to consider whether Gull deals as a consumer (this issue is considered further in relation to the second part of clause 9), since it is clear that Computacon is using written standard terms. The effect of s 3[2] is that Computacon can only exclude or restrict its liability for breach of clause 7 insofar as clause 9 satisfies the requirement of reasonableness. This issue will again be discussed later.

The second part of clause 9 is concerned with the exclusion of liability for breach of implied terms. There is a breach of two of the implied terms under the Sale of Goods Act 1979 here, relating to description (it does not have as big a memory as it should) and satisfactory quality (it regularly breaks down).[3] The relevant provision of UCTA in this situation is s 6. This states that if the buyer is a consumer, then no exclusion of liability for breach of the implied terms is allowed. If, however, the buyer is a business, then a clause may be valid, provided that it satisfies the requirement of reasonableness. What is the position here? At first sight, it appears that Gull buys in the course of a business, but this may not be the answer that the courts give. The relevant authority is *R & B Customs Brokers v UDT* (1988). Here, the plaintiff was a private company which was in the export business. A car was bought for the personal and business use of one of the directors. When the car proved defective, the plaintiff sued on the implied terms, and the defendant relied on an exclusion clause. The Court of Appeal ruled that the exclusion clause was struck down by s 6 of UCTA, because the plaintiff here did not buy the car in the course of a business. This was because the plaintiff's business was not that of buying and selling cars, and there was no evidence that this was done with any regularity. The purchase was thus incidental, and not an integral part of the business' activity. It may well be that Gull can rely on this decision here. He is not in the business of buying and selling computers. Indeed, it seems that this may well be the first time that he has bought one.[4] It seems likely that, on the basis of the *R & B Customs Brokers* decision, he will be treated as a consumer purchaser. Even if this is not the case, he will still be able to plead that the clause is unreasonable.

The final clause to consider, clause 10, is the widest in its scope, in that it potentially applies to all the breaches which we have looked at. It does not directly exclude liability, but says that any claim must be made within 14 days of delivery. Section 13 of UCTA is relevant here. This says that clauses which make enforcement of liability subject to 'restrictive or onerous' conditions must be treated in the same way as exclusion clauses. This would seem clearly to apply to a clause such as clause 10, which severely limits the circumstances in which a claim can be made. This means that clause 10 will be struck down, or will be subject to the requirement of reasonableness, in relation to the various breaches of contract in exactly the same way as clauses 8 and 9, as outlined above.

We must now turn to the 'requirement of reasonableness'. This is set out in s 11 of UCTA, but is, unfortunately, not fully defined. Section 11(1) simply says that the clause must be a fair and reasonable one to have included in the contract, taking into account all the circumstances which the parties knew, or should have known, at the time of the contract.[5] Section 11(4) says that, where liability is restricted to a specific sum (as with clause 9 here), the court should take account of the defendant's resources and the availability of insurance. In relation to clauses subject to s 6, guidelines are set out in Sched 2 to the Act. These guidelines contain factors, such as the bargaining power of each party, which are in fact likely to be relevant to most decisions as to reasonableness, as was confirmed by the Court of Appeal in *Overseas Medical Supplies Ltd v Orient Transport Services Ltd* (1999).

Such decisions as there have been on UCTA are not helpful in setting the parameters of reasonableness. The appellate courts in, for example, *Mitchell v Finney Lock Seeds* (1983) and *Schenkers Ltd v Overland Shoes Ltd* (1998) have shown a reluctance to interfere with first instance decisions on the issue. The following suggestions are therefore only tentative.

First, the blanket exclusions in clauses 8 and 10 are unlikely to be found reasonable. In relation to clause 8, it might be argued that a claimant who wanted to rely on a pre-contractual statement should have insisted that it was included in the contract. But this is unrealistic in relation to a contract where the defendant is almost certainly presenting 'take it or leave it' standard terms. And, in relation to clause 10, two weeks would seem to be far too short a time for the proper evaluation of a complex computer system.

The position with clause 9 is more difficult. The defendant is effectively saying, 'you can have the computer for nothing, but we are not going to compensate you for any consequential loss'. In a situation where the potential losses from a defective business computer may be very difficult to estimate, this may be a reasonable approach, particularly if it would be difficult for the defendant to obtain substantial insurance cover (see s 11(4) of UCTA).

The advice to Gull would therefore seem to be that he has a good chance of recovering his full losses as regards the misrepresentation, and (assuming he is regarded as buying as a consumer) the breaches of the Sale of Goods Act implied terms. As far as the specific breach of clause 7 is concerned, however, clause 9 may operate to limit recovery. In practice, this is unlikely to matter to Gull if he is able to achieve full recovery of his losses under one of the other heads.

Notes

1   It might be possible to argue that failure to meet the terms of clause 7 resulted from negligence, but it is more obvious to deal with this as a breach of a strict liability under the contract.

2   To be precise, s 3(2)(a).

3   See ss 13 and 14(2) of the Sale of Goods Act 1979.

4   The decision in *R & B Customs Brokers* was viewed with some scepticism by the Court of Appeal in the Sale of Goods Act case, *Stevenson v Rogers* (1999). It has also been criticised by various academic commentators (see, for example, Stone, *The Modern Law of Contract*, 5th edn, 2002, p 236). Nevertheless, it has not been overruled, and remains the governing authority as to the meaning of the phrase 'in the course of business' where it occurs in UCTA.

5   Note that the emphasis is on the time of contracting, not what happened as a result of the breach – *Stewart Gill Ltd v Horatio Myer & Co Ltd* (1992).

CHAPTER 7

MISTAKE AND MISREPRESENTATION

Introduction

This chapter is the first of several which look at various arguments which may be used by the parties to a contract to say that the agreement should be regarded as 'void' or 'voidable'. These arguments are often grouped under the general heading of 'vitiating factors'. The two which are considered in this chapter are 'mistake' and 'misrepresentation'.

The reason for linking these two topics is that it will often be the case that a particular set of circumstances gives rise to the possibility of argument in either mistake or misrepresentation. It is useful, therefore, to consider the advantages of one against the other. This issue is dealt with specifically in Question 24. It should not be forgotten, however, that although it is not uncommon to find a contract question that requires an answer covering both mistake and misrepresentation, the issues are not necessarily linked. Indeed, certain aspects of misrepresentation have already been discussed in Chapter 5. Some of those aspects are explored further in Question 27. Question 25, on the other hand, is an example of a question raising mistake issues, but not misrepresentation.

Neither of these areas is particularly easy to deal with. In relation to misrepresentation, the problems arise from the fact that there are remedies under both the common law and statute. In mistake, the complications arise from the fact that the case law on what amounts to an operative mistake is not very clear (particularly the implications of the decision in *Bell v Lever Bros*), and the fact that equity has in some situations stepped in to mitigate the rather strict common law rules. The scope for such intervention has, however, been significantly reduced by the recent decision in *Great Peace Shipping Ltd v Tsavliris Salvage (International) Ltd* (2002), where the Court of Appeal held that there is no power to rescind a contract in equity as distinct from the common law power to hold it void.

There is no easy way to simplify these areas. The advice must be simply to take each question step by step, perhaps in the following order (assuming that it is a problem question):

- is there a misrepresentation?;

- if so, what remedy would the claimant want – that is, rescission or damages?;
- if damages is enough, can the Misrepresentation Act 1967 be used?;
- if rescission is required, are there any bars, such as the involvement of third parties?;
- if misrepresentation cannot provide an adequate remedy, is there an operative common law mistake? Remember that if there is, this will *inter alia* override any third party rights, and allow the recovery of property transferred as a consequence of the mistake; and
- if there is no common law mistake, can equity assist? Equity may take account of less serious mistakes, but can only provide limited remedies (for example, refusal of specific performance) which will not override third party rights.

Note that, for the reasons given in the introduction to Chapter 5, the action in tort for negligent misstatement under *Hedley Byrne v Heller* is not discussed in any detail in this chapter.

Checklist

You should be familiar with the following areas:
- The difference between various types of mistake – for example, common, mutual, unilateral.
- Effects of an operative mistake, both in common law and equity.
- The definition of a misrepresentation.
- Common law remedies for misrepresentation, including the bars on rescission.
- Remedies for misrepresentation under the Misrepresentation Act 1967.

Question 24

'Most situations where either or both parties enter into a contract on the basis of a mistake of fact can nowadays be dealt with quite satisfactorily by the remedies for misrepresentation. There are very few situations where the doctrine of mistake has any practical role to play.'

Discuss.

Answer plan

This question requires you to think about two areas: mistake and misrepresentation. It is not a question which should be attempted unless you have a firm grasp of both. Two particular areas which you will need to consider are:

* are there situations involving a contract being made on the basis of a mistake which do not also involve a misrepresentation?; and
* are there situations in which the remedies for misrepresentation are inadequate, and the remedies for mistake more satisfactory?

The essay will need to start with a description, supported by examples from the case law, of the basic principles operating in relation to misrepresentation and mistake, before going on to discuss the two issues set out above.

Answer

It is certainly true that there are situations where a contract made on the basis of a mistake of fact also involves a misrepresentation. A clear example would be where one of the contracting parties deliberately pretends to be someone other than who they really are, as in, for example, *Lewis v Averay* (1973). The statement 'I am Richard Greene' was a misrepresentation. The subsequent contract was also made on the basis of a unilateral mistake. Even where the mistake is mutual, if one of the parties has been misled by the other's mistake, this may well have involved a misrepresentation. An example might be *McRae v Commonwealth Disposals Commission* (1951), where the invitation for tenders could be said to have amounted to a misrepresentation as to the existence of the oil tanker.[1] Before looking in more detail at the degree of overlap between mistake and misrepresentation, the basic principles of the two areas will be outlined.

A misrepresentation is a false statement of existing fact made by one party to a contract to another, which induces the other party to enter into the contract. It may be made innocently, negligently or fraudulently. The state of mind of the misrepresentor is irrelevant to the issue of whether there is an operative misrepresentation, though it is of considerable importance as regards remedies.

A statement of opinion (*Bisset v Wilkinson* (1927)) or law (*Cooper v Phibbs* (1867)) will not generally be a misrepresentation.[2] A statement of intention may be a misrepresentation if the intention is falsely stated – *Edgington v Fitzmaurice* (1885): 'The state of a man's mind is as much a fact as the state of his digestion.'[3]

The statement must, at least to some extent, induce the contract. It does not have to be the only reason for making the contract, but it must be an operative factor: *Edgington v Fitzmaurice* (1885). The reliance does not, it seems, have to be reasonable. In *Museprime v Adhill* (1990), the unreasonableness of reliance was said to be simply evidence which might suggest that there had been no actual reliance.

Once it has been established that there is an operative misrepresentation, the remedies will depend on whether it was made innocently, negligently or fraudulently. For all three types of misrepresentation, rescission of the contract will be available, unless one of the bars to this equitable remedy exists. If there has been an undue lapse of time, or if it is impossible to restore the parties to their original positions (because, for example, goods have been consumed), or, perhaps most importantly for this essay, if third party rights have become involved, then no rescission is possible. If the misrepresentation is entirely innocent, then the claimant will be left without any remedy. If it was negligent or fraudulent, however, a remedy in damages will still be available. For negligent misrepresentation, this is provided for by s 2(1) of the Misrepresentation Act 1967, which applies where the person making the statement is unable to show that they had reasonable grounds for believing it to be true. Fraudulent misrepresentation is governed by the tort of deceit. In *Royscot v Rogerson* (1991), the Court of Appeal ruled that the assessment of damages is the same under s 2(1) as for fraud. In particular, the wide remoteness rule applicable to the tort of deceit (*Doyle v Olby* (1969)) applies equally to s 2(1). The House of Lords in *Smith New Court Securities Ltd v Scrimgeour Vickers (Asset Management) Ltd* (1996), in confirming *Doyle v Olby*, expressed some scepticism as to whether the same rule should apply to s 2(1). The issue was not directly before the House, however, so *Royscot v Rogerson* must still be regarded as good law.

Turning now to the doctrine of mistake, this is a complex area, and only a brief outline can be given. There are basically three types of mistake, often categorised as common, mutual and unilateral.[4] Common mistake arises where the parties are in agreement, but that agreement assumes some fact to be true when it is not. For example, the parties contract about a cargo, in ignorance of the fact that the ship on which it is being carried has sunk (cf *Couturier v Hastie* (1852), where the cargo had been disposed of by the master of the ship). Mutual mistake arises where the parties are at cross-purposes, but neither is aware of this, as in *Raffles v Wichelhaus* (1864), where there was confusion resulting from two ships of the same name sailing from the same port at about the same time. A unilateral mistake exists where one party is aware of the other's mistake. Many of the cases of mistaken identity, such as *King's Norton Metal Co Ltd v Edridge* (1897), involve unilateral mistake.

In relation to mutual and unilateral mistake, there is no contract because there never was in fact an agreement. The parties were at cross-purposes, or one party was aware that the other party was agreeing on the basis of something which was untrue. In relation to common mistake, there may be an agreement but, if the mistake is operative, then the contract will be declared void from the beginning at common law. In all cases, the mistake, to be operative, must be about something which is fundamental to the contract. The existence of the subject matter is clearly fundamental. The quality of the subject matter (*Bell v Lever Bros* (1932)), or the identity of the person with whom you are contracting, may or may not be fundamental (compare *Ingram v Little* (1961) – identity fundamental – with *Lewis v Averay* (1973) – not fundamental) depending on all the surrounding circumstances.

If a contract is found never to have existed, or is declared void for common mistake, then the whole transaction must be unscrambled. None of the bars to rescission noted in relation to misrepresentation operates, and even third party rights can be overridden. If, on the other hand, there has been a mistake which, while significant, is not so fundamental as to require that the contract be regarded as non-existent or void, the equitable remedies of refusal of specific performance or rectification may be available. The power to rescind a contract in equity, derived from *Solle v Butcher* (1950), has, however, now been firmly rejected by the Court of Appeal in *Great Peace Shipping Ltd v Tsavliris Salvage (International) Ltd* (2002). Where equitable remedies are available, however, they will be subject to third party rights.

What, then, is the relationship between mistake and misrepresentation? Would it be possible, as the question suggests, for misrepresentation effectively to replace the doctrine of mistake in virtually all cases? In answering this, there are two questions to consider:

- are there situations involving a contract being made on the basis of a mistake which do not also involve a misrepresentation?; and

- are there situations in which the remedies for misrepresentation are inadequate, and the remedies for mistake more satisfactory?

We have seen at the beginning of this essay that there are clearly examples of situations where mistake and misrepresentation overlap. This overlap is not, however, complete. It is quite possible to envisage situations involving either common or mutual mistake which did not involve a misrepresentation by either party. In *Bell v Lever Bros* (1932), for example, the validity of the employment contracts was assumed, without there being any representation.[5] Cases of unilateral mistake are much more likely to involve a misrepresentation, but even here it is not inevitable. One party assumes that the painting he is buying is by Constable; the other party knows that the buyer is making this assumption, and knows that it is false. No representation needs to have taken place, but the contract is made on the basis of a mistake, which, even if not operative at common law, may well provide a remedy in equity.

Turning to remedies, the problem with misrepresentation is that, although it now provides damages in the majority of cases, rescission is not always available, because of the equitable bars to it. In cases like *Ingram v Little* (1961), although there had been a clear misrepresentation of identity which had induced the contract, there could have been no rescission for misrepresentation because the car had been sold on to an innocent third party. The remedy of damages was also of little use, because the misrepresenting purchaser had disappeared. Making the contract void for mistake was the only way of providing an effective remedy. Whether the drastic effects on the third party are justifiable may be questionable, but that is a fault of the absence of any remedy allowing losses to be shared, rather than an argument for the abolition of the doctrine of mistake.

The conclusion must be that, although in many situations, misrepresentation can provide a very satisfactory and in some ways more flexible alternative to the doctrine of mistake, there are still a small number of cases where mistake provides the only possible remedy. The number may be small, but it is not so small as to justify being ignored altogether. The doctrine of mistake should be retained to deal with these situations, although there may well be a case for revising the remedies which it provides.

Notes

1   Note that this was held *not* to be an operative mistake.

2   A statement of opinion which is based on false facts may, however, be a misrepresentation.

3   The same argument could apply to a statement of opinion which is not genuinely held.

4   Cf Lord Atkin's 'mistakes nullifying agreement' and 'mistakes negativing agreement'; see Stone, *The Modern Law of Contract*, 5th edn, 2002, pp 282–83.

5   This point is valid even though it was held that there was no operative mistake on the facts.

Question 25

Bernard owns an oil painting and a smaller pencil sketch, which are both thought to be by Daniel, an artist who has recently died, and whose work is fetching increasingly large amounts at auction. Bernard writes to his friend Edwina, offering to sell her 'my little Daniel picture' (meaning the sketch) for £2,000. Edwina, who knows little about modern art, accepts, saying: 'I am pleased to accept your offer. As you may know, I am hoping to build up a collection of modern paintings.' Bernard delivers the Daniel sketch while Edwina is out. Edwina in fact wanted the oil painting, not the sketch. Before she can return it, however, another friend, who is an expert on Daniel's work, tells her that the sketch is of poor quality and not worth more than £50. A good quality sketch would have been worth £700 to £1,000. Bernard, however, who had himself bought the sketch for £1,500, refuses to take it back, and insists that Edwina must pay him £2,000. The oil painting is valued at £7,000.

   Advise Bernard and Edwina.

Answer plan

This question raises two issues in relation to the doctrine of mistake. The first relates to the question of what happens when parties are at cross-purposes as to the subject matter of the contract. This is the kind of mistake which is often referred to as a 'mutual mistake', or a 'mistake negativing agreement'. The cases of *Raffles v Wichelhaus* (1864) and *Smith v Hughes* (1871) are relevant here. The second issue concerns the position where both parties make a mistake as to the value of what they are contracting about. This may be a 'common mistake' or a 'mistake nullifying agreement'. The case of *Bell v Lever Bros* (1932) is the leading authority on this issue as far as the common law rules are concerned, although it may also be necessary to consider the role of equity in this area.

   The order of treatment here will be:

- mutual mistake:
   o   has there been a 'mutual mistake'?;
   o   if so, is the mistake operative?; and
   o   if so, what is its effect?
- common mistake:
   o   has there been a 'common mistake'?;
   o   if so, is the mistake operative?;

○   if so, what is its effect?; and

○   if the mistake is not operative at common law, what is the position in equity?

Answer

In certain situations, where the parties to a contract have made their agreement on the basis of a mistake of fact, the courts will be prepared to say either that the mistake means that there never really was an agreement (and, therefore, there was no contract), or that the mistake is so fundamental that the contract should be set aside. We have the possibility of both types of mistake operating in this question.

The first mistake which we need to consider arises from the fact that Bernard and Edwina seem to be at cross-purposes over the subject matter of the contract. Bernard intends to sell the sketch; Edwina intends to buy the oil painting. Is there a contract here? It is clear that, in some cases of this kind, the courts will say no. In *Raffles v Wichelhaus* (1864), for example, the contract referred to a ship of the name *Peerless* sailing out of Bombay. Unfortunately, there were two ships which matched this description. The court held that the contract could not be enforced. It was impossible to determine which ship was intended.[1]

A misunderstanding of this kind will not, however, always lead to the decision that there is no contract. The approach taken by the courts is an objective one. They will ask not what did these parties intend, but what would a reasonable third party think that they intended, or what would a reasonable offeror think was being offered? In *Raffles v Wichelhaus,* it was not felt possible to give a clear answer even to the objectively stated question, and so no contract existed.[2] In *Smith v Hughes* (1871), however, a different view was taken. The plaintiff had offered to sell oats to the defendant. The defendant thought that he was buying 'old' oats. When delivered, they turned out to be 'new', and of no use to the defendant. The defendant argued that the contract was void for mistake. The court disagreed. Applying an objective test, there was no ambiguity about the contract. The plaintiff had offered to sell, and the defendant had agreed to buy, a specific consignment of 'oats'. The fact that the defendant had mistakenly thought that the oats were of a different type was his own fault, and not a reason for excusing him from the contract.

How should these principles apply to the dealings between Bernard and Edwina? On a subjective approach, it is clear that there was no agreement. Edwina never intended to buy the sketch. Looked at objectively, however, things are not so clear. Although Edwina's reference to building up a collection of 'paintings' might be taken as indicating her mistake, this is fairly vague, and there are a number of things which point in Bernard's favour. First, he refers in his offer to 'my little Daniel picture'. We are told that the sketch is smaller than the painting, and so it can be argued that the objective bystander would assume that the sketch is what Bernard is offering to sell. Secondly, it is clear that an offer to sell the painting at £2,000 would be to undervalue it considerably, given that we are told that its market value is £7,000. But should Edwina have known this? We can probably only hold this point against her if a reasonable person with Edwina's knowledge would have realised that the price was so low that Bernard was very unlikely to have been intending it to apply to the painting as opposed to the sketch.

On balance, it would seem that this is not a case to which *Raffles v Wichelhaus* should apply. Looked at objectively, there was not sufficient ambiguity to mean that there was no contract at all. Edwina cannot therefore escape from the disadvantageous bargain on this basis. The possibility that equity might afford her some relief is considered further below.

Turning to the issue of the mistake as to the value of the sketch, the leading case is *Bell v Lever Bros* (1932). Here, an employee was paid £30,000 compensation on the termination of his contract. It later transpired that the employer would have been entitled to dismiss him without compensation, because of certain previous breaches of contract by the employee. The employer tried to argue that the contract for compensation was void for mistake. The House of Lords, while recognising the possibility of a contract being void where there is a fundamental mistake as to the subject matter, nevertheless held that on the facts the contract was not void. This has led some to argue that virtually the only common mistake which the courts will regard as operative is a mistake as to the existence of the subject matter.[3] This interpretation was not accepted by Steyn J in *Associated Japanese Bank (International) v Credit du Nord SA* (1988). He held that a mistake could make a contract void provided that it rendered the contract 'essentially and radically' different from the one the parties thought they were making. However, even applying this broader doctrine to the facts of the problem, it seems unlikely that Edwina will have any remedy. The contract was for the sale of a Daniel picture, and that is what she got. The fact that it is a less valuable picture than she thought does not make the contract 'essentially and radically' different.

At common law, then, it seems that Edwina will not be able to escape from this contract. In some situations, however, equity will provide relief in relation to both mutual and common mistakes which are not sufficiently serious to render the contract void. This will only apply where the courts feel that it is just that it should do so in all the circumstances, and where there will be no effect on third parties' rights. The scope for equitable intervention has, however, been significantly reduced by the Court of Appeal's decision in *Great Peace Shipping Ltd v Tsavliris Salvage (International) Ltd* (2002), where it rejected the possibility of the remedy of rescission being used in a situation where under the common law the mistake was not sufficiently serious to render the contract void. This approach had previously been adopted in cases such as *Solle v Butcher* (1950) and *Grist v Bailey* (1967). The position now is that where it may be appropriate for equity to intervene, the only remedies that are available are the rectification of a document, or the refusal to grant an order of specific performance. These remedies may also be available as regards mutual mistakes, as shown by *Malins v Freeman* (1837), where a bidder at an auction by mistake bid for one lot thinking that he was bidding for another. The court refused to order specific performance of the contract.[4]

In relation to the facts of this problem, although both Edwina's mistake as to which picture she was buying and the common mistake as to its value might be sufficiently serious to give rise to the possibility of equitable relief, neither rectification nor the refusal of specific performance is of any help to her. Rescission would have been the most useful remedy, but that is no longer available following the *Great Peace* decision. It seems, therefore, that Edwina will be obliged to pay the £2,000 (since Bernard will be able to recover this in an action for debt, rather than through an order for specific performance) for the picture that she did not want, despite the fact that it is only worth £50 at most.

Notes

1   Note that the report of this case, which is often cited as authority for the idea of 'mutual mistake', is in fact very unclear as to the basis on which the court reached its decision.

2   The case of *Scriven Bros v Hindley* (1913) might also be cited here. In this case, a person bidding at an auction mistakenly thought that two lots (which carried the same shipping mark) were both of hemp, whereas one was of less valuable tow. As a result, he bid well over the market price for the tow. He was allowed to escape from the contract on the basis of his mistake.

3   That is, the so called *res extincta* category. Note also *res sua*, that is, the unusual situation where a purchaser attempts to buy property which he or she already owns.

4   Cf *Tamplin v James* (1879), where a mistake was made as to the property included in a lot, but the court held the bidder to the contract, and ordered specific performance.

Question 26

Elvira advertises an antique clock for sale at £500. She receives a letter from a company called Timeless Antiques, which is signed by Frederick, expressing interest in buying the clock. Elvira consults her friend, Dora, who tells her that she, Dora, sold a clock to Timeless Antiques a year before, and that she found it to be a reputable company which would be likely to give Elvira a fair price. Elvira therefore replies to Frederick, inviting him to visit her and to view the clock. Elvira's letter is intercepted by George, one of Frederick's employees. He visits Elvira, pretending to be Frederick, and shows her one of Frederick's business cards, which he has stolen from Frederick's desk. George tells Elvira that the clock is much more valuable than she thought, and is in fact worth £5,000. He writes her a cheque for that amount, drawn on the company's account, and she allows him to take the clock away. The cheque is dishonoured, because the bank realises that the signature on it is a forgery. In the meantime, George has sold the clock to Hazel for £3,000, having realised that although it was not as rare as he had led Elvira to believe, it was worth considerably more than £500. Hazel is unaware of any of George's deceptions. George has now disappeared, and cannot be traced.

Advise Elvira.

Answer plan

The main issue in this question is that of mistake as to identity, and its effect on a contract. There is also a minor issue relating to mistake as to the quality of what is being sold. Note that, while there is clearly on the facts a misrepresentation which might be said to have induced the contract, this is of no help to Elvira since, by the time she discovers this, the clock is already in the hands of an innocent third party, that is, Hazel. Since a misrepresentation makes a contract voidable, rather than void, Elvira will not be able to rely on this to recover her clock.

The order of treatment will be:

- misrepresentation – inability to assist Elvira;
- general issues regarding mistaken identity;
- particular problems of contracts *inter praesentes*; and
- mistakes as to quality of the subject matter.

Answer

The issues raised by this question are those of misrepresentation and mistake, particularly mistake as to identity. It is necessary to consider which, if any, of these will provide Elvira with a satisfactory remedy.

Looking first at misrepresentation, it is clear that George has deliberately misrepresented his identity, and this can fairly be said to have induced the contract. All the elements of fraudulent misrepresentation are present: *Derry v Peek* (1889). Unfortunately, the remedies available for Elvira in these circumstances are limited. In particular, because misrepresentation renders a contract voidable rather than void, it appears that George will have passed a good title to the clock to Hazel. Since Hazel is an innocent third party, Elvira will be unable to claim rescission of the contract on the grounds of misrepresentation. She does have an action in damages against George, in relation to both the misrepresentation and the dishonoured cheque, but this is of little use, since George has disappeared. Elvira needs to find a cause of action which will lead to the contract with George being held to be void at common law. This will then override any rights Hazel may have. To do this, Elvira will have to argue that the contract was based on a mistake.

The first type of mistake on which Elvira might attempt to rely is mistaken identity. She thought that she was dealing with Frederick as a representative of Timeless Antiques, whereas she was in fact dealing with George, who was acting for his own purposes. This is a unilateral mistake as to the identity of the other contracting party. The attitude of the courts to such a mistake is that it will operate to render the contract void, if the mistake can be shown to have been fundamental. An example is *Cundy v Lindsay* (1878). Here, a fraudulent individual named Blenkarn, operating from Wood Street, induced the plaintiffs to contract with him. They thought that they were dealing with a reputable firm called 'Blenkiron & Co' which also had premises in Wood Street. Blenkarn received goods which he then sold to the defendant. It was held that the offer of the contract was made exclusively to Blenkiron & Co, and so could not be accepted by Blenkarn. In other words, the identity of the other contracting party was fundamental to the contract. As a result, since there was no contract with Blenkarn, the defendant had acquired no title to the goods, and was obliged to return them to the plaintiffs.

This decision will clearly operate in Elvira's favour, if it applies. A complication arises, however, from the fact that Elvira here deals with George face to face, rather than by letter. The courts have been much stricter in applying the doctrine of mistake to *inter praesentes* contracts, taking as their starting point a presumption that you intend to do business with the person standing in front of you. A good example of this is the case of *Lewis v Averay*

(1973). The plaintiff in this case had advertised his car for sale. He was approached by a 'rogue', who offered to buy it. The rogue produced an identity card for Pinewood Studios in the name of Richard Greene, who was a well known actor. The plaintiff allowed the rogue to pay by cheque, and take the car away. Before the plaintiff was able to rescind the contract, the rogue had sold the car to an innocent third party. The court refused to hold the contract void for mistake. The plaintiff intended to contract with the rogue: his mistake was not as to the rogue's identity but as to his attributes, that is, his creditworthiness.[1]

Although it is difficult to overturn the presumption, it is not impossible, as is shown by *Ingram v Little* (1961). The plaintiffs again advertised a car for sale and were approached by a rogue. On this occasion, however, on being offered a cheque in payment, the plaintiffs demurred, and only agreed to take it once they had checked in the telephone directory that a person with the name and address that the rogue gave was listed. The Court of Appeal found for the plaintiffs against the defendants who had bought the car in all innocence from the rogue, on the basis that there had been a mistake as to identity which rendered the contract void.

These two cases are difficult to reconcile and difficult to apply. It should be noted, however, that Elvira's case is slightly different from both *Lewis v Averay* and *Ingram v Little*, in that, prior to the meeting with George, there had been correspondence between Elvira and Frederick. Elvira thought that she was meeting a representative of Timeless Antiques, a firm which she had checked on as being reputable. In this respect, the case is closer to that of *Hardman v Booth* (1863). Here, the plaintiff had thought that he was dealing with a person acting as an agent for a firm, Gandell & Co, whom he, the plaintiff, had approached, whereas in fact the rogue was acting on his own behalf. It was held that the mistake of identity was sufficiently fundamental to render the contract void.

Applying all this to Elvira's case, it seems that she may well be able to argue that, although she did not make the first approach to Timeless Antiques, by the time that George came to visit her it was of considerable importance to her that she was dealing with that particular firm. This could be so even if the identity of the person acting on behalf of the company was not material. Thus, if George for some reason was pretending to be Frederick, but was nevertheless genuinely acting on behalf of his employers, Elvira would not have been able to claim fundamental mistake. She would still be dealing with Timeless Antiques. Because, however, she was intending to deal *only* with Timeless Antiques, the fact that George was acting on his own behalf might well constitute a mistake as to identity rather than attributes, which would render the contract void, and enable Elvira to recover her clock from Hazel.[2]

If, as is argued above, Elvira can rely on mistake of identity to avoid the contract, then this provides her with a complete remedy. In case this argument fails, however, the question of the mistake as to the value of the clock must be considered. It is unlikely, however, to be of much assistance to Elvira. First, the leading House of Lords' decision on this type of mistake, *Bell v Lever Bros* (1932), emphasises that the mistake to be operative must be as to some fundamental quality of the thing contracted about, which renders it something different in kind from that which it was thought to be.[3] A mistake as to value is unlikely to be sufficient on its own. Secondly, the mistake here is that, at the time of the contract with George, Elvira thinks that the clock is more valuable than it in fact is. It is hard to see the courts agreeing that a seller who has disposed of goods at an overvalue should be allowed on that ground to call the contract of sale void.

In conclusion, it seems that Elvira's best course of action is to rely on the mistake as to identity, and to argue that her situation is analogous to that of the plaintiffs in *Ingram v Little* and *Hardman v Booth*. If successful, this will allow her to recover her clock. The only alternative is to trace George, who can obviously be sued for the £5,000 which he agreed to pay for the clock, plus any consequential damages.[4]

Notes

1   This followed the approach taken in the earlier case of *Phillips v Brooks* (1919).

2   Hazel would then be left with the problem of tracing and suing George.

3   Note that *Bell v Lever Bros* was concerned with a 'common' mistake, whereas this is a 'unilateral' mistake; the same principle is, however, thought to apply – see Stone, *The Modern Law of Contract*, 5th edn, 2002, p 292.

4   There is a possibility that an argument could be made here in agency or negligence for liability on the part of Timeless Antiques. It is unlikely, however, that the setter of this question had these issues in mind, since the way the facts are presented clearly directs the person answering to think in terms of the doctrine of mistake.

Question 27

Stitch plc is a clothing manufacturer, with a factory in Nottingborough. Menders Ltd are negotiating with Stitch plc for a contract to service Stitch's Hummer sewing machines. During the course of a telephone conversation, Button, Menders' Sales Director, says that they have three 'well satisfied' existing customers in the Nottingborough area. He also says that Menders have a stock of Hummer machines which can be supplied if any of Stitch's machines have to be taken away for repair. In fact, this stock of machines has recently been replaced by inferior Grinders models, though Button is unaware of this. The day after this telephone conversation, two of the three of Menders' existing Nottingborough customers cancel their contracts, because of poor quality work. A week later, having made no checks on the truth of Button's statements, Stitch enters into a contract with Menders by exchange of letters. The contract is to service 'all machines at Stitch plc's factory in Nottingborough' at a price of £5,000 per annum. When Menders' engineers arrive to start carrying out the contract, they find that Stitch has 50 machines at the factory: Button had misheard this as '15'. The usual price for servicing 50 machines would have been £15,000 per annum. Three of the machines have to be taken away for repair, and are replaced by Grinders. The factory is that day visited by a representative of A1 Fabrics, who has recently placed a very valuable order, which will produce a profit to Stitch of £30,000. Unfortunately, it is a condition of this contract that Stitch only uses Hummer machines. When the representative of A1 Fabrics sees the Grinders machines on the premises, she immediately cancels this contract.

What actions based on misrepresentation, or mistake, might arise from these facts? What would the remedies be?

Answer plan

This answer will mainly be concerned with the possibility of actions for misrepresentation as regards Button's statements, that is:

- can an expression of opinion be a misrepresentation? (*Bisset v Wilkinson* (1927); *Smith v Land & House Property Corp* (1884));

- what is the effect of changed circumstances (that is, the cancellation of the existing contracts)? (*With v O'Flanagan* (1936));

- does reliance on a misrepresentation have to be reasonable? (*Museprime Properties v Adhill Properties* (1990)); and

- what remedies are available at common law or under the Misrepresentation Act 1967?

There is also the possibility that Menders could raise a counter argument that the mistake as to the number of machines is a mutual mistake, negativing consent, and thereby preventing any contract from coming into existence (as in *Scriven Bros v Hindley* (1913)).

Answer

This essay is concerned with problems which arise in connection with false statements, or mistakes, which form the basis of a contract. It requires, in particular, consideration of the rules relating to misrepresentation and mutual mistake.

A misrepresentation is a false statement of existing fact. It becomes actionable when it is made by one party to a contract to the other, and induces the contract. There are two statements in the problem which may amount to misrepresentations. Both are made by Button. They are that Menders have three 'well satisfied' customers, and that the spare machines held by Menders are 'Hummers'. The two statements will be considered in turn.

The statement about the customers does not at first sight appear to be a misrepresentation. For one thing, it may well be regarded as a statement of opinion rather than fact, and, as such, not a misrepresentation (*Bisset v Wilkinson* (1927)). Secondly, it may be true at the time it is made (though it is unlikely that the customers become dissatisfied overnight). The combination of two cases, however, provides a clear basis for bringing the statement within the category of misrepresentation. In *Smith v Land & House Property Corp* (1884), it was held that a statement of opinion can be treated as a misrepresentation if the maker of the statement is aware of facts which make it unsustainable. Furthermore, although silence does not generally constitute a misrepresentation, if the maker of a statement which was true at the time subsequently becomes aware of facts which make it untrue, there is a duty to disclose this (*With v O'Flanagan* (1936)). Taking these two principles together, Button's statement about the customers can be seen to have the characteristics of a misrepresentation by the time the contract is made. Does it induce the contract? There is a week's delay between the statement and the contract, and Stitch makes no attempt to check its accuracy. Neither of these factors is fatal to Stitch's claim. Partial reliance on the statement is enough (*Edgington v Fitzmaurice* (1885)), and there is no obligation to take any opportunities that may occur to check its truth (*Redgrave v Hurd* (1881)). In this case, the plaintiff was offered the chance to examine accounts which would have revealed the falsity of statements about the value of a solicitor's practice. His failure to do so did not preclude an action for misrepresentation. It seems, then, that Stitch may well be able to base an action on the statement about the customers. The possible remedies will be considered below.

The second possible misrepresentation is that concerning the stock of 'Hummer' machines. This is clearly a statement of fact, and is false at the time it is made. On the issue of inducement, Menders might try to argue that the make of the replacement machines would not generally be an issue of crucial importance, and that Stitch would be unreasonable to rely on it. The decision in *Museprime Properties v Adhill Properties* (1990), however, indicates that reliance does not have to be reasonable. Given the terms of the contract with A1 Fabrics, Stitch should have little difficulty in showing that there was actual reliance in this case, even if Menders would not have expected there to be. This statement would therefore also be actionable. We must now consider the possible remedies.

The remedies available for misrepresentation depend on whether it was made innocently, negligently or fraudulently. In relation to all types of misrepresentation, the basic remedy is that of rescission of the contract, but this will be lost if full restitution is impossible, if the contract has been affirmed, if third party rights would be affected, or if there has simply been too long a lapse of time. In the problem, rescission may be available in relation to the statement about the customers, unless the contract is too far advanced for full restitution to be possible. This remedy is, however, unlikely to be available in respect of the statement about the machines. By allowing the 'Grinders' to be installed, Stitch may be taken to have affirmed the contract, and thus to have lost the right to rescind (*Long v Lloyd* (1958)).

In any case, Stitch is more likely to be seeking damages than rescission. The easiest way to obtain this will be to argue for negligent misrepresentation under s 2(1) of the Misrepresentation Act 1967. This allows damages to be recovered for misrepresentation unless the maker of the statement can prove that 'he had reasonable grounds to believe and did believe *up to the time the contract was made* that the facts represented were true'. Button will have great difficulty in proving this, and so Stitch's chances of recovering damages on this basis are high. Moreover, since the decision of the Court of Appeal in *Royscot v Rogerson* (1991), the measure of damages under s 2(1) is the same as for fraud. This means that all consequential losses are recoverable (*Derry v Peek* (1889)), including lost profits (*East v Maurer* (1991)). The lost profit on the contract with A1 Fabrics would thus appear to be recoverable.

Given the favourable burden of proof under s 2(1), and the extent of the damages recoverable, there is little point in Stitch arguing for fraudulent misrepresentation (which might be applicable as regards the customers' statement). Nor is there any need to consider an action for negligent misstatement under *Hedley Byrne v Heller* (1964), which requires the proof of both a 'special relationship' and a failure to take reasonable care on the part of the maker of the statement (although the statement does not need to be one of fact).

The arguments so far have gone in favour of Stitch. Menders might seek to counterclaim by saying that the contract should be set aside on the basis of a mutual mistake (referred to in *Bell v Lever Bros* (1932) as a mistake which 'negatives consent'). This arises where the parties are at cross-purposes about some important aspect of the contract, so that they were never truly in agreement. An example is the case of *Raffles v Wichelhaus* (1864), where the existence of two ships with the same name meant that it was impossible to determine exactly what was intended. Here, the argument would be that the parties were at cross-purposes over the number of machines to be serviced. The courts take an objective approach to this issue, asking whether a reasonable third party would have realised that there was a problem (*Smith v Hughes* (1871)). Menders may seek to argue here that the price is so low that a reasonable person in Stitch's position should have realised that it could not have been intended to apply to 50 machines. A similar argument was successful in *Scriven Bros v Hindley* (1913), where there was confusion over the lots in an auction, with an unusually high price being bid. If Menders succeed in this argument, the effect will be that the whole contract will be set aside (although they would still be likely to be able to claim on a *quantum meruit* basis for the work already done). Even if the mistake is not operative at common law, equity may sometimes grant relief. Of the possible equitable remedies, however, refusal of specific performance (*Malins v Freeman* (1837)) would not seem appropriate (since specific performance would be unlikely to be awarded anyway), and rectification is not available as regards mutual mistakes (*Riverlate Properties Ltd v Paul* (1975)). Menders will thus only be likely to achieve success with the mistake argument if it is regarded as sufficiently serious to render the whole 'agreement' a nullity under common law.

It should be noted at this stage that although there is a slight possibility of an argument based on common or unilateral mistake in relation to the issues of the 'satisfied customers' and the spare machines, these are unlikely to be regarded as sufficiently serious to render the contract void. Moreover, they offer Stitch less attractive remedies than the action for misrepresentation under s 2(1) of the 1967 Act.

In conclusion, then, Stitch's best course of action is to sue for damages under s 2(1) of the 1967 Act in relation to both of Button's statements. Menders may counter with a claim of mutual mistake at common law, which, if successful, would render the whole contract non-existent.

CHAPTER 8

DURESS AND UNDUE INFLUENCE

Introduction

The vitiating factors covered in this chapter are the related concepts of duress and undue influence. Duress is a common law concept, based on threats made to a contracting party. Undue influence developed in equity to deal with situations where there was improper pressure, without necessarily any specific threats. Because the two concepts are closely related, questions raising one will often require discussion of the other. The fact that both areas have widened in scope in recent years also raises the issue of a general principle attacking 'unconscionability' in contracts, and this not infrequently appears in questions on these topics.

In dealing with a problem question on duress, the following questions should be considered:

- was there a threat to carry out an unlawful (not necessarily criminal) act?;
- was the threat 'operative' – that is, did it cause the person threatened to enter into the contract?;
- did the threat involve, or itself constitute, a criminal offence?; and
- if not, did the person threatened have any reasonable alternative to compliance?

In relation to undue influence, the questions should be:

- was the relationship between the parties one of those which automatically raises a presumption of influence?;
- if not, had the particular relationship developed in such a way that influence should be presumed?;
- if 'yes' to either of the above, was entering into the contract disadvantageous to the person influenced?; and
- if influence cannot be presumed, do the circumstances surrounding the contract suggest that undue influence was in fact operating?

In relation to both concepts, if either is found to be operative, the question of remedies will then have to be discussed. The most likely remedy to be sought in both cases will be rescission of the contract. But, as with misrepresentation, the right to rescind may be lost, by lapse of time, affirmation of the contract, etc.

Checklist

You should be familiar with the following areas:

- The meaning of 'duress'.
- Development of the concept of 'economic' duress.
- Remedies for duress at common law.
- The concept of 'undue influence' and its development.
- Differences between duress and undue influence.
- Equitable remedies for undue influence.

Question 28

What are the differences between 'duress' and 'undue influence'? Do the two concepts together constitute a law against unconscionable contracts?

Answer plan

There are three parts to this answer:

- description of the concepts of 'duress' and 'undue influence';
- indication of the differences between them; and
- consideration of whether the two concepts preclude unconscionable contracts in general, or whether they amount to only a partial prohibition.

The third part is obviously the most difficult, but it is an issue which is quite often raised. The issue of substantive versus procedural fairness will need discussion. The views of Lord Denning in *Lloyds Bank v Bundy* (1974) will need to be noted, along with the adverse reaction to them in later cases. The cases involving allegations of undue influence, such as *National Westminster Bank plc v Morgan* (1985), are probably more relevant to this issue than the cases on duress.

Answer

The concepts of duress and undue influence are related, in that they both deal with the situation where a person enters into a contract when, if left to his or her own devices, he or she probably would not have done so. In other words, the contract is made as the result of some external pressure or interference. On the other hand, there are significant differences between them, and it is probably not accurate to regard them as simply aspects of a more general principle attacking unconscionable bargains.

Duress involves a threat, for example, 'if you do not make this contract, I will hit you'. A contract made in such circumstances will be voidable. There is no true agreement, and so the person subject to the threat should not be held to the contract.[1] Unlawful threats of physical violence are clearly going to have this effect, but in recent years the courts have extended the concept far beyond this. Any threat of criminal behaviour will apparently amount to duress, but the courts have also recognised the category of so called 'economic duress'. One of the earliest examples of this was in *Universe Tankships Inc v International Transport Workers Federation* (1983), where industrial action was threatened to force the owners of the ship to improve the working conditions of the crew. To escape the action, the owners made a payment to the union's welfare fund. They then brought an action to recover this as a payment made under duress.

The court held that the threatened industrial action was unlawful under English law, and the payment was held to have been made under duress.

From this and subsequent decisions, it seems that any threat of an unlawful act, such as a tort or breach of contract, can amount to duress. Where the threat is not of a crime, however, there is an additional requirement, which is that the person threatened has no reasonable alternative but to agree. This derives from Lord Scarman's speech in *Pao On v Lau Yiu Long* (1979), where he was attempting to distinguish between duress and legitimate commercial pressure. Where the person threatened with a breach of contract, for example, can expect to be fully compensated by damages or specific performance, then there is no reason to bring in duress. If, however, as was the case in *Atlas Express v Kafco* (1989), the carrying out of the threatened breach of contract would effectively put the other party out of business, there may be no reasonable alternative to compliance. In this situation, the courts will be prepared to intervene on the basis of duress. The Court of Appeal, in *CTN Cash and Carry v Gallaher* (1994), suggested that in certain circumstances a threat to carry out a *lawful* act (for example, to withdraw credit facilities) could amount to economic duress. This statement was *obiter*, however, and it is difficult to see how the boundaries between legitimate and illegitimate pressure would then be drawn.

Turning to undue influence, it is important to note that here there are two categories: presumed undue influence and actual undue influence. In both cases, the essence of the defence is that one of the parties to a contract has been in such a position of influence over the other that there is a danger that the person subject to the influence has been led into making a disadvantageous agreement. The difference between the two categories is that there are certain relationships where it is presumed that such influence will exist. Where no such presumed influence arises, the party seeking to escape from the agreement will have to prove that as a matter of fact he or she was acting under the influence of the other party.

The relationships where influence is presumed include parent/child, doctor/patient, solicitor/client, religious adviser/disciple, but not, it should be noted, husband/wife. The relationships are ones where one person places trust and confidence in another, and so is liable to act on their suggestions without seeking independent advice. Outside these general categories, a particular relationship may develop in such a way over a period of time that influence will be presumed. In *Lloyds Bank v Bundy* (1974), the relationship was that of banker and customer. Mr Bundy had placed great reliance on the bank over a number of years. When the bank was relied on to provide advice on a business transaction, there was held to be a presumption of influence.[2]

The category of actual undue influence covers situations falling outside the presumption. Here, the burden of proof is on the person alleging influence. It can apply between husband and wife, as recognised in *BCCI v Aboody* (1989). The nature of the influence is, however, the same as for presumed undue influence. In other words, the person influenced must have acted out of their trust in the influencer, without seeking or obtaining advice from elsewhere.

In relation to presumed influence, whether such influence is to be regarded as undue will turn in part on whether the transaction was disadvantageous to the person influenced. This test derives from the case of *National Westminster Bank v Morgan* (1985) and was at one time applied in a fairly rigid manner as a test of 'manifest disadvantage'. The House of Lords in *Royal Bank of Scotland v Etridge (No 2)* (2001), however, adopted a rather more flexible approach. If a transaction is disadvantageous, then it will raise suspicions that undue influence has been used, which it will be up to the alleged influencer to dispel. In relation to situations of actual undue influence, however, the question of the disadvantageous nature of the transaction has no relevance: *CIBC Mortgages v Pitt* (1993).

What, then, are the differences between these two related concepts of duress and undue influence? One is that duress is a common law concept, whereas undue influence originates in equity. This does not seem to result in any great practical distinction between the two. In both cases, the consequence of a successful argument for the existence of the concept is that the resulting contract is regarded as voidable.

It is also clear from the above descriptions that duress results from a specific threat, made on a particular occasion, whereas undue influence is more likely to arise from a continuing relationship. What has happened in the past between the two parties may be just as important as the events surrounding the making of the particular contract about which there is a dispute.

More significant is the difference between the position of the party who has benefited from the contract in each case. In relation to duress, it is clear that he or she must have acted improperly.[3] Subject to the statement in *CTN Cash and Carry v Gallaher* mentioned above, the threat must generally be to carry out some unlawful act, either a crime or a civil wrong. Where undue influence is concerned, however, there is no need for the influencer to have acted with an improper motive. Particularly in the category of presumed influence, it may be that he or she was simply over-enthusiastic, and did not realise the effect of his or her influence. Provided that the resulting agreement is disadvantageous, however, the other party will be able to escape from it.

A further difference is that the contract which results from duress does not have to be disadvantageous to the person who is persuaded to enter into it. The court is here concerned with the procedural impropriety rather than the issue of substantive fairness. In relation to presumed (though not actual) undue influence, as we have seen, the unfairness of the transaction is a prerequisite for a successful plea. This difference is clearer when the duress results from a criminal threat, for, again as we have seen, where a civil wrong is threatened there is the additional requirement of 'no reasonable alternative'. This perhaps comes close to saying that the contract must be disadvantageous.

Finally, the relationship of the two concepts to a general rule of 'unconscionability' must be considered. This would require a general ban on 'unfair' contracts, whenever the unfairness was such that a court could not in all conscience allow it to stand. Duress and undue influence do not equal unconscionability for a number of reasons. First, both concepts place more stress on procedural fairness than substantive fairness. Unconscionability would require the courts to focus more directly on the nature of the contract itself, rather than the events which led to it being formed. To that extent, the concepts are clearly narrower than an approach based on unconscionability.

Secondly, in relation to duress, it is clear that this concept can be looked at as being wider than unconscionability, in the sense that a contract which is substantively fair can be struck down simply because it was made under duress.

It is also significant that attempts by some judges, most notably Lord Denning in *Lloyds Bank v Bundy*, to argue for a general rule against unconscionable contracts have not gained favour, and indeed have been specifically disapproved in later cases.[4] This ties in with an indication of reluctance to allow the concept of economic duress to expand too rapidly, and to overlap into the area of legitimate commercial pressure.

This reluctance probably results in part from a desire for certainty. The occurrence and consequences of procedural unfairness are relatively easy to predict. If the courts were having to look at the substance of contracts in every case to see if they were 'fair', then there would be great increases in uncertainty in the commercial world, and far more litigation. The current approach of the English courts may at times seem cautious, but it is probably the right one.

Notes

1   This concept is often expressed in the cases by a reference to the threatened person's 'will' being 'overborne', or that they acted 'involuntarily'. Commentators have pointed out that this is not strictly accurate, in that the person has decided to make the contract, and in doing so has exercised a choice. This is not the same as the involuntary act of an automaton – cf, in the criminal law context, *DPP for Northern Ireland v Lynch* (1975).

2   Which, on the facts, the bank failed to rebut.

3   Though it is not necessary to show that the party guilty of the duress was aware that the other party was acting under it: *Universe Tankships Inc of Monrovia v International Transport Workers Federation and Laughton* (1983).

4   For example, by Lord Scarman in *National Westminster Bank plc v Morgan* (1985).

Question 29

Answer both parts:

(a) Apex plc have a contract with Nadir Ltd. Apex tell Nadir that unless Nadir enter into a five year contract with Apex's subsidiary, Crux Ltd, on terms which are particularly advantageous to Crux, they (Apex) will 'terminate their agreement' with Nadir. Despite the fact that the terms suggested mean that Nadir will make a loss on the deal with Crux, they agree because of the value which they place on their contract with Apex. Two years later, Apex go out of business. Nadir now want to escape from the contract with Crux.

Advise Nadir.

Would it make any difference if Apex's threat, rather than being to terminate their agreement, was not to renew their contract with Nadir?

(b) Maria, an orphan, married Harold four years ago when she was 17 and he was 30. She has a valuable collection of jewellery which she inherited from her mother. Harold, whose business is in debt, asks her to guarantee a loan of £20,000. Maria refuses. Later, Harold brings his bank manager home, and presents Maria with papers to sign, guaranteeing the loan of £20,000 and using Maria's jewellery as security. The bank manager tells her that she may consult her solicitor if she wishes, but that there is little danger of her losing her jewellery. Maria signs the guarantee. Harold's business collapses, and the bank wants to enforce the guarantee.

Advise Maria.

Answer plan

Part (a) of this question deals with duress, and part (b) with undue influence. The issues raised are quite distinct, and so the two parts should be looked at separately:

Part (a):

- We are dealing here with 'economic' duress. The threat by Apex plc is to break their contract with Nadir. In looking at the cases on economic duress, of which *Atlas Express Ltd v Kafco (Importers and Distributors) Ltd* (1989) is perhaps the most relevant, the issue of whether Nadir had any reasonable alternative to compliance will need to be considered. A further issue is the question of the two year delay before Nadir attempt to avoid the contract.

The alternative scenario will not need lengthy consideration. The threat here appears not to be to do anything unlawful, and so, subject to the Court of Appeal's *obiter* comments in *CTN Cash and Carry v Gallaher* (1994), there will be little possibility of pleading duress.

Part (b):

- The two types of undue influence, presumed and actual, will both need discussion. The issues are:
    - ○ Has the relationship between Harold and Maria developed in a way which creates a presumption of undue influence? (Remember that there is no automatic presumption between husband and wife.)
    - ○ If not, has Harold exercised actual undue influence (as in *BCCI v Aboody* (1989))?
    - ○ If Harold has influenced Maria, is the bank affected by this on the basis of the tests laid down in *Barclays Bank v O'Brien* (1993) and *Royal Bank of Scotland v Etridge (No 2)* (2001)?
    - ○ Has the bank itself used undue influence over Maria (as in *Lloyds Bank v Bundy* (1974))?

Answer

Part (a)

If Nadir wish to escape from the contract with Crux, the only possibility would seem to be a plea of duress. There may be problems for them, however, as to whether the threat was sufficiently serious, and as to the delay of two years before they attempt to avoid the agreement.

Duress is a common law concept, which enables a person who has entered into a contract as a result of threats to treat the contract as voidable. Not all threats will have this effect, however, and the right to rescind the contract may in any case be lost in certain circumstances.

Originally, the concept of duress was based on threats of criminal activity – for example, if you do not make this contract, you will get beaten up (see *Barton v Armstrong* (1976) for a modern example). Over the past 25 years, however,[1] it has been recognised that in certain situations commercial pressure can go beyond what is legitimate between businesses, and itself amount to duress. For this to be the case, there are two main requirements:

- the threat, although not of a crime, must be of some action which is improper. This has generally been taken to mean an act which is unlawful,[2] involving at least a civil wrong, such as a tort or breach of contract. There is an *obiter* statement by the Court of Appeal in *CTN Cash and Carry v Gallaher* (1994) which suggests that in certain circumstances a threat of a lawful act can amount to duress, but this has not as yet been developed in subsequent cases; and

- the person threatened must have no practical alternative to compliance: *Pao On v Lau Yiu Long* (1979).

In the problem, the first requirement seems clearly to be satisfied. Apex plc are threatening to break their contract with Nadir, which is sufficiently unlawful to give rise to the possibility of duress. The difficulty arises with the second requirement. When can it be said that the person threatened has no real alternative but to comply? The cases talk of the person's will being 'overborne', but this is not particularly helpful, since they are still in fact making a choice of compliance, even if they do so to avoid some other consequences.[3] An example where this requirement was satisfied was *Atlas Express v Kafco* (1989). The defendants, Kafco, were a small manufacturing company who had a very valuable contract with Woolworths, a store with branches nationwide. They employed Atlas, a national firm of carriers, to make deliveries to Woolworths. Atlas found that they had, through their own mistake, entered into the contract with Kafco on uneconomic terms. They told Kafco that they must agree to an increase in the charge for carriage, or otherwise Atlas would not make the deliveries. Kafco could not risk being in breach of their contract with Woolworths, and so agreed to the change under protest. When Atlas brought an action to recover the increased charges, Kafco resisted on the grounds of duress. It was held that losing the contract with Woolworths, or being sued by them, would be so disastrous for Kafco that they had no real alternative but to go along with Atlas' suggestion. They were not obliged to pay the additional carriage costs.

Does the same argument apply here? The alternative to making the contract with Crux is for Nadir to lose the contract with Apex. We are told that they place great value on this contract, but it is not clear just how vital it is to their business.[4] If it was felt that Nadir could be adequately compensated for the loss of the contract by suing Apex for damages for breach, then they would not be able to rely on duress to escape the agreement with Crux.

A final problem for Nadir is that it is now two years since the contract with Crux was made. Duress renders a contract voidable at the option of the person subject to the duress, but it is also clear that the right to rescind can be lost. In *The Atlantic Baron* (1978), this occurred when the party threatened was held to have affirmed the contract, and failed to raise their claim until over six months after the ship which was the subject of the contract had been delivered. Here, there is a delay of two years between the threat and the attempt to avoid the contract. It is likely that, because of this, Nadir will not be allowed to rescind the contract.

The alternative scenario, where the threat is of non-renewal rather than termination, is that it is most unlikely that it will amount to duress, because the threat involves nothing unlawful. Although the Court of Appeal (in *CTN Cash and Carry v Gallaher* (1994)) has suggested that in certain circumstances a threat of a lawful act could amount to duress, there is no reason to think that it would apply to a straightforward situation such as this.[5] Nadir are therefore highly unlikely to have a remedy as a result of this threat.

Part (b)

Maria has not entered into the guarantee agreement as a result of any threats made to her, so her claim to be able to escape from it will have to be based on undue influence. There are two possible arguments for this to exist on these facts. The first will be based on the fact that her husband may be in such a dominant position over her that she is unduly influenced by him. The second will relate to the relationship between banker and client, since she signs the agreement as a result of the involvement of the bank manager.

Looking first at Harold's influence over Maria, the relationship of husband and wife does not automatically raise a presumption of influence. The particular relationship, however, may have developed in a way which gives rise to a presumption. There is little evidence of this from the facts. Although Harold is much older than Maria, there is no evidence of any regular pattern of Maria signing documents presented to her by Harold. Indeed, in relation to the guarantee, she at first refuses to sign. This might well indicate that she is taking an independent decision, and does not simply fall within her husband's wishes. Could Maria prove *actual* undue influence? A case which illustrates the principles operating in this area, and which bears a close factual resemblance to the problem, is *Bank of Credit and Commerce International SA v Aboody* (1989). Mrs Aboody married her husband when she was quite young. He was 20 years older than her. For many years, she signed documents relating to her husband's business, of which she was nominally a director, without reading them or questioning her husband about them. She signed guarantees and charges relating to the matrimonial home, to support loans by the bank to the business. She had taken no independent advice, though she had on one occasion been encouraged to do so by the bank's solicitor. It was found that, although Mr Aboody had not acted with any improper motive, he had unduly influenced his wife. Will the same argument apply here?

There are significant differences between Maria's case and that of Mrs Aboody. Although, as has been noted above, there is a similar age difference between husband and wife in the two cases, there is no clear evidence that Maria was on this occasion intimidated by Harold. Moreover, there is no evidence that Harold was present at the signing of the document, whereas Mr Aboody was.[6] If he had been, this might well have strengthened Maria's claim. As it is, without further evidence of the way in which Harold may have exercised influence over Maria, it seems unlikely that she will succeed on this ground.

If Harold has not influenced Maria, then the bank cannot be affected by Harold's actions. If Harold *is* found to have influenced her, however, the question is whether the bank had notice (actual or constructive) of this: *Barclays Bank v O'Brien* (1993). The bank should be put on inquiry if the transaction is not to Maria's financial advantage, and it is a transaction of a type in relation to which there is a substantial risk that a husband will have committed a legal wrong in getting the wife to agree. Since the transaction provides no direct financial assistance to Maria, and being a guarantee or surety is regarded as falling within the second condition, it seems that these requirements are satisfied. The bank can only protect itself by taking reasonable steps to ensure that the wife is fully aware of the nature of the transaction, and has had every opportunity to take legal advice. Recent case law has been fairly lenient to the lender in relation to the issue of legal advice. The leading authority is *Royal Bank of Scotland v Etridge (No 2)* (2001), where it was said that in this type of situation the bank must insist on the wife receiving independent legal advice, with the solicitor confirming to the bank that the documentation and its implications have been explained to her. On the facts given here, it appears that the bank has not satisfied these requirements, since Maria has simply been told that she may consult a solicitor if she wishes. Nor does there even seem to have been much of an attempt to explain the transaction by the bank. Assuming, therefore, that Harold has unduly influenced Maria (which is not very likely), the bank would not be allowed to enforce the guarantee.

A further possible argument for Maria is based on what the bank manager said to her. It is clear that in some cases the relationship between banker and customer will be such as to give rise to a presumption of undue influence: *Lloyds Bank v Bundy* (1974). But this will not always be the case,[7] as was illustrated by *National Westminster Bank v Morgan* (1985). Here, a wife had again signed a charge relating to the matrimonial home, in order to obtain a loan to avoid the house being repossessed by the building society to which it was mortgaged. The bank manager who called at the house to obtain the wife's signature had innocently misrepresented the scope of the charge.[8]

The House of Lords, however, took the view that the wife knew what she was doing, and there was no undue influence.

Is Maria's situation best regarded as being like that of Mr Bundy or Mrs Morgan? As was the case with Harold's influence, there is no indication here that she has relied on the bank manager over a period of time, which had been the case with Mr Bundy.[9] It is a one-off event, apparently, as with Mrs Morgan. There is perhaps slightly more influence being used here than in *Morgan*, but it must be doubtful whether it is sufficient to raise the presumption.

Even if it does, there is a further problem. Where presumed influence is being alleged, the courts will only be likely to find the influence 'undue' where the transaction is disadvantageous to the person influenced: *National Westminster Bank v Morgan* (1985), as reinterpreted in *Royal Bank of Scotland v Etridge (No 2)* (2001). So, even if Maria can establish that she was influenced by the bank manager to sign the guarantee, she will not be able to avoid it unless it is to her clear disadvantage. In one sense, this is so, in that she puts her jewellery, which is probably of sentimental as well as commercial value to her, at risk. On the other hand, the survival of her husband's business is to her benefit, and if this is the only way it is likely to be achieved, then it cannot be said to be a totally disadvantageous arrangement. For this to be so it would probably have to be shown that there never was a real chance of Harold's business being saved by the extra money from the bank.

In conclusion, then, it seems that on the basis of the facts given, and in particular in the absence of any long term influence exercised by either Harold or the bank, Maria must be advised that she has little chance of avoiding the guarantee on the basis of undue influence.

Notes

1   At least since *The Siboen and The Sibotre* (1976).

2   Either a threat to do something unlawful in itself, for example, a tort or breach of contract, or a threat to do something lawful where the threat itself is unlawful – as in the case of blackmail.

3   In other words, they are not simply acting as an 'automaton', without any control over their actions.

4   Note that Apex are a 'plc' (that is, a public limited company), whereas Nadir are simply 'Ltd'. This almost certainly indicates that Apex are a much larger organisation than Nadir, which may mean, as in *Atlas Express v Kafco*, that Nadir are very dependent on this one contract.

5   The Court of Appeal referred to Professor Birks' view that 'those who develop outrageous but technically lawful means of compulsion' ought not to 'always escape restitution' (*An Introduction to the Law of Restitution*, 2nd edn, 1989, p 177). It seems unlikely that Apex's threat could be regarded as sufficiently outrageous to fall within this category. See also Stone, *The Modern Law of Contract*, 5th edn, 2002, pp 312–13.

6   Indeed, he came, in a state of some agitation, into the room where Mrs Aboody was being advised by the bank's solicitor, and reduced Mrs Aboody to tears.

7   Unlike relationships such as parent/child, doctor/patient, solicitor/client, where influence will always be presumed: *Goldsworthy v Brickell* (1987).

8   He said that it would not relate to the husband's business debts to the bank. This was untrue, though the charge was never in fact used in this way.

9   The fact that a relationship of influence had been established over a period of time was also regarded as significant in *Goldsworthy v Brickell* (1987), although here it was over a matter of months rather than years.

Question 30

Harry, who is 25, lives in a large house which was left to him by his parents. In 1995, his gay friend Tom, aged 40, comes to live with him. Harry allows Tom to take all the decisions about the organisation of the household, and most of the time they live together happily. At times, however, Tom becomes violent, and Harry knows that in the past he has served a prison sentence for assault. When, therefore, Tom tells Harry that he thinks that Harry should sell him a half share of the house for £10,000, Harry agrees, even though the house is worth about £200,000, as he fears what Tom's reaction would be if he refused. The transfer takes place. One year later, Tom's business is running into difficulties, and he suggests that the house should be used as security for a loan which he is negotiating from the bank. Tom tells Harry that the limit of the security will be £75,000. This is untrue, as the security is in fact unlimited. Harry goes to the bank with Tom, where the papers are presented to him for signature. As he is about to sign, the bank's employee says: 'Are you sure you don't want to think about this a bit longer, or take legal advice?' Harry says: 'No thank you, I am happy to trust Tom.'

Tom's business has now, a year after the loan was made, collapsed with debts of £500,000, and the bank is seeking to enforce the security by taking possession of the house.

Harry wishes to avoid: (a) the transfer of the half share in the house to Tom; and (b) the security transaction with the bank. Advise Harry.

Answer plan

This question is clearly designed to raise the issues dealt with by *Barclays Bank v O'Brien* (1993), where a debtor tries to escape liability by arguing undue influence or misrepresentation by a third party. Note, however, that this only arises in relation to part (b). The first part requires a consideration of duress (because of the possibility of Tom's violence) and undue influence as between Tom and Harry.

You will need to discuss:

Part (a):

- the requirements for duress; and
- the requirements for actual and presumed undue influence.

Part (b):

- the effect of Tom's influence, or misrepresentation, on Harry's liability to the bank;
- in that context, the doctrine of 'notice', as explained in *Barclays Bank v O'Brien*, and applied in *CIBC Mortgages v Pitt* (1993);
- the requirements for legal advice set out in *Royal Bank of Scotland v Etridge (No 2)* (2001); and
- the possibility of the bank itself having unduly influenced Tom.

In other words, part (a) requires the discussion of the basic principles of duress and undue influence, and part (b) the application of the latter in the particular context of three-party relationships.

Answer

Harry is seeking to escape from contractual obligations which he has undertaken in respect of Tom and his bank. One way of persuading a court to set aside an agreement is to show that it was made as a result of duress or undue influence. Duress is a common law concept, whereas undue influence has developed in equity. Can Harry use either of these to avoid his contractual obligations?

Let us consider first the transfer of the half share in the house at a gross undervalue (approximately one-tenth). It is well established that, if a contract is made as a result of threats of physical violence, it will be vitiated (for example, *Barton v Armstrong* (1975)). The reason is said to be that the threatened party is not truly consenting to the agreement, and that therefore one of the essential elements of a binding contract is missing. If, therefore,

Tom had said to Harry, 'Sell me your share for £10,000, or I will break your legs', there is no doubt that Harry would not be bound to the agreement. This is not what happened, however. We do not have any indication of specific threats by Tom. Harry complies simply because he is frightened by the possibility of a violent reaction following his refusal. There is nothing in the cases to suggest that this is sufficient to found a plea of 'duress'. Unless there has been something more specific in the way of a threat, therefore, it seems that any argument based on duress must fail.

Can Harry argue that he has been unduly influenced by Tom into entering into this agreement? Undue influence is divided into two categories in English law: actual and presumed. The difference is primarily concerned with the burden of proof. In relation to actual undue influence, the party alleging that he or she has been influenced must prove this on the balance of probabilities. If the influence is presumed, however, it is the alleged influencer who must prove (again, on the balance of probabilities) that no undue influence was used. Whether there is a presumption of influence depends on the relationship between the parties. Certain types of relationship, for example, solicitor/client, parent/child, doctor/patient, will automatically be presumed to involve influence. Tom and Harry do not fall into any of these categories. If, however, there is a clear dominant party in any relationship, and the other party regularly acts in accordance with that person's wishes, then again, influence may be presumed (for example, *Lloyds Bank v Bundy* (1975)). Whether the relationship has developed in this way is of course a question of fact. Here, it seems that Harry is very much the subservient partner in the relationship. We are told that he 'allows Tom to take all the decisions about the organisation of the household', which might well indicate that he has become accustomed to doing what Tom says. It is likely, therefore, that a court would be prepared to presume influence, and put the burden on Tom to show that Harry acted entirely freely in entering into the agreement. There is a difficulty for Harry, however, in that the remedy which he is seeking will be 'rescission'. This equitable remedy is subject to certain bars, one of which is lapse of time. Thus, in *Allcard v Skinner* (1887), a woman who had given much of her property to a religious order while under the influence of that order was not able to recover, because she did not start her action until six years later. The position is not quite so clear cut here, in that it is only two years since the transfer took place. It still seems likely, however, that a court would have expected Harry to act more quickly to avoid this transaction.

In conclusion on this part of the problem, then, it seems that although there is some evidence that Harry entered into the contract on the basis of undue influence, it is unlikely that he will be able to get it rescinded.

Turning to the second transaction from which Harry wishes to escape, it may again be argued that he has been influenced by Tom. What is even more clear, however, is that Tom has misrepresented the extent of the liability, in that he has told Harry that the limit of the security is £75,000, whereas in fact it is unlimited. As against Tom, therefore, any agreement would be rescindable on the basis of misrepresentation. The contract which Harry has made, however, is not with Tom, but with the bank. Can he avoid this transaction on the basis of Tom's influence or misrepresentation?

The normal answer would be no, in that the actions of a third party (Tom) will not normally operate to vitiate a contract between two other people (Harry and the bank). This area is, however, one in which the courts have developed some special rules. The basis of the current approach is to be found in the case of *Barclays Bank v O'Brien* (1993). This concerned a wife who had been misled by her husband as regards an agreement to use the matrimonial home as security for a loan. The House of Lords ruled that the same principles applied whether the surety had entered into the agreement on the basis of undue influence or misrepresentation.[1] The approach of the courts should be based on the doctrine of notice, which is very important in equity. In other words, the question of whether the creditor was affected by the misrepresentation or undue influence of the third party should depend on whether he or she had actual or constructive notice of it. Actual notice will arise where the creditor has witnessed, or has become aware of, specific instances of influence or misrepresentation. This is largely a question of fact. More difficulty exists in identifying constructive notice. In the House of Lords' view in *Royal Bank of Scotland v Etridge (No 2)* (2001), wherever the relationship between a surety and a debtor is 'non-commercial', the lender should be put on inquiry. This is not limited to, but clearly includes, relationships between cohabitees (married or unmarried, heterosexual or homosexual). If the creditor is aware of the relationship, and the transaction is one which is not, on its face, to the financial advantage of the surety,[2] the creditor should be put on inquiry, and will be 'infected' by any misrepresentation or undue influence of the debtor, unless certain steps are taken. These are that the creditor must warn the surety (not in the presence of the debtor) of the risks involved in the transaction, and advise him or her to take independent legal advice.

Applying these principles to the facts of the case, does the bank have constructive notice of the risk of misrepresentation or undue influence by Tom? It appears that Harry and Tom are a cohabiting homosexual couple, but even if their relationship is simply one of friendship, it is clearly personal and not 'commercial'. If the bank is aware of this, then one element of the constructive notice is satisfied. The transaction is not to Harry's financial advantage, so this requirement would also be satisfied. The bank's position therefore seems to turn on its knowledge of the relationship between Harry and Tom. Since the bank must almost certainly be aware that Tom and Harry live at the same address, then this will be a clear indication that their relationship is a personal one, and that Harry's role in acting as a surety is not part of a business transaction. They will, therefore, be put on inquiry. If this is so, then the rather tentative suggestion of 'more time' or 'legal advice', made in Tom's presence, would almost certainly be insufficient to satisfy the requirements as to the steps which creditors should take to protect themselves.

These requirements were reviewed and restated by the House of Lords in *Royal Bank of Scotland v Etridge (No 2)* (2001). They said that in this type of situation, where there is a 'non-commercial' surety, the bank must insist on the surety receiving independent legal advice. The solicitor giving the advice must confirm to the bank that the documentation and its implications have been explained to the surety. On the facts given here, it appears that the bank has not satisfied these requirements. The bank's employee has simply asked Harry, 'are you sure you don't want to take legal advice?'. This is clearly inadequate, and Harry may well be able to resist the enforcement of the security against him.

One final possibility which must be considered is whether the bank itself is guilty of using undue influence on Harry. This possibility was recognised in *Lloyds Bank v Bundy* (1975), where an elderly farmer was held to have been unduly influenced by a representative of a bank with which the farmer had had a long relationship, and in which he placed his trust and confidence. There is no evidence here, however, that Harry's relationship with the bank is of this kind. It seems unlikely, therefore, that he would be able to escape from the security transaction on this basis.

In conclusion, then, it appears that there is little Harry can do about the transfer of the half share of the house. He may, however, be able to resist the enforcement of the security by the bank, if it can be shown that the bank should have had constructive notice of the likelihood of Harry's being unduly influenced by Tom, or being affected by Tom's misrepresentation.

Notes

1 On the facts, they found that Mrs O'Brien had not been unduly influenced by her husband, but she had been misled by his misrepresentation.

2 Stress was laid on this requirement in the subsequent case of *CIBC Mortgages v Pitt* (1993), where a straightforward mortgage of the matrimonial home was not regarded as being of obvious financial disadvantage to a wife.

Question 31

'It is not clear that the House of Lords has yet managed to find a satisfactory balance between the need to protect those vulnerable to undue influence, and the need to ensure that banks and other financial institutions remain willing to lend money to small businesses in situations where domestic property may provide the only realistic security.' (Stone, *The Modern Law of Contract*, 5th edn, 2002, p 336.)

Discuss.

Answer plan

This essay focuses on one particular aspect of the law on undue influence – that is, the extent to which those lending money on the security of domestic property (probably the matrimonial home) can be prevented from enforcing the debt because of undue influence (by the creditor or a third party) over the person providing the security. Two decisions of the House of Lords dominate this area, namely *Barclays Bank v O'Brien* (1993) and *Royal Bank of Scotland v Etridge (No 2)* (2001). You should not attempt the question unless you are confident that you have a firm grasp of both cases. Note that the question does not merely require an exposition of the law derived from these cases, but also requires you to adopt a critical perspective, addressing the issue of whether the balance of rights between the various parties is being struck correctly.

The suggested order of treatment is:

- outline the problem;

- explain the principles to be derived from *Barclays Bank v O'Brien* (1993);

- explain how those principles have been modified by subsequent case law, and in particular *Royal Bank of Scotland v Etridge (No 2)* (2001); and

- consider critically the question of whether the balance between the rights of creditors and the rights of those providing security has been struck satisfactorily – that is, protecting the vulnerable while not 'scaring off' prospective lenders.

Answer

Over the past 10 years, the English courts have been grappling with a difficult problem involving the interaction of the law of contract with an area of social and economic sensitivity. It is important for the economy that small businesses flourish. Such businesses often cannot do so without significant and substantial borrowing. Creditors will only be willing to lend the sums concerned on the basis of some appropriate security. The only available security will often be the house in which the borrower is living with his or her partner. The danger is that the partner, having a legal interest in the house, may be persuaded by undue influence or misrepresentation to allow it to be used for security without a full appreciation of the risks involved. The courts may then be asked to prevent the creditor from enforcing the security, in order to protect the rights of the partner. The situation most commonly arises where the borrower is a man and the person supplying the security is his wife, though as the House of Lords has now made clear, care needs to be taken wherever the relationship between borrower and surety is 'non-commercial'.

The starting point for discussion of the modern law applying to this area is the House of Lords' decision in *Barclays Bank v O'Brien* (1993). In this case, Mrs O'Brien had been misled by her husband as to the extent of the security being supplied to support his business overdraft with the bank. The jointly owned matrimonial home was used as security for the debt. The relevant documents were presented for her signature by an employee of the bank, who did not explain the transaction or suggest that she should take independent legal advice. When the bank subsequently tried to enforce its security, the question arose as to whether it was prevented from doing so by Mr O'Brien's misrepresentation to his wife. While the case was thus primarily concerned with misrepresentation, the House of Lords made it clear that the same principles should apply where the allegation was that the borrower had used undue influence on the surety.

There was no suggestion in the *O'Brien* case that the bank itself had been guilty of undue influence or misrepresentation (unlike, for example, *Lloyds Bank Ltd v Bundy* (1975), where the bank itself was at fault). The question was rather whether the bank was 'infected' by Mr O'Brien's wrongdoing in the form of the misrepresentation. The House of Lords rejected arguments that this type of situation was best analysed in terms of agency (with the husband acting as agent for the bank), or on the basis of some kind of 'special equity' protecting wives. Instead, it held that the governing principle should be that of actual or constructive notice. Was the bank aware ('actual notice') of any wrongdoing by Mr O'Brien which would have entitled Mrs O'Brien to set aside any transaction as against her husband? If not, should it have been aware ('constructive notice') of the risk of such wrongdoing, and taken steps to negate its effect? On the facts, the House found that although Mrs O'Brien had not been unduly influenced by her husband, she had been materially misled by his misrepresentation, so that she would have had a right to set aside the transaction vis à vis her husband. The bank was obviously aware of their relationship, and aware that the transaction was one which was risky from Mrs O'Brien's point of view. The bank should, therefore, have taken steps to advise Mrs O'Brien separately and to ensure that she was fully aware of the nature and extent of the security being provided. As it had not done so, Mrs O'Brien was entitled to set aside the security transaction vis à vis the bank.

Cases subsequent to *O'Brien* accepted the general approach laid out there, but became somewhat confused over when exactly the creditor should be put on notice, and what steps needed to be taken to protect its position. In particular, there were queries as to what the position was when the surety received legal advice, but from the same lawyer as was acting for the borrower. These issues were thoroughly reviewed by the House of Lords in *Royal Bank of Scotland v Etridge (No 2)* (2001).

The first question concerns when the creditor is put on notice. The House of Lords decided that this could not be limited to transactions involving husband and wife, cohabitees and sexual partners (as had been suggested in some of the earlier cases). The case of *Credit Lyonnais Bank Nederland NV v Burch* (1997) indicated that this was too narrow an approach, since here the 'victim' of the undue influence was a junior employee in the borrower's firm. In *Etridge*, therefore, the view was taken that the creditor should be put on notice wherever the relationship between the borrower and the surety was 'non-commercial'. To this extent, the House has extended the protection given by the law, by requiring that all non-commercial sureties should receive proper independent advice.

As regards the steps which should be taken by the creditor to ensure that proper advice is given, the House moved away from the position in *O'Brien*, which put the emphasis on the creditor itself providing advice. The House recognised, as had been shown by many of the cases post-*O'Brien*, that it was often preferable and more practical for the advice to be given by a solicitor. In relation to this, the creditor should communicate directly with the surety to determine whom he or she wishes to use as a legal adviser. This can be the same solicitor that is acting for the borrower, as long as the surety is happy with this. The legal adviser must be provided with all the relevant information, including any confidential financial information provided by the borrower to the creditor, and any suspicions that the creditor may have that the surety may have been misled or unduly influenced. The surety must then have the transaction fully explained by the legal adviser. The surety should then be asked to sign a document indicating that the transaction and its implications have been fully explained and understood. Once it has been confirmed to the creditor by the legal adviser that all these steps have been taken, then the creditor will be fully protected from any subsequent claim that the surety was misled or unduly influenced.

What is the position if these steps are not taken? This will mean that the validity of the security transaction is vulnerable to challenge, but it does not necessarily mean that the transaction will be set aside. The surety will still need to show that there was some misrepresentation or influence from the borrower (or from the creditor) which justifies the court treating the transaction as voidable. It is in this area that *Etridge*, while extending the situations in which the creditor needs to take steps to protect itself, has probably narrowed the situations where undue influence will be found. One of the factors which will be relevant to a finding of such influence is whether the transaction is disadvantageous to the surety. The House was clear that it did not regard the most common situation which arises in this area, that is, one where the wife provides security for her husband's business debts, as being one which as a matter of course would give rise to a presumption that the husband's influence was undue. Wives may well be willing to support their husbands' businesses in this type of situation, not least because the business may provide the main family income, and so be prepared to take risks to achieve this. This does not in itself mean that they have been unduly influenced.

It may be questioned whether, in taking this line, the House of Lords has in fact given appropriate weight to the pressures which will be placed on a wife in this type of situation. If she is asked by her husband to support his business, it may be very difficult for her to say no. A refusal would be likely to put a severe strain on their relationship, which she will presumably wish to continue. Her ability to resist would be assisted if she has received independent legal advice which has emphasised the risks involved. The focus in *Etridge* is on the importance of such advice in protecting the position of the creditor. It is just as important that sureties in this situation should receive such advice, both for their own protection and to provide support for a decision not to proceed with the transaction. It is likely to be easier to say, 'I am not going ahead because the solicitor advised me of the risks involved', as opposed to, 'I am not going ahead because I don't trust you to make a success of the business'. Even with such support, however, the decision to refuse to provide the necessary security is likely to be a difficult one.

At the moment, the law in this area seems to be weighted in favour of the creditor, despite the fact that *O'Brien* was seen as a 'victory' for wives who act as sureties. This is indicated by the fact that a significant majority of the cases which have subsequently come before the appeal courts have resulted in a decision against the surety. The House in *Etridge*, while providing welcome clarification of various issues, and in particular the steps which a creditor needs to take to protect itself, has done nothing to change this imbalance. The risk of shifting it too far in favour of the surety is, of course, that creditors will become reluctant to lend money where the security is domestic property in which someone other than the borrower has an interest. It is submitted, however, that there is scope for more protection to be provided to sureties in this type of situation, without the risk of scaring off the majority of potential lenders.

CHAPTER 9

ILLEGALITY

Introduction

The vitiating factor which is considered in this chapter is 'illegality'. Although there are a variety of ways in which a contract can be deemed to be 'illegal' and thus unenforceable, modern contract courses tend to focus on the issue of 'restraint of trade'. This is reflected in the balance of the questions in this chapter. Part of Question 32 deals with 'immoral' contracts, and the first part of Question 33 with the effects of illegality, but the rest of the questions deal with various aspects of the restraint of trade doctrine.

The rules which apply in this area are reasonably well settled, and questions on restraint of trade should not provide too much difficulty. One problem in answering them, however, arises from the fact that whether a restraint is enforceable or not will depend on whether it is regarded as 'reasonable' in all the circumstances. This means that it is difficult to give a firm and definite answer. What must be done, however, is to give some answer, albeit qualified, and to back it up with reasons drawn from past decisions, or the facts of the problem itself, or both.

The main points to be remembered in relation to restraint of trade are that:

- restraints are *prima facie* void;
- they will, however, be valid if:
  o there is a legitimate interest to protect; and
  o the restraint goes no further than is reasonable to protect that interest.

One aspect of restraint of trade which is of growing importance, but is beyond the scope of most contract courses, is the effect of Art 81 of the EC Treaty. This applies where the restraint has an effect on cross-border trade within the European Union. All the questions in this chapter, as is usual in most undergraduate contract examinations, relate to restraints which affect simply domestic UK trade.

Nor is there any attempt here to deal with the legislative regime contained in the Competition Act 1998. This area, like the European element, is more commonly part of a specialist course on competition law.

Checklist

You should be familiar with the following areas:

- General concept of 'illegal contracts'.
- Contracts for 'immoral purposes'.
- General doctrine of restraint of trade.
- Rules applying to employment contracts.
- Rules applying to sale of a business.
- 'Solus' agreements.
- Effects of illegality.

Question 32

Consider the likely attitude of the courts to *both* the following situations:

(a) Bertha is a prostitute. She attracts her clients by sitting on a high stool near the downstairs bay window of her house. The window has been broken by someone throwing a brick through it. Bertha engages Conrad, a glazier, to replace the window with specially toughened glass, and at the same time to enlarge it, so as to give prospective clients a better view. Conrad does the work, but Bertha refuses to pay.

(b) Jack is a DJ employed by Noyz Clubs Ltd, which run clubs in Extown and the surrounding area. Jack has built up a considerable following among the young people of the area. The result is that the number of people attending the clubs at which he is the DJ is considerably greater than the number attending other clubs in the area. His contract of employment contains a clause to the effect that if he leaves the employment of Noyz Clubs Ltd he will not appear as a DJ at any clubs in Extown or Fartown (six miles away) for the next five years. Jack now wishes to work as a DJ for another firm which runs clubs in the area.

Answer plan

Two aspects of the doctrine of illegality are dealt with here:

Part (a):

- In this part, the question concerns the extent to which the courts will enforce contracts made for immoral purposes. The relevant principles will need to be outlined at the start of the answer. The case of *Pearce v Brooks* (1866) will then be the main authority to consider. A contract to replace a window for a prostitute would not generally be an 'illegal' contract, but since the use of the window is connected with her work, the answer may be different. It may also be relevant to know whether Conrad was aware of Bertha's profession.

Part (b):

- This part of the answer should start with an outline of the main rules relating to contracts in restraint of trade, as they apply to employment contracts. The restrictive term in Jack's contract will be *prima facie* void. It will then be up to Noyz to show:
  - that there is a valid interest for them to protect;
  - if there is, that the restraint is reasonable as between the parties in the protection of that interest; and
  - that the restraint is not contrary to the public interest.

The issue of 'reasonableness' is always at some stage going to be a matter of opinion, but that should not deter you from discussing it, and expressing your own opinion as to which way the decision should go.

Answer

Part (a)

At first sight, the contract between Conrad and Bertha appears perfectly valid, and there seems to be no reason why Conrad should not recover his money for carrying out the repair. In some situations, however, the courts deem a contract to have been made for an illegal purpose, and will for that reason refuse to allow it to be enforced. This extends beyond contracts to perform criminal or tortious acts, to those which are frowned on for reasons of public policy, because, for example, they interfere with the institution of marriage[1] or promote sexual immorality. It is this last category with which we are concerned here.

There is no doubt that, despite the relaxation of attitudes towards sexual morality over the last 30 years,[2] prostitution, although not in itself illegal, would be regarded as an immoral activity. A contract with a prostitute for the provision of sexual services would clearly be unenforceable. The question is to what extent will contracts which are ancillary to the purposes of prostitution also be struck down? There are two cases which require consideration, showing the two sides of the issue.

In *Pearce v Brooks* (1866), there was a contract under which the plaintiffs supplied the defendant with a coach. One instalment on the purchase price was paid, and then the coach was returned in a damaged condition. The plaintiffs sued for compensation under the contract. There was evidence, however, that the defendant was a prostitute, and that the coach was used by her in order to attract clients. It was held that if the plaintiffs knew that the defendant intended to use the coach for this purpose, then this was an illegal contract, and the plaintiffs could not recover under the contract or for the damage. On this basis, it would appear that Bertha might be able to resist any action by Conrad to recover the costs of replacing the window. But the courts have made it clear that not every contract made with a prostitute will be illegal. In *Appleton v Campbell* (1826), the plaintiff sued the defendant for board and lodging. The defence was that the defendant was a prostitute, and used the room for the purposes of prostitution, to the plaintiff's knowledge. It was held that, if this was indeed the case, then the contract was unenforceable. If, on the other hand, the prostitute entertained her clients elsewhere and simply used this room for herself, then the plaintiff could recover, since even a prostitute had to be allowed to make a valid contract for somewhere to live.[3]

Two issues need to be explored to determine the possibility of Conrad's being able to enforce his contract with Bertha. First, did he know that she was a prostitute? From the facts, it seems likely that he would have realised the purpose for which Bertha used her front room, but if he did not know, then it seems, from *Pearce v Brooks*, that he would be able to enforce. The knowledge of the coach builders was regarded as a relevant issue in that case. Secondly, was the contract one which fell within the scope of the approach in *Appleton v Campbell*? It must surely be allowable in the normal course of events for prostitutes to have the windows in their houses repaired, and to make valid contracts to do so. Protection against the elements should be regarded in the same way as the need for shelter.[4] The problem for Conrad is that this particular window is used by Bertha in connection with her prostitution. As with the coach in *Pearce v Brooks*, the window is used as a means of attracting clients.[5] The point is emphasised by the fact that the contract is not simply for the replacement of the broken glass, but also for the enlargement of the window. If Conrad was aware of all this, it may well be that he will be unable to recover anything from Bertha.

It is hard to see exactly what purpose is served by the approach adopted to contracts made by prostitutes. While it is understandable that contracts for prostitution themselves should be unenforceable, there seems to be little justification in striking down ancillary contracts of the kind in *Pearce v Brooks* or in the problem.

An indication that the courts may be prepared to move in this direction may be found in the decision of the Court of Appeal in *Armhouse Lee Ltd v Chappell* (1996). The contracts here were for the placing of advertisements in magazines relating to telephone 'sex lines'. It was held that they did not involve any criminal offence, nor did they offend against any generally accepted moral code. The contracts were therefore enforceable. This decision does not, however, overturn the principles stated in *Pearce v Brooks* (1866) as regards contracts with prostitutes. As a consequence, unless Conrad is able to plead ignorance, he is likely to find himself without a remedy.

Part (b)

The term in the contract between Jack and Noyz which attempts to restrict whom Jack may work for after leaving Noyz's employment appears to be 'in restraint of trade'. Such provisions are regarded as *prima facie* void, as being contrary to public policy: *Nordenfelt v Maxim Nordenfelt* (1894). Such a provision in a contract of employment may, however, be valid if three conditions are satisfied. These are that:

* the person imposing the restraint has a valid interest to protect;
* the restraint is reasonable, having regard to the interest to be protected; and
* the restraint is not contrary to the public interest.

These three requirements, and the way in which they apply to the problem, will now be considered in more detail.

First, we must look at the question of the existence of a 'valid interest' which Noyz may protect. In contracts of employment, the interest to be protected has generally been related to trade secrets to which the employee has had access, or influence over customers, either as a result of reliance on the employee's skill and judgment or because the customers have dealt exclusively with the employee. It has been said that the categories of interest are not closed (in *Grieg v Insole* (1978)),[6] but here it would seem that Noyz could argue that Jack's influence over those attending the club was the relevant factor. The position is not identical to that of the tradesman (for example, the milkman) who visits customers on behalf of his employer. The club customers come to Jack rather than him going to them. Nor does he have personal contact with each customer, unlike the sales representative. His position is also not identical with another category of employee where restraints have been upheld, that is, the solicitor who may have built up the client's trust. Jack may wish to argue that his success is simply a result of his own skill as a DJ. Other than originally employing him, his employers have not done anything to develop the situation where Jack is so popular. The only interest which Noyz have is in preventing attendances at their clubs from falling. That in itself cannot be a legitimate interest worthy of protection. Noyz, on the other hand, may say that they have provided the investment in equipment, advertising, etc, which has enabled Jack to become a success. He should not now be allowed to use his position of influence over the young people of the area in a way which harms Noyz.

As can be seen, the argument is quite finely balanced. It is submitted that Noyz will have an interest worthy of protection, if they can establish that they have substantially contributed to Jack's success. Assuming this to be the case, the other requirements for a valid restraint need to be considered.

In looking at the reasonableness of the restraint between the parties, three main factors must be considered, namely area, time and type of activity.

As regards area, the restriction must relate to the scope of the restrainer's interest. In *Mason v Provident Clothing* (1913), for example, a restraint on a canvasser, who had been employed to sell clothes in Islington, not to enter into similar business within 25 miles of London was held to be too wide. Here, the restraint appears to be limited in area to the places where Jack has previously been working, so it may well be that this is reasonable.

Again, as regards the type of activity restricted, this is limited to work 'as a DJ', which would seem to be reasonable, given that this is precisely the role in which Jack has been employed by Noyz. Even if more general words had been used, the courts have recently seemed prepared to regard them as limited by the 'factual matrix' within which the restraint was imposed.[7]

Finally, there is the question of time. What is reasonable here will depend on the type of contract. For example, in *Fitch v Dewes* (1921), a lifelong restraint on a solicitor's managing clerk was upheld. The business was one to which clients were likely to return over a long period. In the case of Jack, however, different considerations would surely apply. Fashions and attractions amongst young people change very rapidly, particularly in the area of music. In five years' time, a whole new generation of club attenders would have arrived. It seems unlikely that Noyz would need to keep Jack out of circulation for this long in order to protect their interest. The five year restraint is almost certainly unreasonable – six months or a year would have been sufficient.

If the restraint is unreasonable between the parties, there is no real need to consider the question of whether it is more generally contrary to the public interest. It seems unlikely, however, that in this case the public interest would be sufficient to prevent the restraint operating.[8]

In conclusion, then, it seems that Jack will be able to work as he wishes, because the restraint on the part of Noyz Ltd is unreasonable as regards the length of time for which it is to operate, and is therefore unenforceable.

Notes

1   This covers contracts in restraint of marriage (*Baker v White* (1690)) and marriage brokage contracts (*Hermann v Charlesworth* (1905)).

2   See, for example, the acceptance in *Somma v Hazlehurst* (1978) that a contract, under which an unmarried couple living together as husband and wife were granted a licence to occupy furnished premises, could not be struck down on grounds of immorality.

3   As Abbott CJ put it: '... if the defendant had her lodgings there, and received her visitors elsewhere, the plaintiff may recover, although she be a woman of the town, because persons of that description must have a place to lay their heads.' That is, a prostitute can validly rent a room in which to lay her head, but not her clients.

4   A comparison might be drawn with the concept of 'necessaries' in minors' contracts: see Chapter 4.

5   Note that soliciting prostitution is not only immoral, but also illegal, which strengthens the argument for illegality.

6   Where Slade J recognised a possible interest of the cricket authorities in ensuring that the game should be properly organised and administered. On the facts, however, he found that the attempted restraint was unreasonable.

7   See, for example, *Littlewoods v Harris* (1978) and *Clarke v Newland* (1991).

8   The relevant cases are *Wyatt v Kreglinger & Fernau* (1933) and *Bull v Pitney Bowes* (1966).

Question 33

Answer both parts:

(a) What is the general rule about recovery of money or property transferred under an illegal contract? What are the exceptions?

(b) Sid owns a shop in Westbridge, a large town. His business mainly consists of selling and repairing Easifly lawnmowers. His is the only shop in Westbridge which deals in this type of lawnmower. Sid is now considering opening another shop in Eastchester, where he lives. Eastchester is a small town some five miles from Westbridge. Sid plans to sell his shop in Westbridge. The prospective purchaser is Greengrass plc, a national firm which owns a chain of garden centres, and which specialises in Easifly lawnmowers. This firm wants Sid to agree not to open another shop selling 'Easifly lawnmowers, or any other make of lawnmower, or any other garden equipment, anywhere in the United Kingdom', for the next 10 years.

Advise Sid.

Answer plan

Part (a):

- The answer to this part of the question will be largely descriptive. The general rule of non-recovery can be stated quite briefly, though at least one example should be given from the cases. The main part of the answer will be concerned with the exceptions, that is:
    - illegal purpose not carried out;
    - oppression;
    - fraud;
    - no reliance on illegal transaction; and
    - class-protecting statutes.

Part (b):

- The problem is concerned with the enforceability of restraints on the seller of a business. These will be permissible, provided that the restraint:
    - protects a legitimate interest;
    - is reasonable in its scope; and
    - is not contrary to the public interest.

An additional factor which will need to be considered is whether the restraining clause, if unreasonable as it stands, can be cut down, using the 'blue pencil' test, to make it reasonable.

Answer

Part (a)

If the courts have found that a contract is unenforceable because it is illegal, they are reluctant to allow it to be used in any way as the basis of a legal action. The basic rule, therefore, is that money or property transferred under an illegal contract cannot be recovered.[1] A good example of this principle in operation is *Parkinson v College of Ambulance* (1925). The plaintiff had made a contribution to a charity on the basis that he would get a knighthood in return. When no such honour was forthcoming, the plaintiff brought an action to recover his contribution. It was held that a contract to purchase a title is illegal and the plaintiff knew this. He could not therefore recover his money.

There are, however, a number of exceptions to this general principle. The first is where the contract is still executory, and the claimant is allowed to withdraw from his illegal purpose. This derives from *Taylor v Bowers* (1876), where the plaintiff had transferred goods as part of a scheme designed to defraud his creditors. At the point where he sought to recover the goods, however, no creditors had been defrauded, and so he was allowed to recover. For this argument to succeed, there must be a genuine withdrawal, not just a frustration of the claimant's purpose through inaction on the other side (as in *Parkinson v College of Ambulance* (1925)). Nor must there be any substantial performance of the contract (*Kearley v Thomson* (1890)).[2]

A second exception arises where the illegal contract has been made as a result of 'oppression'. In *Atkinson v Denby* (1862), for example, a creditor refused to accept a composition agreement unless he was paid an additional £50. The debtor paid the money, but then sought to recover it. It was held that, although the agreement to pay the money was a fraud on the other creditors, and therefore illegal, the debtor could recover because he had virtually been forced to agree because of his weak bargaining position. The rationale of this exception is that the parties are not equally at fault.[3] This will also be the case where the contract is made as a result of a fraudulent misrepresentation that it is lawful (*Hughes v Liverpool Victoria Legal Friendly Society* (1916)).

If a claimant can establish a right to possession of the property concerned without relying on the illegal transaction, recovery will be allowed. For example, in *Bowmakers v Barnet Instruments* (1945), the plaintiff was allowed to recover possession of machines transferred under illegal hire purchase transactions. Since the hire purchase agreements had not transferred ownership of the goods, the plaintiff was held to be allowed to recover on the basis of his basic rights of ownership, without relying on the agreement.[4]

A similar approach was taken by the House of Lords in *Tinsley v Milligan* (1993), where a resulting trust in relation to a house was held to be unaffected by the illegal purpose which had led to the house being put into the name of the trustee alone.[5]

The final exception is to be found in the area of so called 'class-protecting statutes'. This concerns the situation where a statute making an agreement illegal was passed to protect the members of a particular class (for example, tenants under the Rent Acts). A member of that class may be able to recover property given under the agreement notwithstanding the illegality. If, for example, a tenant paid a premium in order to obtain a tenancy, and such an agreement was unlawful under the Rent Acts, the tenant would be allowed to recover the premium (*Kiriri Cotton Co Ltd v Dewani* (1960)).[6]

Here, again, the basis of the exception is that there is not equal fault between the parties. The statute indicates a recognition by Parliament that some contractors may be taken advantage of by others who are in a stronger position. It would be wrong to then apply the statute in a way that penalised the weaker party. In fact, all the exceptions, apart from the first (illegal purpose not carried out), appear to be based on the application of this principle, which therefore provides a unifying theme to most of the rules operating in this area.

Part (b)

This scenario is concerned with an attempt to impose a restriction on the vendor of a business. Such a restriction will be regarded as being 'in restraint of trade' and therefore *prima facie* illegal. Sid will only be bound by it, therefore, if Greengrass can overturn the presumption of illegality by showing that the restraint is reasonable to protect a legitimate interest. Even if it is unreasonable as worded, the court may be prepared to enforce it if the scope can be narrowed by cutting out some part of the restriction.

The starting point for this kind of restraint is the decision of the House of Lords in *Nordenfelt v Maxim Nordenfelt* (1894), which held that all covenants in restraint of trade are *prima facie* contrary to public policy and therefore void. It was recognised, however, that the presumption could be rebutted if the restraint could be shown to be reasonable with reference to both the interests of the parties and the public interest. For the restraint to be reasonable, Greengrass will have to show that they have a legitimate interest to protect, that the scope of the restraint does not extend further than is reasonable to protect that interest, and that there is no more general public interest in preventing the restriction.

Looking at these requirements in turn, the first – the requirement of a legitimate interest – is easily satisfied. Where a person sells a shop as a going concern, an important element in the sale is likely to be the 'goodwill'. This means the fact that people know of the existence of the shop dealing with a particular type of goods, and the fact that there may well be a regular clientele. Reputation and established customers are both commercially valuable assets. It is almost certain that Sid will wish to increase the price of his business by including these elements in its valuation. It is well established that the protection of the goodwill in a business being bought is a legitimate interest which can be protected by a reasonable restrictive covenant. This indeed was the situation in *Nordenfelt v Maxim Nordenfelt* itself. The approach benefits the vendor as well as the purchaser, in that if the vendor were not able to accept a binding obligation not to compete, then he might have difficulty selling the business at all, and would certainly have to do so at a much lower price than would otherwise be the case.[7]

So, it would seem that Greengrass do have an interest to protect. Is the restraint reasonable to protect that interest? It covers the sale of any make of lawnmower and other garden equipment, anywhere in the UK, for 10 years. It will have to be considered reasonable in respect of scope, area and time if it is to stand. On the face of it, the clause seems likely to fail on each count. Sid's business has been mainly concerned with Easifly lawnmowers, whereas the restraint extends to other lawnmowers and other garden equipment. It will be a matter of fact as to the extent to which Sid's existing business deals in these other items but, on the facts given, the suggestion would seem to be that the business relating to Easifly lawnmowers is by far the most important element. A restraint which extends, as this one does, far beyond this area is likely to be regarded as unreasonable. The purchasers must tailor the restraint to the scope of the business which they are acquiring, not the scope of their own business (*British Reinforced Concrete Engineering Co Ltd v Schelff* (1921)).

As to area, it must be noted that in *Nordenfelt* a worldwide restriction was held to be reasonable. Here, the restriction applies simply to the UK. But, as with the scope, the area must relate to the interest being protected. It seems unlikely that Sid could do serious harm to Greengrass by opening up a shop in an area in which he was unknown. Moreover, there are very likely to be some areas of the UK where Greengrass do not have any existing shops which might be affected by Sid's competition. In the circumstances, the area, like the scope, would appear too wide.

Finally, the length of the restriction must be considered. It is stated to last for 10 years. This is a period which could rarely be regarded as reasonable in relation to a restriction on employment, but different considerations will apply in relation to a business. The question to be asked is presumably whether, if at any point within the next 10 years Sid were to open a shop in competition to Greengrass, he would be likely to recover any of his previous customers, so as to reduce the value of the goodwill sold to Greengrass. It is difficult to provide a clear answer to this, but it may well be that this aspect of the restraint is reasonable.

It has been suggested above that the restraint is probably unreasonable as regards scope and area. This is not the end of the story, however. The courts may be prepared to sever unreasonable parts of the restraint, and give effect to what is reasonable. Thus, in *Goldsoll v Goldman* (1915), a restraint which listed a number of countries where the vendor of a business was not to compete was held to be unreasonable as to area. It was, however, made reasonable by cutting out those countries where there was no real risk of competition and letting the rest stand. The test is sometimes called the 'blue pencil' test, in that what the courts are supposed to do is simply strike out the offending words. What is left should still make sense, without the need to add anything or rewrite anything. The excision must also not change the whole nature of the restraint: *Attwood v Lamont* (1920). In this case, a list of activities in an employment contract could not be cut down to the one in which the defendant had been engaged, since it was held that the whole point of the restraint had been to protect the entire range of the plaintiffs' business.[8]

Applying this to the facts of the problem, it would seem relatively easy to narrow the scope of this clause by cutting out the phrases 'any other make of lawnmower, or any other garden equipment'. The question of area (or time, if this is thought unreasonable) is more difficult, in that no list of places is included which can be cut down. Excising 'anywhere in the United Kingdom' would not narrow the area, but leave it entirely open. The courts might be prepared to do this, however, if they combined it with another approach, used in *Littlewoods v Harris* (1977) and *Clarke v Newland* (1991), where it was held that a wide restraining clause has to be interpreted in the context in which it was put forward. In *Littlewoods*, this meant the area of the business in which Harris had been employed, and, in *Clarke v Newland*, the type of medical practice concerned. The area of operation would then be related to the area in which Sid had been carrying on his business.[9] If this approach can be combined with the 'blue pencil' test, it may be possible for the clause to become reasonable.

The final possibility is that the restraint, while reasonable between the parties, is contrary to the general public interest. There does not seem to be any reason why this should operate on these facts.

In the light of the above discussion, the advice to Sid should be that if he agrees to the suggested clause, it is unlikely to be enforced as it stands. If, however, by the methods outlined above, it is found to be reasonable to a limited extent, it almost certainly would prevent him opening an 'Easifly' shop in Eastchester. His repair business, however, would not seem to be affected, and it is unlikely that he would be prevented from dealing in other lawnmowers or other garden equipment. To that extent, Sid may have a viable business prospect, even if his range of activities is slightly restricted by the covenant.

Notes

1 This area of law used to be said to be governed by the principle *in pari delicto potior est conditio defendentis*, or *in pari delicto* for short. This Latin tag translates roughly as 'if both parties are equally at fault, the defendant is in the stronger position'. Although the Latin is not so much in general use nowadays, the underlying principle remains the same.

2 There is disagreement amongst the textbook writers as to the precise effect of *Kearley v Thomson*. Cf Treitel, *The Law of Contract*, 10th edn, 1999, p 456, with Cheshire and Fifoot, *The Law of Contract*, 14th edn, 2001, p 435. See also Stone, *The Modern Law of Contract*, 5th edn, 2002, p 355.

3 That is, not *in pari delicto*; see note 1 above.

4 Note that this decision has been criticised as being inconsistent with *Taylor v Chester* (1869). See Stone, *The Modern Law of Contract*, p 356.

5 Cf also *Skilton v Sullivan* (1994), where an attempt to avoid VAT was held not to render a contract unenforceable.

6 Note that the Rent Act 1977 makes specific provision for the recovery of such a premium: s 125.

7 An argument which might be raised here is whether the position would be different if Sid was happy to sell the premises without the goodwill. It almost certainly would be. The purchaser would then have no interest to protect, and the restraint could not be allowed to stand.

8 This case is in fact difficult to reconcile with *Goldsoll v Goldman* (1915) but, since the issue does not directly arise on the facts of the problem, it is not discussed further here.

9 It is difficult to see how this could work in relation to the time restraint, should that be regarded as unreasonable.

Question 34

Peter owns a garage where he sells and repairs Sporta cars. He has a contract with Sporta plc under which he is obliged to buy from Sporta all the spare parts required for his repair business. This agreement was entered into last year, and is to last for 15 years. It is linked to a mortgage agreement under which Sporta lent Peter £20,000 to refurbish the garage. Peter has just discovered that Sporta are supplying Delia, who is the Sporta dealer in the next town (five miles away), with spares at a 10% discount. As a result, Peter's repair business is unable to run at a profit. He would be able to buy spares from other suppliers much more cheaply.

Two years ago, Peter employed Edith as a salesperson in the car showroom. It was a term of her contract that if she left Peter's employment she would not participate in the business of selling cars within 10 miles of Peter's garage for a period of three years. Edith resigned last month, and Peter has now discovered that she is working for Delia, selling Sporta cars.

Advise Peter as to his rights in relation to:

(a) the contract with Sporta plc; and

(b) the restriction on Edith's employment.

Answer plan

Although the facts of this problem are presented as a continuous narrative, in effect there are two separate problems to be discussed, as indicated by the instructions at the end of the question. The two aspects can be clearly separated in the answer.

(a) As regards the contract with Sporta, we are here concerned with a 'solus' agreement, in which a retailer is tied to a particular supplier. These types of restraint are most common in relation to public houses and petrol stations, as is shown by the case law, but there is no reason why they should not extend to other areas, as in the problem.

The two cases which will need most discussion are *Esso Petroleum v Harpers Garage* (1968) and *Shell v Lostock Garage* (1977). These suggest that the agreement in the problem will be regarded as *prima facie* void as being in restraint of trade, but that it may nevertheless be enforced if it is shown to be reasonable as between the parties and in the public interest (assessed at the time of the contract).

(b) This problem is a standard one in relation to restraints in employment contracts. The restrictive term in Edith's contract will be *prima facie* void. It will then be up to Peter to prove:

o   that there is a valid interest for him to protect;

o   if there is, that the restraint is reasonable as between the parties in the protection of that interest; and

o   that the restraint is not contrary to the public interest.

Answer

Part (a)

It was not clear prior to 1968 whether agreements for exclusive dealing, or 'solus' agreements, were within the scope of the doctrine of restraint of trade.[1] In that year, the House of Lords, in *Esso Petroleum v Harpers Garage* (1968), took the view that an agreement under which a garage owner was compelled to buy petrol from a particular supplier over a period of years was in restraint of trade and *prima facie* void. The presumption of unenforceability that this raised, however, could be rebutted by showing that:

• the person imposing the restraint had a legitimate interest to protect;

• the restraint was reasonable in protecting that interest; and

• the restraint was not contrary to the general public interest.

These are the standard tests which are also applied to restrictive covenants imposed on employees or on the sale of a business, but they may operate in slightly different ways. In particular, it may be more difficult in exclusive dealing arrangements to identify an interest which is being protected by the person imposing the restraint.

In *Esso Petroleum v Harpers Garage*, there were two agreements, in relation to two garages. The owners of the garages had to buy all their petrol from Esso, and they also had to agree to open at all reasonable hours. One of the agreements was to last for four and a half years. The other, which was linked to a mortgage over the premises, was to last for 21 years. The House of Lords considered that there was a legitimate interest to protect, in, for example, the maintenance of Esso's network of outlets for their petrol.[2] As to the reasonableness of the restraint, the shorter restraint was held to be reasonable and the 21 year one unreasonable.[3] The precise basis for this decision is not all that clear, though a number of their Lordships clearly felt that the longer restraint was contrary to the general public interest.

Before attempting to apply this decision to the problem, one other case needs consideration: *Shell v Lostock Garage* (1977). In this case, there was again a restraint which required the garage owner to buy all petrol from the plaintiff. The length of the restraint was probably short enough to be valid. During a petrol price 'war', however, Shell supplied petrol at lower prices to two garages which were competitors of the defendants. They started to buy petrol elsewhere, claiming that Shell's action had rendered the exclusive dealing contract unreasonable and unenforceable. This argument was accepted at first instance, and by Lord Denning in the Court of Appeal. The majority of the Court of Appeal, however, held that the reasonableness or otherwise of the restraint must be assessed at the time of the contract, and cannot be altered by subsequent events.[4]

What then is the position as regards Peter's contract with Sporta? It is clearly an exclusive dealing contract which, on the basis of the decision in *Esso v Harpers,* is *prima facie* in restraint of trade. It also follows from the decision in *Shell v Lostock* that the fact that Sporta are supplying Delia with spares at a discount is irrelevant in assessing the reasonableness of the restraint. This must be judged at the time the contract was entered into.

The first question, however, is whether Sporta have a legitimate interest to protect. The answer would clearly seem to be yes. They have put money into the business in terms of the loan to refurbish the garage, and may reasonably wish to protect that investment by making sure that the additional business which the improved premises will attract does not end up benefiting a rival supplier.

Given that there is a legitimate interest, is the restraint reasonable to protect that interest? The main issue here is likely to be the length of the restraint, but other factors, such as the terms of the mortgage, may be relevant. If, for example, the money was lent at an interest rate below the normal commercial mortgage rates, this would add to the reasonableness of the restraint. Conversely, if the rate is penal, this may make the whole agreement unreasonable. As to the length, it is greater than the four and a half years approved in *Esso,*[5] but considerably less than the 21 years which was disapproved. Fifteen years is still a considerable time, however. The effect of the refurbishments is not really going to last that long. On balance, assuming that the agreement is not terminable at any point within the 15 years, it is suggested that the restraint would be likely to be found unreasonable on this ground. Even if it is not, however, it is probable that Sporta's favoured treatment of Delia will make it unlikely that they will be able to get specific performance of the agreement with Peter. This was the view of the majority in *Shell v Lostock Garage.* It seems relatively safe, therefore, for Peter to buy his spares from elsewhere, though he runs the risk of having to pay damages to Sporta.

Part (b)

Edith has been employed as a salesperson by Peter, and he now wishes to prevent her from working in a similar position for Delia. The question of whether he will be able to do so depends on the enforceability of the provision in Edith's contract of employment with Peter. Such a clause is, like the exclusive dealing agreement considered in the first part of the question, regarded as being in restraint of trade and *prima facie* unenforceable. Again, like the solus agreement, it may, however, be enforced if it is 'reasonable'. The test of reasonableness has the same three elements as were outlined above – that is, there must be an interest to protect, the scope of the clause must be reasonable as between the parties, and it must not be contrary to the public interest.[6]

It is well established that, in relation to certain types of employee, an employer will have an interest to protect in preventing that employee working for a rival. In particular, if the employee has been employed in a position which put him into direct contact with the employer's customers, there is a danger that those customers will be 'poached' by the employee for his new employer. Alternatively, the employee may have had access to trade secrets, which the employer may legitimately wish to protect.[7] In either of these situations, there will be a legitimate interest which the employer can protect.

In the present case, it is likely that Peter's argument for restraining Edith will be based on the fact that she has established relationships with Peter's customers and that they may follow her to her new job, which is only five miles away. In other cases, a legitimate interest of this kind has been recognised in relation to, for example, a hairdresser (*Marion White Ltd v Francis* (1972)), a sales representative (*T Lucas & Co v Mitchell* (1974)) and a tailor (*Attwood v Lamont* (1920)). Does this apply here? An important distinction may be that buyers of new cars do not make their purchases very frequently. There is likely to be a gap of at least a few years between transactions. When they do make a purchase, it is likely to be based on questions of price and the characteristics of the car, rather than any relationship with the salesperson. By way of contrast, the hairdresser meets each customer every few weeks, and will much more quickly build up a rapport with them. There must at least be a possibility that Peter's argument may fail at this point, in that in the circumstances there is no real interest which needs to be protected. Edith may well be a good and effective salesperson, but that is not in itself enough to allow Peter to stop her working for somebody else.

Assuming that a legitimate interest is found, the restraint will have to be found to be reasonable as regards time, scope and area. This is a question of fact in each case. The reasonableness of the restraint must be looked at in the light of the interest being protected. The question is: 'Is this particular restraint reasonable to protect this particular interest?' On the facts of the problem, the time of the restraint may well be reasonable. It is only three years, and that is just the sort of time period that people may leave between the purchase of one car and the next. Similarly, the area of restriction does not seem unreasonable, since people may well travel to a nearby town in order to find the car they want. The most difficult aspect of the restraint for Peter to argue is reasonable is the scope. The term in Edith's contract appears to prevent her from selling any make of car, whereas Peter's business relates solely to Sporta cars. The fact that Edith is in fact selling Sporta cars is irrelevant. As noted above in the answer to the first part of the question, *Shell v Lostock Garage* makes it clear that the clause must be assessed at the time of the contract, not in the light of subsequent circumstances. Peter may, however, get some help from the cases of *Littlewoods Organisation v Harris* (1978) and *Clarke v Newland* (1991). In the *Littlewoods* case, a clause covered all aspects of the plaintiffs' business, whereas the defendant was only employed in the mail order business. It was held that the context in which the clause was imposed should be used to interpret it as only applying to mail order. Similarly, in *Clarke v Newland*, the broad agreement 'not to practise' was held to mean 'practise as a general medical practitioner' since that was the role in which the defendant had previously been employed. Peter might thus argue that the general words of the clause should be limited by the context, and be taken to apply only to Sporta cars.

It is unlikely, however, in view of the arguments set out above about the interest which Peter is trying to protect, that these issues will ever come to be considered. Peter should be advised that it is unlikely that he will be able to stop Edith working for Delia.

Notes

1   See, for example, *Foley v Classique Coaches* (1934).

2   This was the view of Lord Pearce. The speeches of the other Lords are less clear in identifying the protectable interest.

3   Another case which might be mentioned here is *Alec Lobb (Garages) Ltd v Total Oil (Great Britain) Ltd* (1985), where a 21 year restraint was held to be reasonable because it was terminable after seven or 14 years.

4   They managed to find other ways, however, of refusing Shell relief: by finding an implied term (Bridge LJ), or ruling that it would be inequitable to grant specific performance (Ormrod LJ, with whom Lord Denning agreed).

5   Or the seven years in *Alec Lobb* – see above, note 3.

6   This element was used to strike down a restraint in *Wyatt v Kreglinger Fernau* (1933) and *Bull v Pitney Bowes* (1967), though its precise scope remains very uncertain.

7   For example, *Littlewoods Organisation v Harris* (1978). Note that the law of breach of confidence may also be used to protect trade secrets or other confidential information: *Faccenda Chicken Ltd v Fowler* (1987).

CHAPTER 10

FRUSTRATION

Introduction

The doctrine of frustration is one of the more straightforward areas of the law of contract. Although it involves a mixture of common law rules and statute (in the form of the Law Reform (Frustrated Contracts) Act 1943), which can sometimes cause difficulties (for example, regarding exclusion clauses), in this case the two fit together fairly comfortably. This is probably because the Act is primarily concerned with the effects of frustration, whereas the question of what amounts to a frustrating event is left to the common law. Both common law and statute must be understood, however, before attempting questions on this topic.

Of the questions in this chapter, Question 35 is primarily concerned with what amounts to a frustrating event, whereas Question 36 concentrates more on the consequences of frustration. Question 37 brings the two aspects together.

In dealing with the meaning of 'frustration', the following issues are likely to be important:

- has the event deprived the other side of the entire benefit of the contract? *Krell v Henry* and *Herne Bay Steam Boat Co v Hutton* are useful contrasting decisions on this area; and

- what is the meaning of 'self-induced' frustration? The case of *The Super Servant Two* is an interesting one to add to the older decision in *Maritime National Fish Ltd v Ocean Trawlers Ltd*.

On the consequences of frustration, you will need to be familiar with:

- the decision in the *Fibrosa* case;

- the provisions of s 1(2) and (3) of the Law Reform (Frustrated Contracts) Act 1943; and

- the decision in *BP Exploration v Hunt*.

The *BP v Hunt* decision and its implications is probably the most difficult area within the topic of frustration. It is not an easy case to understand, but some work on it will pay dividends, in that whenever you need to discuss s 1(3) of the Act your answer will be greatly improved if you can make some attempt to explain the effects of the decision.

Checklist

You should be familiar with the following areas:

* Historical development of the doctrine of frustration.
* The definition of a 'frustrating event'.
* The meaning of 'self-induced' frustration.
* Effects of frustration at common law.
* The effects and limitations of the *Fibrosa* case.
* The Law Reform (Frustrated Contracts) Act 1943: its effects and limitations.

Question 35

Martina owns two houses in Loughchester. In the summer of 2002, she entered into a contract with Loughchester University for it to rent the houses for the coming academic year for use as student accommodation. The University paid Martina £500 straight away, with the rent to be paid to Martina by the University monthly in arrears. Martina then engaged Roger Roofers Ltd to carry out repairs on the roofs of the houses, to be completed by 23 September, in time for the arrival of the students. She paid Roger Roofers £1,000, with the balance of £3,000 to be paid on completion of the work. Consider the effect on Martina's contracts of the following events:

(a) On 1 September, when Roger Roofers had completed work on the first house, but not started on the second, the second house was struck by lightning, causing a fire which destroyed both houses.

(b) As in (a), but only the second house was destroyed. The first house escaped damage.

(c) As a consequence of an unexpected restriction on student numbers imposed by the government, Loughchester University recruited fewer students for its courses than it had expected and had a surplus of accommodation. It told Martina on 20 September that it would not need to use her houses, and regarded their contract as at an end. It also requested the repayment of the £500 already paid.

Answer plan

There are two contracts to be considered: the one between Martina and the University, and the one between Martina and Roger Roofers. In each case, you will need to consider whether the events which have occurred in each of the three situations have led to the frustration of the contract. If there is frustration, you will need to go on to consider the effects of the Law Reform (Frustrated Contracts) Act 1943 on the parties' obligations.

The suggested order of treatment is:

- introduction – outlining the concept of 'frustration';

- situation (a) – both contracts have been frustrated. As regards the University contract, note that a contract for the lease of land can now be frustrated, as confirmed by *National Carriers Ltd v Panalpina (Northern) Ltd* (1981). In relation to the roofing contract, you will need to consider the application of the 1943 Act, and in particular s 1(3);

- situation (b) – the roofing contract has again probably been frustrated. The application of s 1(3) of the 1943 Act may, however, be different in this situation. Has the University contract been frustrated? Since it can still be performed in part, it may be that it has not – cf *Herne Bay Steamboat Co v Hutton* (1903);

- situation (c) – is the non-availability of students a frustrating event? Although government intervention can frustrate a contract, in this situation the University's non-allocation of students to Martina's houses may well be treated as 'self-induced frustration', in which case Martina will be able to claim against the University for breach of contract.

Answer

This problem is concerned with the doctrine of frustration, which arises where an external event, which is not the responsibility of either party, renders further performance of the contract impossible, or at least radically different from what had been contracted for.[1] The kind of events which have been recognised as giving rise to frustration include natural disasters (*Taylor v Caldwell* (1863)), government interference (*BP Exploration v Hunt* (1982)), supervening illegality (*Denny, Mott and Dickson v James Fraser* (1944)), strikes (*The Nema* (1982)) and ill health (*Condor v Barron Knights* (1966)).

The approach of the common law, when it finally recognised the possibility of frustration in *Taylor v Caldwell* (1863), was simply to say that all future obligations were discharged. Money paid was irrecoverable (*Chandler v Webster* (1904)), as was compensation for benefits provided but for which payment was not yet due (*Appleby v Myers* (1867)). This was mitigated to some extent by the decision in *Fibrosa Spolka Akcyjna v Fairbairn* (1943), where the House of Lords held that money paid could be recovered if there was a total failure of consideration. Further flexibility as regards the consequences of frustration was introduced by the Law Reform (Frustrated Contracts) Act

1943, which applies to most, though not all, contracts. There are, however, still some areas where the rules can operate harshly. In particular, although in certain circumstances s 2(3) of the Act allows recovery for benefits conferred prior to the frustrating event, the approach to this section adopted in *BP Exploration v Hunt* (1982) means that the scope for such recovery is narrower than might be thought at first sight.

Turning to the facts of the problem, there are two contracts which need to be considered in each of the three situations – the one between Martina and the University, and the one between Martina and Roger Roofers Ltd. We are told very little about the contents of these contracts. It is assumed, however, that neither of them contains any provisions directly relevant to the circumstances which have arisen, and that the situations will be dealt with simply by the common law rules and the provisions of the 1943 Act.

Situation (a)

In the first situation, the two houses have been destroyed. This is clearly an event which is capable of frustrating the contracts. The destruction of the subject matter is one of the clearest examples of frustration, and was in fact what was involved in the first case in which the principle was recognised by the English courts – that is, *Taylor v Caldwell* (1863). As regards the contract with the University, at one time it was thought that a contract for the lease of land could not be frustrated – *Cricklewood Property Investment Trust v Leighton's Investment Trusts Ltd* (1945). This view was rejected, however, by the House of Lords in *National Carriers Ltd v Panalpina (Northern) Ltd* (1981), where the majority held that there was no reason in logic or law why a lease could not be frustrated if the intended use of the land became impossible. That would seem to apply here, since the use of the land for the accommodation of students can no longer take place. Although the decision in *National Carriers* might be said to be *obiter*, in that the House held that on the facts the contract was not frustrated, there is no reason to doubt that it would be followed where necessary. What is the consequence of the contract being frustrated? The University's obligation to pay rent will be discharged. Can it recover the £500 which it has already paid? This is dealt with by s 1(2) of the 1943 Act. This provides that money paid prior to a frustrating event can be recovered. It is subject to the proviso, however, that if the party to whom the money was paid has incurred expenses, such amount as the court considers just may be retained to cover these. Martina will no doubt wish to argue that she has spent money preparing the houses for student accommodation, and that she should therefore be able to retain the £500. In *Gamerco SA v ICM/Fair Warning Agency* (1995), it was made clear, however, that just because expenses have been incurred this does not automatically mean that retention of money paid will be allowed. The court should take a broad view, looking at all the circumstances, before deciding what is a just result. On the facts given, there does not seem to be any particular reason why Martina should not be allowed to retain some or all of the £500 towards her expenses. It should be noted, however, that s 1(2) does not allow her to be awarded more than the £500 which has already been paid, even if her expenses exceed this amount.

In relation to the contract with Roger Roofers, this again will be frustrated, in that the work cannot be completed. Martina will wish to recover the £1,000 which she has paid. This would not have been possible under the common law, since there was not here a total failure of consideration, as required by the *Fibrosa* case. Roger Roofers had done half the work on the contract. As we have seen, however, s 1(2) does allow for recovery of the £1,000, subject to the Roger Roofers expenses. In this situation, it is likely that Roger Roofers will wish to claim that their expenses far exceed the £1,000 and that the full amount should be retained. Moreover, they may wish to argue under s 1(3) that they have conferred a valuable benefit on Martina, by the work done on the first house, and that it would be just for them to be awarded a sum to compensate for this. Under the common law this would not have been possible, because the decision in *Appleby v Myers* (1867) confirmed that where the obligation to pay for work does not arise until after the frustrating event, no compensation for work done is recoverable. Although at first sight s 1(3) appears to alter this position, the way in which the section was interpreted by Goff J in *BP Exploration v Hunt* (1982) means that it probably will not do so. Goff J held that the reference in s 1(3) to a 'valuable benefit' referred to a benefit assessed in the light of the frustrating event. If the consequence of the frustrating event was that the benefit was destroyed, then nothing could be recovered in relation to it. The object of the Act was to prevent unjust enrichment, rather than to apportion losses. If the party concerned had not been 'enriched' at the end of the day, there was no need for the Act to intervene. Applying this approach here, it means that Roger Roofers will not be able to recover anything under s 1(3), despite the fact that they have done half the work under the contract.

Situation (b)

This again involves the destruction of the subject matter, and therefore potentially frustration of the contract. In relation to the contract with the University, however, the contract is not completely impossible. One house survives, and there is no reason why it could not be used to accommodate students. The question is, therefore, whether the contract has become 'radically different' from what was intended by the parties (see *Davis*

Contractors Ltd v Fareham (1956)). A comparison might be drawn with *Herne Bay Steam Boat Co v Hutton* (1903), where the hiring of a boat to tour the royal fleet and to watch the King's review of it was held not to be frustrated when the review was cancelled. The fleet remained, so it was possible for the tour to go ahead. Although the circumstances here are different, it might still be argued that enough of the contract survives for it not to be frustrated. Martina, on the other hand, will wish to argue that the contract is frustrated, since otherwise she may be liable for breach in providing only one house, rather than two. On balance, it is suggested that the contract is in fact 'radically different', since only half of it can be performed. If this is so, then the position will be the same as in situation (a) as regards the application of the 1943 Act.

The position with regard to Roger Roofers is much clearer. Since the completion of their work is impossible, the contract is frustrated. There is an important difference from situation (a) here, however, in that this time the house on which the roofing work has been completed has survived the frustrating event. This means that Roger Roofers will have a strong argument for some compensation under s 1(3) of the 1943 Act. Martina has obtained a valuable benefit, in that she now has a house with a repaired roof. If she were allowed to retain this without paying anything to Roger Roofers, she would be 'unjustly enriched'. On this occasion it is likely that a court would consider it just that she should pay something to Roger Roofers in addition to the £1,000 already paid. Since presumably about half the work has been done, the starting point might well be a further £1,000, to bring her payment up to half the contract price. The courts' discretion is broad, however, and can take into account all the circumstances in deciding what is the appropriate sum to be awarded.

Situation (c)

The alleged frustrating event here is the government's restriction on student numbers. This only affects Martina's contract with the University, so we do not need to consider Roger Roofers' contract here. There is no doubt that government intervention can lead to the frustration of a contract as, for example, in *Metropolitan Water Board v Dick Kerr* (1918), which involved the requisitioning of property in war time. The problem for the University here is that it has some students requiring accommodation, but has allocated them to premises other than Martina's houses. In this respect the case seems similar to *Maritime National Fish Ltd v Ocean Trawlers Ltd* (1935), where a company obtained fewer trawling licences than it had hoped for, and failed to allocate one of them to a boat hired from the other party. It was held here that the alleged 'frustration' was in fact 'self-induced', because the company had decided which trawlers should have a licence. Even if the decision involves deciding which of two contracts to break, as in the *The Super Servant Two* (1990), the courts have still held that the fact that it was in the hands of one of the parties to decide whether the contract went ahead or not meant that the contract was not frustrated. It seems, therefore, that Martina has a strong case here for arguing that her contract with the University has not been frustrated by the government's action. She is entitled to retain the £500 already paid, and indeed can sue the University for breach of contract in relation to the rent which she was due to be paid.

Note

1   Note that parties can provide for the consequences of frustration in their contract, for example, by a *force majeure* clause. If so, the courts will give effect to this. It is assumed here that there is nothing in the contracts which covers the events which have occurred.

Question 36

Answer both parts:

(a) 'The decision in the *Fibrosa* case meant that the reform contained in s 1(2) of the Law Reform (Frustrated Contracts) Act (1943) was unnecessary.'

Discuss.

(b) 'If the facts of *Appleby v Myers* (1867) were to occur again today, the outcome would be exactly the same.'

Do you agree?

Answer plan

Both parts of this question are concerned with the doctrine of frustration. The particular area they raise is the consequences of frustration, and the impact of the Law Reform (Frustrated Contracts) Act 1943. It is not necessary in answering these questions to give a full account of the whole doctrine of frustration. The concentration should be on the particular issues raised, that is:

Part (a):

- what was the common law position on the effects of frustration prior to the *Fibrosa* decision?;
- what was the effect of *Fibrosa*? That is, it allowed, in certain situations, the recovery of money paid under a contract that became frustrated;
- how does the 1943 Act deal with this situation? That is, the situations in which s 1(2) allows recovery; and
- what are the differences between *Fibrosa* and s 1(2)?

Part (b):

- what happened in *Appleby v Myers*? That is, no recovery for the benefit of work done;
- how does the 1943 Act deal with this? That is, s 1(3): recovery for a 'valuable benefit'; and
- does s 1(3) meet the criticisms of *Appleby v Myers*? Here, the decision of *BP v Hunt* will need to be considered in some detail.

Answer

Part (a)

This question is concerned with the consequences of a contract being frustrated, that is, coming to an end,[1] as a result of some external factor which is not the fault of either party. The common law, once the possibility of frustration had been accepted (*Taylor v Caldwell* (1863), reversing the line taken in *Paradine v Jane* (1647)), took the view that the loss must lie where it fell at the time of the frustrating event. All actions taken up to that point were to have legal effect, since the contract was at that time still subsisting. Once the contract was frustrated, however, rights and liabilities were frozen at that point. In particular, money paid or payable under a frustrated contract before the time of frustration could not be recovered.

The strict application of this rule led to some anomalous results, with the position of the parties depending on the precise wording of their contract. Virtually identical factual situations could result in very different legal consequences. The cases of *Krell v Henry* (1903) and *Chandler v Webster* (1904) were both concerned with the hire of a room to view the coronation procession of King Edward VII. The procession was cancelled due to the King's ill health, and both contracts were held to be frustrated. In *Krell v Henry*, the hirer had paid a deposit, with the balance payable after the event. In *Chandler v Webster*, however, the full amount was payable before the contract was frustrated (though in fact only part of the amount had been paid). The result of applying the rule outlined above was that in *Krell*, the hirer lost his deposit, but was not obliged to pay the balance of the hire, whereas in *Chandler*, the hirer not only received no refund of the money already paid, but had to pay the balance as well, even though he had received no benefit under the contract.

This consequence of the strict rule, with its clear potential for injustice, was reconsidered by the House of Lords in the *Fibrosa* case. Here, an English company had a contract to sell machinery to a Polish company. A proportion of the price had been paid in advance, and further payment was due. The outbreak of the Second World War led to the contract being frustrated. Under the rule applied in *Chandler v Webster*, the Polish company would not have been able to recover anything, and would have had to pay the amount which was due prior to the frustration. The House of Lords, however, overruled *Chandler*, and held that the Polish company were not only relieved of payment of the outstanding sum, but could also recover the money that had actually been paid. The reason for the decision was that here there had been a 'total failure of consideration'. In other words, the buyers had received nothing at all in exchange for their money. In such a situation, the House felt that they should be able to be put back into the position they were in prior to the contract.

Fibrosa was an improvement on *Chandler*, but it still left two potential areas for injustice to arise. First, the approach could only be used where the failure of consideration was total. If the buyers had received any part of the performance, no matter how small, the rule would not apply, and they would have to pay everything due prior to the frustration. Secondly, the rule could operate harshly on the other side. The English company in the case, for example, were left without any compensation for expenses which they might have incurred in connection with the contract prior to the frustration.

The Law Reform (Frustrated Contracts) Act 1943 addressed both these issues in s 1(2). This section states that whenever a contract to which the Act applies is frustrated, money paid under it is to be returned, and money payable shall cease to be so. This applies even where there is no total failure of consideration, that is, where some performance has been tendered. This deals with the first deficiency in the *Fibrosa* rule. Secondly, however, s 1(2) allows the party to whom the sums were paid or payable to retain, or recover, an amount to cover expenses incurred in relation to the contract. The operation of this is subject to the supervision of the court, which is to allow it to operate only to the extent to which it is just to do so.[2] In *Gamerco SA v ICM/Fair Warning Agency* (1995), for example, although some expenses had been incurred, the plaintiffs' losses were so substantial that in the circumstances the judge made no deduction in ordering the return of the full amount which they had paid.

Was the 1943 Act unnecessary? Clearly not. The *Fibrosa* decision, while a step in the right direction, did not go far enough. The further reform contained in the 1943 Act was necessary to meet the two limitations to the decision outlined above. It has done so in a way which, on the whole, seems fair and sensible.

Part (b)

The case of *Appleby v Myers* (1867) concerned a contract for the manufacture of machinery by the plaintiffs on the defendants' premises. Payment was due on completion of the work. When some of the work had been done, the factory and the partly constructed machinery were destroyed by fire. The contract was clearly frustrated, but could the plaintiffs recover any compensation for the work that they had done? The answer was no. The common law approach to frustration was, as has been indicated above, that losses should lie where they fall at the time of the frustrating event, so there was no basis for a claim by the plaintiffs.

The 1943 Act attempted to deal with this situation in s 1(3), which states that where a party to a frustrated contract has obtained a 'valuable benefit' before the time of discharge, the other party can obtain compensation for this. As with s 1(2), this is subject to the supervision of the court, which must decide what is the just amount in the light of all the circumstances of the case.[3]

At first sight, this appears to provide a remedy for the plaintiff in *Appleby v Myers*. The work which they had done could be argued to constitute a 'valuable benefit', for which compensation could be paid. On closer inspection, however, the position is not so simple. How could the defendants be said to have received any benefit when (a) the machinery was not completed, and (b) after the fire it was totally worthless?

These issues were considered in some detail by Goff J, as he then was, in the only reported case on the 1943 Act, *BP Exploration v Hunt* (1982). Looking carefully at the statutory wording, he came to the conclusion that 'benefit' means the 'end product' of what the plaintiff has provided, not the value of the work itself. This is supported by the requirement in s 1(3) for the court to take account of the effect on the benefit of the circumstances of the frustration. Using an example similar to the facts of *Appleby v Myers*, he came to the conclusion that a plaintiff who has carried out work which has been destroyed by fire cannot claim any compensation for this. The defendant has in the end received no benefit, because all the work has been destroyed.[4]

Goff J's interpretation of the section is not the only possible one,[5] but it has not been criticised or doubted in any subsequent decision, and so we must take it as representing the current law on this issue. If that is the case, then the statement in the question is correct, and *Appleby v Myers* would be decided the same way today as it was in 1867.

Notes

1   Or, more precisely, performance becoming impossible, or radically different.

2   The rule can still operate harshly in that no more can be recovered than was due prior to the frustration of the contract. For example, if on a contract worth £5,000 a deposit of £500 has been paid, but the other party has incurred expenses of £750, the maximum that can be recovered is £500. The remaining £250 is irrecoverable, unless s 1(3), which is discussed in the answer to part (b), can be brought into play.

3   Taking account, for example, of expenses incurred by the party providing the benefit.

4   There is also the issue of whether half completed machinery is of any benefit. This might depend on the costs of getting the work completed.

5   Treitel, for example, argues forcefully that the issue of the effect on the benefit of the frustrating circumstances should be taken to refer to the assessment of the 'just sum' rather than the valuation of the benefit: *The Law of Contract*, 10th edn, 1999, p 853; cf Stone, *The Modern Law of Contract*, 5th edn, 2002, p 401.

Question 37

Raminder has entered into a contract to have a combined central heating and air conditioning system installed into his house by Coolflo Ltd, at a cost of £9,000. He pays £1,000 and the work starts. Consider the rights and liabilities of Raminder and Coolflo in relation to this contract if the following alternative events occur when the work is two-thirds complete:

(a) Raminder's house accidentally catches fire, and is totally destroyed.

(b) The government announces that, because of a scare about legionnaires' disease, air conditioning systems of the kind that Raminder is having installed will become illegal, with immediate effect. The change will not, however, affect the central heating part of the system.

(c) The firm making parts which are essential to complete the system goes out of business, and there is no other source of supply. Coolflo uses the few remaining parts which it has to complete a system for another customer.

Answer plan

In answering this question it is necessary to ask the following questions in relation to each event:

- is the contract frustrated?; and
- if so, what are the effects on the parties?

In part (a), there is no doubt that the contract is frustrated. The concentration will therefore be on the second question, that is, what are the effects on the parties? One particular issue which will need discussing is whether Coolflo can claim anything under s 1(3) of the Law Reform (Frustrated Contracts) Act 1943. The views of Lord Goff as expressed in *BP Exploration v Hunt* (1982) suggest that it will not be able to do so.

Part (b) requires discussion of government intervention making the performance (or part of it) illegal (cf *Denny, Mott and Dickson v James Fraser* (1944)). It must also be considered whether a sufficient amount of the contract survives (that is, the central heating system) for the principle in *Herne Bay Steam Boat Co v Hutton* (1903) to apply, and thus prevent frustration. If the contract is frustrated, there is more chance here that s 1(3) will allow Coolflo some compensation for the work done.

In part (c), the central issue is that of 'self-induced' frustration (cf *Maritime National Fish v Ocean Trawlers* (1935)). To what extent can it be said that it is a result of Coolflo's own actions that it is unable to complete the contract? (Cf *The Super Servant Two* (1990).)

Note that it will not be necessary to repeat discussion of similar points in the different parts. Reference back to earlier discussion is quite acceptable.

Answer

This question is concerned with the doctrine of frustration. This provides that where, as a result of events outside the control of the parties, a contract becomes impossible (for example, *Taylor v Caldwell* (1863)), or at least radically different from what had been agreed (*Davis Contractors Ltd v Fareham UDC* (1956)), it will come to an end. All future obligations will cease, and there may be some redistribution between the parties to take account of money, property or services which have been transferred prior to the frustrating event. This process is governed by a combination of common law rules and the provisions of the Law Reform (Frustrated Contracts) Act 1943.

The three alternative situations will now be considered in turn.

Part (a)

There is no doubt that destruction of the subject matter of the contract can result in frustration. Indeed, the first case to recognise the doctrine, *Taylor v Caldwell* (1863), involved such a situation. A music hall had been hired for some performances, but burnt down before they began. It was held that the contract was frustrated, and that all future obligations were discharged. There seems little doubt that the same will apply as between Raminder and Coolflo, so that there will be no further responsibilities under the contract.

More difficulty arises, however, in relation to the £1,000 that Raminder has already paid, and the fact that Coolflo has completed two-thirds of the work. Under the common law, money paid under a frustrated contract cannot generally be recovered (*Chandler v Webster* (1904)). The one exception is where there has been a total failure of consideration on the part of the recipient of the money. Here, since the House of Lords' decision in the *Fibrosa* case,[1] the courts will allow recovery of what has been paid. If there has been any performance, however, this is not possible. Coolflo has certainly performed part of the contract, and Raminder will not therefore be able to recover his £1,000 under common law. The strict approach of the common law is, however, mitigated by the provisions of the Law Reform (Frustrated Contracts) Act 1943, and in particular s 1(2). This provides that, where money has been paid under a contract which is then frustrated, it is recoverable. The other party, however, may deduct expenses, up to the value of what was paid.

This is subject to what a court may think is just and reasonable in the circumstances. In *Gamerco SA v ICM/Fair Warning Agency* (1995), for example, although some expenses had been incurred, the plaintiffs' losses were so substantial that in the circumstances the judge made no deduction in ordering the return of the full amount which they had paid. There is nothing in the facts to indicate that this discretion should be exercised against Coolflo here. Coolflo, therefore, may well be able to argue that it should retain all or part of Raminder's £1,000 to cover expenses.

The maximum amount that Coolflo will be able to retain under s 1(2) is £1,000. We are told, however, that it has performed two-thirds of a contract for which the total price is £9,000. It may well wish to argue, therefore, that it should be entitled to more than this, because of the work that has been done. The only basis for such a claim is s 1(3) of the 1943 Act. This provides that, where a 'valuable benefit' has been conferred by one party on the other before the time of discharge, the court can award a sum which it considers just in all the circumstances to compensate for this. The precise meaning of this section fell to be considered in *BP Exploration v Hunt* (1982). At issue was the question of whether the 'valuable benefit' had to be considered as it stood before, or after, the frustrating event. In Goff J's opinion (and the appeal courts did not disagree), the answer is that the benefit must be considered after the frustrating event.[2] Thus, he felt that if a building on which work has been done is destroyed by fire, then nothing can be awarded under s 1(3). The work is in the end of no value, and so cannot be considered a 'valuable benefit'.[3] Applying this to the problem, that is almost exactly the position here, so, assuming that Goff J's view prevails (and there is no judicial authority which contradicts it), Coolflo will not be entitled to any compensation under s 1(3).

The most that Coolflo will be entitled to on the facts in part (a) is therefore £1,000.

Part (b)

The alleged frustrating event here is the government ban on the system being used for the air conditioning. There is no doubt that government action which renders the performance of a contract illegal can be regarded as frustrating the contract. In *Denny, Mott and Dickson v James Fraser* (1944), the contract concerned trade in timber. This was made illegal in 1939 and, as a consequence, the whole contract was held to be frustrated. The only difficulty here is that the contract for the air conditioning and the central heating seems to be 'entire'. That is, it is not severable, and one payment is to be made to cover all the work. The central heating system remains legal. Can it be said that, nevertheless, the contract as a whole is frustrated? A relevant authority is *Herne Bay Steamboat Co v Hutton* (1903). Here, the contract was for the hire of a boat to go for a day's cruise around the royal fleet, and to watch the King's review of it. The King's illness meant that the review was cancelled. The contract was held not to be frustrated, however, because it still had some purpose. The tour of the fleet was something worth doing in its own right, and so the effect on the contract was not sufficiently fundamental to frustrate it. Using this case, it might be argued that because the installation of the central heating system can go ahead there is still some point to the contract, and it is therefore not frustrated. Alternatively, it might be argued that the answer to the question, 'will the performance be radically different from what the parties agreed?' should be 'yes'. The situation is distinguishable from *Herne Bay*, where the use of the boat was still possible, although there was less to see. Nor is it like the Suez Canal cases, such as *Tsakiroglou & Co v Noblee Thorl* (1962), where the closure of the canal made performance more difficult and more expensive. Here, an important element of the contract cannot be performed at all.[4] The argument is finely balanced, but it is submitted that it should be regarded as being frustrated.

If this is so, then the consequences of frustration must be considered. The common law provisions, and s 1(2) of the 1943 Act, will operate in exactly the same way as in (a). There is an argument here, however, that Coolflo should be able to recover something under s 1(3), at least as far as the central heating system is concerned. The work that has been done on this can presumably be completed under a new contract with Coolflo, or someone else, and so can be regarded as a 'valuable benefit'. It would then be up to the court to decide what amounted to a just sum to be awarded for this benefit.

Part (c)

In this case, it is the unavailability of parts essential to the completion of the system which may be said to frustrate the contract. If it is true that there is no other source of supply, and no other way of adapting parts to complete it, then this is the type of event which might bring the doctrine of frustration into play. We are told, however, that Coolflo has, in fact, used parts of the required type to complete another system. This almost certainly means that it will not be able to plead frustration of the contract with Raminder. The relevant authorities are *Maritime National Fish v Ocean Trawlers* (1935) and *The Super Servant Two* (1990). In the former case, the hirers of a trawler decided to use certain fishing licences which they had obtained for boats other than the one hired. The licences were essential for them to be able to use the hired boat. They therefore alleged that the contract was frustrated. It was held that this was not the case, because it was their decision as to which boats should be licensed, and the so called frustration was therefore 'self-induced'. This case left open the issue of whether a party who is left with the option of choosing which of two contracts to break, because of some potentially frustrating event, would also be unable to use the doctrine. In *The Super Servant Two* (1990), the sinking of one of only two vessels capable of performing a contract meant that the defendants had to decide whether to perform their contract with the plaintiffs, or perform another contract to which the other suitable vessel was already assigned. It was held by the Court of Appeal that the fact that the defendants chose to perform the other contract meant that the 'frustration' of the contract with the plaintiffs was 'self-induced', and so did not operate to relieve the defendants of their obligations. The same argument would apply to Coolflo. It has decided to use the parts for the other contract. Its contract with Raminder will not therefore be frustrated. On the contrary, Coolflo will be in breach of contract for failure to complete, and Raminder will be able to sue for damages.

Notes

1   That is, *Fibrosa Spolka Akcyjna v Fairbairn Lawson Combe Barbour Ltd* (1942).

2   This is because the Act is concerned not with distributing losses, but preventing unjust enrichment. Raminder is not unjustly enriched, because he ends up with nothing of value.

3   Note, however, the contrary view expressed by Treitel, *The Law of Contract*, 10th edn, 1999, p 853; cf Stone, *The Modern Law of Contract*, 5th edn, 2002, p 401.

4   The force of this argument may depend on the precise terms of the contract. Does it provide simply for the installation of 'an air conditioning system', or for a system of the particular type which has been made illegal? If the former, then it is arguable that it is like the Suez Canal cases: Coolflo can still install a system, but this will be more difficult and more expensive for it. The answer given in the text assumes that the contract does specify the particular system.

CHAPTER 11

PERFORMANCE AND BREACH

Introduction

The topics of performance and breach have links with two other areas. First, the issue of whether a particular term is a 'condition' or a 'warranty' ties in with discussion of the contents of the contract (dealt with in Chapter 5). Indeed, contract texts will often deal with the issue at that point. Secondly, the question of what the consequences are of breaking a contract, and in particular whether there is a right to treat the contract as repudiated, has obvious connections with the whole topic of remedies (which is covered in Chapter 12). Questions may well, therefore, overlap with these other two areas.

The main issues dealt with in this chapter are:

- the distinction between conditions, warranties, and innominate terms – how the courts decide into which category to put a particular term, and why this is important; and

- the distinction between 'entire' and 'severable' contracts or obligations, as in, for example, *Cutter v Powell*; and the doctrine of 'substantial performance', as in *Hoenig v Isaacs*.

The first of these issues is a complex one, requiring you to deal with questions of the parties' intentions, and how these should be assessed, as well as looking at the requirements of the commercial world. The case law is not straightforward, with different courts apparently taking differing approaches. You need to understand where the difficulties lie, but you cannot hope to explain them all satisfactorily in the space available.

The topic of what amounts to performance of a contract is probably easier, in that the case law is less complicated. There is some uncertainty as to what precisely is the difference between incomplete performance and complete but defective performance, but this is an issue which turns as much on the facts of the situation as on any clear principles of law.

Checklist

You should be familiar with the following areas:

- Distinction between 'conditions' and 'warranties': categorisation under common law and statute.

- Consequences of breach of either type of term.
- The meaning of 'innominate' terms, and the effects of breach.
- Distinction between 'entire' and 'severable' contracts or obligations.
- The doctrine of 'substantial performance'.

Question 38

'There are ... many contractual undertakings of a more complex character which cannot be categorised as being "conditions" or "warranties".' (Diplock LJ, in *Hong Kong Fir Shipping Co Ltd v Kawasaki Kisen Kaisha* (1962).)

Following the recognition of the category of 'innominate' or 'intermediate' terms in the *Hong Kong Fir* case, would it not be better to place all contractual terms in this category, and thus give the courts greater flexibility in dealing with breaches of contract?

Answer plan

The approach to answering this question is quite straightforward. First, the meaning of the terms 'condition' and 'warranty' should be explained, and their significance. This, of course, relates to the consequences of breach, with a breach of condition giving the right to repudiate as well as to claim damages. Next, the reason for the recognition of the intermediate category should be explained. The main argument comes from the need to recognise that some terms can be broken in a variety of ways, some more serious than others.

The second part of the answer, with the explanations of the terminology out of the way, will need to concentrate on the particular issue raised in the question. There are at least two arguments in favour of retaining the categories of condition and warranty:

- certainty – particularly in commercial contracts it may be important to be able to predict the effect of a breach on a contract, without having to wait to see what the precise consequences of it are; and
- consumer protection – the labelling of some terms as 'conditions' in the Sale of Goods Act 1979, for example, provides a strong remedy for consumers who have been sold defective goods.

The conclusion is likely to be that, although the 'innominate' term category allows a desirable degree of flexibility in some situations, there is still scope for applying the more rigid approach derived from classifying terms as conditions and warranties.

Answer

The English law of contract recognises that not all breaches of contract are of equal seriousness. Some will be so serious that they will in effect bring the contract to an end, or should entitle the innocent party to do so. Others will be capable of being adequately dealt with simply by an award of damages to cover losses. For example, in a contract for the hire of a room, failure by the hirer to pay the rent may well mean that the contract can be terminated. On the other hand, failure by the landlord to fulfil an obligation to clean the windows every month would be likely to result only in a remedy in damages.[1] This question is concerned with the methods by which the courts decide which breaches of contract will lead to which consequences.

One of the approaches which has been used is to label particular terms in a contract as conditions or warranties. A condition is an important term of the contract, any breach of which will lead to the right to repudiate. A warranty is a less significant term, any breach of which will only ever give a right to damages. One of the clearest examples of this use of terminology is to be found in the Sale of Goods Act 1979, where the various implied terms as to title, quality, etc, are specifically labelled as either conditions or warranties. In other contracts, it may be more difficult to decide which category a term should fall into.

The courts will sometimes take the view that it is accepted in the commercial world that certain clauses, or types of clauses, should be regarded as conditions. In *Bunge Corp v Tradax Export SA* (1981), for example, it was stated that time clauses in mercantile contracts should usually be treated as conditions. In the absence of such guidance from custom, however, the court is left with trying to decide the importance of the term. Lord Diplock suggested in *Hong Kong Fir Shipping Co Ltd v Kawasaki Kisen Kaisha* (1962) that a condition was a clause, the breach of which would deprive the other party of 'substantially the whole benefit' of the contract. Later cases have not followed this, however, preferring to apply a vaguer test of whether the term is central to the contract.[2] This will depend to some extent on the intentions of the parties when they made the contract. If they have actually spelt out in the agreement that a particular term is a condition, and stated that breach of it will give rise to a right to terminate the contract, then it is likely that the courts will give effect to that intention.[3] Simply labelling a term as a condition, however, is not necessarily conclusive. In *Schuler AG v Wickman Machine Tool Sales Ltd* (1973), the parties had stated that it was a 'condition' of the agreement that the defendants should make weekly visits to six named firms over a period of four and a half years. If this clause was truly a condition, the effect would be that failure to make any one of those visits would amount to a repudiatory breach, giving the plaintiffs the right to terminate the contract. The House of Lords refused to accept that this was what the parties had intended when they made the contract. Despite the fact that the label 'condition' had been used, the House ruled that this clause had to be treated as either a warranty or an innominate term. The decision does not mean that the labels used by the parties are unimportant. They clearly give a strong indication of what the parties may have intended. But, where the result would be as surprising as it would have been in *Schuler v Wickman*, the courts will be prepared to substitute their own interpretation of the intention of the parties.[4]

One problem with the classification of terms into conditions and warranties is that it is an 'all or nothing' approach. If a term is a condition, any breach of it, no matter how apparently trivial, will give the other party the right to terminate. Conversely, if it is a warranty, no breach of the term, no matter what the consequences, will do more than give a remedy in damages. This was the problem confronted by the Court of Appeal in *Hong Kong Fir Shipping Co Ltd v Kawasaki Kisen Kaisha* (1962). The clause that they were considering was the obligation of 'seaworthiness' in a time charter. This obligation could be broken in any number of ways. For example, the failure to have proper medical supplies on board would render the vessel 'unseaworthy' just as much as if the whole ship was in danger of sinking at any moment. Some of the possible breaches would be of a kind which could clearly be remedied very easily, or if not remedied could be adequately compensated for by an award of damages. Other breaches of the term, however, would go to the root of the contract, and justify termination. Faced with this situation, the Court of Appeal, with Lord Diplock[5] giving the fullest analysis, decided that there were certain intermediate terms where the question of the right to terminate would depend on the consequences of the breach of contract. In other words, the court's focus of attention shifts from the making of the contract and the parties' intentions at that time, to the breach which has in fact occurred, and the consequences of it. If those consequences are that the contract is substantially affected by the breach, then the innocent party will have the right to terminate. On the facts of the case before them, the court held that the breach was not sufficiently serious to be treated in the same way as a breach of condition, and that the charterers had no right to terminate.

The approach taken in *Hong Kong Fir* has been followed in later cases.[6] Would it not be sensible, then, to do as the question suggests, and apply it as the general rule for all contractual terms? The advantage of doing so would of course be, as the question suggests, the greater flexibility that this would allow. The courts would be able to look at the position as between the parties and provide a remedy appropriate to the seriousness of the breach. It is true, as well, that in some circumstances fairly unmeritorious claims of breach of condition have allowed a party to escape from a contract. For example, in *Arcos Ltd v Ronaasen & Son* (1933), there was a sale of goods contract for the supply of some wooden staves to be used in making barrels. The staves supplied were of a thickness one-sixteenth of an inch different from the contractual description of 'half an inch'. Compliance with description is a condition under s 13 of the Sale of Goods Act. The buyers were held to be entitled to reject the staves, despite the fact that they would have been perfectly usable for making the barrels.[7] An approach based on 'innominate' terms would almost certainly have come up with a different result. It is clear, however, that even outside the area of the labels applied by the Sale of Goods Act, the concept of the condition and the warranty has survived.

A good example of this is the case of *The Mihalis Angelos* (1970). The clause being considered here was that of a vessel being 'expected ready to load' at a particular date. It was held that this was a condition, in the strict sense, and that the charterers were able to terminate for delay without needing to show that the breach had serious consequences. The reasons for adopting this approach given in this case[8] are of more general application. It was pointed out that in the commercial world there are great advantages in certainty. Parties to a contract like to know what the consequences of their actions are going to be. If they break a contract, will the other side be able to terminate or not? If a party terminates for breach, will it run the risk that a court will subsequently say that it had no right to do so? The categorisation of terms into conditions and warranties enables clear predictions to be given, and reduces the degree of uncertainty. This in turn will improve efficiency, and should reduce costs. The suggestion is that, for the business community, the benefits of certainty outweigh the risks of a certain amount of injustice.

There is a second argument for conditions and warranties, which relates to the consumer contract. This is that it is better in the context of trying to establish standards of quality in consumer contracts, which is one of the aims of the Sale of Goods Act implied terms, to have strict rules which make the supplier liable if the goods do not meet a particular standard. The consumer who buys an item which turns out to be defective will generally wish to return it and reclaim his or her money. It is better in this situation to impose a strict liability on the supplier, rather than leave the issue of the availability of termination to be decided on a case by case basis depending on the seriousness of the breach. Such an approach would undoubtedly work to the advantage of the supplier, who, through standard form contracts or superior bargaining power, would be likely to be able to force the consumer to accept a lesser remedy than is available under the law at the moment.

The case of *Hong Kong Fir* was a significant development in the law relating to the consequences of breach of contract. It has opened up the possibility of a flexible approach which in many cases will make it easier to do justice between the parties. It does not provide the right answer for all situations, however. The parties themselves should have the freedom, if they wish, to construct their contract in such a way as to benefit from the certainty provided by the concepts of 'condition' and 'warranty'. Moreover, the consumer continues to need to have strong remedies available against the supplier of goods which turn out to be defective.

Notes

1   An example from decided cases could be used here, by contrasting *Poussard v Spiers* (1876) with *Bettini v Gye* (1876).

2   See, for example, *Bunge v Tradax* (1981).

3   *Financings Ltd v Baldock* (1963) might be mentioned here, in that in this case the courts refused to regard a right to terminate set out in the contract as automatically being a right to terminate for breach of condition. Cf *Lombard North Central plc v Butterworth* (1987).

4   A similar approach was adopted by the Court of Appeal in its recent decision in *Rice v Great Yarmouth BC* (2000).

5   Strictly, Diplock LJ, as he then was.

6   For example, *Cehave NV v Bremer Handelsgesellschaft mbH, The Hansa Nord* (1975), where it was applied, perhaps somewhat surprisingly, to a sale of goods contract.

7   It should be noted that the position under the Sale of Goods Act 1979 has been affected by the addition in 1994 of s 15A, which reduces the right to rescind for minor breaches of ss 13 or 14 in non-consumer contracts.

8   See the judgment of Megaw LJ: [1970] 3 All ER 125, p 138.

Question 39

In September 2002, Arthur bought a large and draughty house which had a greenhouse in the garden. He engaged Confirm Ltd to fit double glazing to each of the 60 windows in the house, at a price of £500 per window. The total price of £30,000 was to be payable on completion of the contract. He also engaged Tom, a local glazier, to fit new glass, 5 mm thick, to the greenhouse, at a price of £3,000, again payable on completion of the work.

On 30 October 2002, Confirm informed Arthur that its work had been completed, but, upon inspecting it later the same day, Arthur discovered that one of the windows had not been double glazed at all, and that 30 of them still let in draughts. At the same time, Arthur noticed that Tom had completed work on the greenhouse, but found, on inspecting some spare panes of glass, that they were only 4 mm thick.

Confirm, while agreeing that further work needs to be done, is insisting on a payment of £14,500 in relation to the 29 windows which are satisfactory before doing any further work. Arthur is insisting that all the work must be completed in accordance with the contract before he makes any payment.

Advise Arthur as to his rights under his contracts with Confirm and Tom.

Answer plan

The first part of this problem, dealing with the contract between Arthur and Confirm, is concerned with performance, and when the contract price is earned. The issues are:

* is the contract 'entire', as in *Cutter v Powell* (1795) and *Sumpter v Hedges* (1898), or is it severable?; and

* if it is entire, has there been 'substantial performance', entitling Confirm to some payment, as in *Hoenig v Isaacs* (1952)?

The second contract, that between Arthur and Tom, raises the issue of the remedies for breach. The use of the incorrect thickness of glass will amount to a breach of one of the implied terms under the Supply of Goods and Services Act 1982. The issue is then whether Arthur is entitled to repudiate the contract for this breach, or whether he can only claim damages (or a reduction in price) from Tom.

Answer

Arthur has made two contracts, neither of which has been performed to his satisfaction. Slightly different issues relating to performance and remedies arise in relation to each of them, however, and so they will be looked at separately.

Looking first at the contract with Confirm, it is seeking payment for the work it has done towards the double glazing contract. Arthur is resisting until all the work is complete. Whether he is entitled to do so will depend on whether his contract with Confirm is regarded as an 'entire' contract (as in *Sumpter v Hedges* (1898), for example) or severable, and on whether what Confirm has done can be regarded as 'substantial performance' (as in *Hoenig v Isaacs* (1952)).

Is the contract with Confirm an 'entire' contract?[1] A good example of the concept of the entire contract is the case of *Cutter v Powell* (1795). This concerned a contract under which a sailor was contracted to serve on a ship sailing from Jamaica to Liverpool, for a sum of 30 guineas.[2] He died before the voyage was completed, and his widow sued for his wages for the time he had served. It was held that she could not recover anything, because the contract was an entire one. In other words, the obligation to pay the 30 guineas only arose when the voyage was completed. There was no obligation to pay wages on a periodic basis.[3] The same approach was taken in *Sumpter v Hedges* in relation to a building contract, where the work was left incomplete and was finished by the owner. It was held that the builder was not entitled to any payment for the work he had done, because the contract was an entire one.

Applying this to the present case, the answer is not clear cut. It is possible to identify a price for each window double glazed but, on the other hand, it is stated that the entire sum is payable on completion. What was the intention of the parties? It seems likely that it was intended to be an entire contract. The position would clearly have been different if payment was to be made in stages, according to the number of windows completed, but that is not the situation here. It is submitted that, although it is possible to put a value on the proportion of the work completed by Confirm, because the contract was made on the basis of a price per window, the statement about payment on completion should override this and preclude a claim of the kind which Confirm is making.[4]

This does not conclude this part of the question, however. In certain situations, the entire contracts rule can operate harshly, and it has to some extent been mitigated by the development of the rule of 'substantial performance'. This was recognised in the case of *Hoenig v Isaacs* (1952). This case concerned a contract to furnish and decorate a flat for a fixed sum. When the work was completed, it was found to be defective in various ways, though it would only have taken a small sum to put the matters right. The defendant refused to pay anything, because the plaintiff had failed to complete what should be regarded as an entire contract. It was held that there had been 'substantial performance' of the contract, despite the fact that it was defective in various ways. The plaintiff was allowed to recover the contract price, less the amount that it would take to put the defects right.[5] The distinction that needs to be drawn is between a contract that is completed, albeit defectively, and one that has not been completed at all. In *Bolton v Mahadeva* (1972), an argument for substantial performance failed. The contract was for the installation of a central heating system. The system as fitted gave out much less heat than it should have done, and caused fumes in one of the rooms. It was held that there was not substantial performance. Although the complete system had been fitted, it did not fulfil its primary function of heating the house, and so the installer was not allowed to recover.[6]

Looking at what has been done in this case, has there been substantial performance? On the one hand, all but one of the windows have had double glazing fitted. On the other, half the windows are still defective in that they do not keep out the draughts, which was presumably a primary reason for installing the double glazing. The answer will depend on whether the case is regarded as being closer to the situation in *Hoenig v Isaacs*, or that in *Bolton v Mahadeva*. It is submitted that the extent of the defects in this case, affecting over half the windows, means that the case is closer to *Bolton v Mahadeva* and that therefore the contract should not be regarded as being substantially performed.

Thus, as regards the contract with Confirm, the advice to Arthur should be that he is not obliged to make any payment to it, but can retain the full contract price, pending Confirm's substantial completion of the contract.

The problem with Tom's contract with Arthur is rather different. The issue here is not a question of entire or severable contracts, or substantial performance. Assuming that the glass which Tom has used for re-glazing the greenhouse is 4 mm rather than 5 mm thick, as specified in the contract, there is no doubt that there is a breach. The question is, what are the effects of this breach on the contract?

By virtue of s 3 of the Supply of Goods and Services Act 1982, there is an implied obligation in a contract such as this to supply goods which match their contractual description. Here, the contract description states that the glass should be 5 mm thick, whereas what has been fitted is only 4 mm thick. There is then a breach of this implied obligation. Moreover, the obligation is stated by the Act to be a 'condition' of the contract. The consequences of breaking a condition are that this amounts to a repudiatory breach of contract, entitling the other side to reject performance and treat the contract as at an end. It might be argued by Tom that the difference between what he has supplied and what he should have supplied is small, and that the glass fitted will do its job just as well as the slightly thicker panes. All that he should be obliged to do is to deduct from the contract price an amount equivalent to the difference in price of the two types of material. The courts, however, have approached the issue of breaches of such implied conditions strictly. In *Arcos v Ronaasen* (1933), for example, they were considering the implied condition as to description in a sale of goods contract.[7] The contract was for the supply of wooden staves for making barrels, which were supposed to be half an inch thick. Those supplied, although perfectly satisfactory for making barrels, were one-sixteenth of an inch out. The court held that they did not match their description, and that the buyer was therefore entitled to reject them. Similarly, in *Re Moore & Co and Landauer & Co* (1921), the fact that tins of fruit were supplied in cases containing 24 tins each, as opposed to 30 tins each as specified in the contract, was held to be sufficient to entitle the buyer to reject the whole consignment. In some later cases, this very technical approach has been disapproved,[8] and s 15A of the Sale of Goods Act 1979 and s 5A of the Supply of Goods and Services Act 1982 now restrict the right of a business purchaser to reject for minor breaches of this kind. Since Arthur is a consumer purchaser, however, he can still rely on the principles set out in *Arcos v Ronaasen* and *Moore and Landauer*. Moreover, the use of the incorrect thickness of the glass seems more significant than the deviations in those cases. Although the thinner glass will serve just as well in allowing light into the greenhouse, it will not, for example, provide such good insulation, which may be important to Arthur.

It seems, therefore, that Arthur is entitled to treat the contract as repudiated by Tom's breach. This means that he can refuse to pay anything, and can indeed insist that Tom removes all the glass that he has installed. If Tom wants to be paid, he will have to do all the work again, using the correct thickness of glass. On the other hand, Arthur does not have to do this. Where there is a repudiatory breach, the other party always has the choice of whether to terminate or not. It may be that Arthur will decide that the 1 mm difference is not sufficient reason to go to all the trouble of having the work done again. Instead, he could, by way of damages, set off against the contract price both the difference in the cost of the glass and any other additional expenses, for example, extra heating, that might arise from having the thinner glass installed. This may well be his preferred solution.

It seems, then, that Arthur is in a strong position in relation to both these contracts. He is entitled to insist on full performance, without making any payment, and is thus in a good bargaining position as regards reaching any compromise with either Confirm or Tom.

Notes

1   The courts regularly talk in terms of entire 'contracts', but some commentators suggest that they should be considering entire or divisible obligations: see further Stone, *The Modern Law of Contract*, 5th edn, 2002, pp 409–12.

2   A guinea was the equivalent of 21 shillings or, in decimal currency, £1.05.

3   One reason for this apparently rather harsh decision seems to have been that the sum of 30 guineas was higher than the normal rate for such a voyage. The sailor was regarded as having taken the opportunity of earning more than normal against the risk of receiving nothing if the voyage was not completed.

4   It might be possible here to introduce a reference to *Williams v Roffey* (1989), where the revised version of the contract did seem to be on the basis of a payment per flat completed, thus changing what appeared originally to be an entire contract into one containing divisible obligations.

5   *Hoenig v Isaacs* has been little used in subsequent cases, and it may be that the doctrine of substantial performance is of no great practical significance. Indeed, Treitel (*The Law of Contract*, 10th edn, 1999, p 730) doubts that it exists at all; cf Stone, *The Modern Law of Contract*, 5th edn, 2002, pp 409–12.

6   Note that this decision was criticised in the 1983 Law Commission Report No 121, *Pecuniary Restitution for Breach of Contract*, para 2.32.

7   That is, under s 13 of the Sale of Goods Act 1893; see now s 13 of the Sale of Goods Act 1979.

8   For example, *Ashington Piggeries v Christopher Hill* (1972) and, in particular, *Reardon Smith Line Ltd v Hansen Tangen* (1976).

Question 40

In August 2001, Sprocket Ltd entered into a contract with Quikclean Ltd, under which Quikclean agreed to provide cleaning services at Sprocket's office premises for a period of five years. The cleaning was to take place each day, between 7 pm and 9 pm. The contract stated in clause 8 that: 'In the event of Quikclean's failure to clean all offices as required, Sprocket Ltd will be entitled to terminate the contract with immediate effect.' On 10 occasions between August 2001 and July 2002, Quikclean's cleaners failed to turn up to clean Sprocket's offices. Quikclean blamed this on a staffing problem, and claimed in July 2002 that the problem had now been solved. On 9 August 2002 Sprocket found that the managing director's office had not been cleaned, although all the other offices had been. Sprocket thereupon purported to terminate Quikclean's contract, relying on clause 8.

Advise Quikclean.

Would your answer be different if the problem was that Quikclean's employees had left the premises insecure, so that vandals had gained entry and started a fire which caused extensive damage to Sprocket's premises?

Answer plan

This question is concerned with the rights of an innocent party to terminate a contract following a breach by the other party. The issues that need to be discussed include the differences between conditions, warranties and innominate terms, and the situations where a breach will be held to be serious enough to justify termination of the contract. The suggested order of treatment is as follows:

- introduction to the issues;

- consideration of the status of clause 8 of the contract. Does it mean that every breach of contract can be treated as a breach of 'condition'? Relevant cases are *Schuler v Wickman Machine Tool Sales Ltd* (1973) and *Rice v Great Yarmouth Borough Council* (2000);

- if clause 8 does not have this effect, when will the right to terminate arise? Again, *Rice v Great Yarmouth Council* will be relevant;

- consideration of the alternative scenario. Discussion of the principles derived from the case of *Hong Kong Fir Shipping Co v Kawasaki Kisen Kaisha* (1964) will be relevant here.

Answer

This question is concerned with the rights of an innocent party to terminate a contract for breach. There are two ways in which such a right may arise. In some situations, the party may have broken a term which is of particular importance. The courts will treat this as a breach of 'condition', giving rise to the right to terminate, whatever the effects of the particular breach which has occurred. An example of this type of term is the implied condition of correspondence with description under the Sale of Goods Act 1979. Where the clause concerned is not a condition, it may be a warranty (breach of which will not give rise to a right to terminate, whatever the consequences) or an innominate term (in respect of which the right to terminate will depend on the effects of the breach).[1] A serious breach of an innominate term is therefore the second way in which a right to terminate may arise.

In this case, Sprocket has purported to terminate for what seems to be a fairly minor breach – that is, the failure to clean one office. It is probable, however, that this will need to be looked at in the light of the overall dealings between the parties, and Quikclean's earlier breaches.

The courts' starting point is generally an attempt to discern the intentions of the parties. To that end, they will look closely at precisely what the parties have said in the contract itself. If, for example, they have labelled a particular clause as a 'condition', then this may be an indication that they intended any breach to give rise to the right to terminate. Such labelling is not conclusive, however, as is shown by the case of *Schuler AG v Wickman Machine Tool Sales Ltd* (1973). The contract in this case contained a clause, described as a condition, which required that representatives of Wickman should visit six potential named customers of Schuler's goods each week throughout the duration of the contract. Wickman's representatives missed some visits, and Schuler purported to terminate for breach of condition. The House of Lords held that they were not entitled to do so. They said that it was necessary to look beyond the label used by the parties, even though this was relevant evidence of their intentions, and to consider the consequences of categorising a term as a condition. The effect would be that any breach, however small, would entitle the other side to terminate. In relation to the contract under consideration, they could not accept that failure to make just one of several thousand visits could have been intended to be grounds for termination.

In that case, the label of 'condition' was used. In the problem, that is not the case. Instead, the clause specifically states that there should be a right to terminate for a 'failure to clean all offices'. In *Rice v Great Yarmouth Borough Council* (2000), the Court of Appeal had to consider a clause of this kind in relation to a contract for the provision of maintenance services to a local authority. The court adopted a similar approach to that taken in *Schuler v*

Wickman, and held that it could not have been the parties' intention that any breach of contract, no matter how minor, should lead to the right to terminate. The clause had to be interpreted within the overall context of the contract and in line with common sense. It was only where there was a breach, or accumulation of breaches, serious enough to be regarded as repudiatory that the right to terminate would arise.

Applying this approach to the problem, we have a clause which, if read literally, means that a failure to clean just one office on just one occasion would lead to a right to terminate the whole contract. It seems unlikely that a court would regard this as accurately representing the parties' intentions. It will be appropriate to advise Quikclean, therefore, that it is unlikely that their failure to clean one office on 8 August 2002 would in itself entitle Sprocket to terminate the contract.

That is not the end of the story, however. Although clause 8 almost certainly does not have the effect of turning every breach of contract into a breach of condition, a breach, or accumulation of breaches, which is sufficiently serious will give a right to terminate. There are two possibilities to consider here. The office which has not been cleaned is that of the managing director. We do not know exactly what state it was in, or what the managing director's schedule was for 9 August. Suppose that the office had been used for a social occasion on the afternoon of 8 August; suppose also that the managing director had early meetings on 9 August with important clients who needed to be impressed and there was no other appropriate office which could be used. In that situation it is just possible that a court would regard the effect of the breach on 8 August as being sufficiently serious to justify termination. This would be adopting the approach taken in *Hong Kong Fir Shipping Co v Kawasaki Kisen Kaisha* (1962), which will be discussed further below, in connection with the alternative set of facts.

The other possibility is that Sprocket can refer back to the previous breaches by Quikclean (which appear to have been more serious) and argue that, taken together with the breach of 8 August 2002, termination is justified. In other words, the breach of 8 August would be treated as 'the last straw': not sufficient in itself to justify termination, but adding to the accumulated breaches of the previous year. This was the approach taken by the Court of Appeal in *Rice v Great Yarmouth*. In that case, the contract was to last four years. The court suggested that it was relevant to look at the contractor's performance over a full year, with a view to judging whether the council had been deprived of a substantial part of what it had contracted for. In that context, previous breaches were relevant as indicating what might be likely to happen in the future. If it was likely that there would continue to be problems, then this would add to the arguments justifying termination. On the facts, however, the court refused to interfere with the judge's decision that the contractor's breaches were not sufficiently serious to justify termination. It seems likely that a similar conclusion would be drawn from the facts in the problem. The fact that there had been a failure of performance on 10 days out of, say, 250 working days during the previous year is unlikely to be regarded as depriving Sprocket of a substantial part of what it had contracted for. The breaches can surely be adequately dealt with by the payment of compensation, or a reduction in charges for the future. A far greater degree of unreliability would be needed to justify the immediate termination of the contract.

Turning to the alternative situation, Quikclean's staff have here failed to secure the premises, and this has led to severe damage to Sprocket's offices. It is assumed that it was an express or implied term of the contract that Quikclean's staff were responsible for ensuring that the building was secure when they left. Quikclean will therefore be in breach of contract. There is not, however, apparently any provision equivalent to clause 8, purporting to set out the consequences of such a breach. It will fall to the courts to decide, therefore, whether this is to be treated as a breach of a condition, a warranty or an innominate term. It is possible that it could be argued that keeping the building secure is sufficiently important that any breach should entitle the other side to terminate the contract. If that is the case, then Sprocket will be justified in bringing the contract to an end immediately. On the other hand, it might be argued that the obligation as regards security is more like the term as to 'seaworthiness' in *Hong Kong Fir Shipping Co v Kawasaki Kisen Kaisha* (1962). In this case, it was held that the term as to seaworthiness was neither a condition nor a warranty, but an intermediate or 'innominate' term. In relation to such terms, the question of whether the innocent party can terminate for breach depends on the seriousness of the breach and its consequences. If that approach is adopted in the dispute between Sprocket and Quikclean, however, it still seems that the arguments will go in Sprocket's favour. The failure to secure the building has had serious consequences, with significant damage having been caused to Sprocket's premises. This will no doubt have caused disruption to Sprocket's business. In the circumstances, even if the term as to keeping the building secure is treated as an innominate term rather than a condition, the particular breach which has occurred is sufficiently serious to entitle Sprocket to terminate the contract with immediate effect.

Note

1 It might be noted here that some commentators argue that there are in effect only two categories of term – conditions and innominate terms: see, for example, Reynolds (1981) 97 LQR 541 and Stone, *The Modern Law of Contract*, 5th edn, 2002, p 421.

CHAPTER 12

REMEDIES

Introduction

There are two main remedies for breach of contract, namely damages and specific performance. Questions 41 and 43 concentrate on the former, and Question 42 deals with both.

The issues that arise in damages questions tend to centre around the principles used to decide what type of damages to award, rather than how the precise figure to be awarded is arrived at. Thus, the questions will raise issues about:

- the principle behind the award – that is, generally compensation rather than punishment, putting the parties into the position they would have been in had the contract been performed properly;

- the difference between the expectation interest and the reliance interest;

- the possibility of a 'restitutionary' remedy (not based on compensation), as recognised by the House of Lords in *AG v Blake*;

- the rule of remoteness. What is meant by a loss being 'within the reasonable contemplation of the parties' (*The Heron II*)? Again, some comparison with the tortious rule of remoteness may be called for; and

- the situations where non-pecuniary losses may be recoverable – as recently reviewed by the House of Lords in *Farley v Skinner*.

There are relatively few questions that can be asked about specific performance. Again, the question is more likely to be an essay than a problem, and will almost certainly involve some variation on the issues raised in Question 42, that is:

- what is the basis for the award of an order of specific performance?; and

- in what situations will the courts regard it as being an appropriate remedy?

The possibility of using an injunction as a contractual remedy may also arise (though not in Question 42).

Checklist

You should be familiar with the following areas:

- The award of damages: general principles of compensation.
- The meaning of, and distinction between, 'expectation', 'reliance' and 'restitutionary' interests.
- The rule of remoteness, its development and current status.
- The situations in which non-pecuniary losses may be recoverable.
- The availability of specific performance.

Question 41

The main object of damages for breach of contract is to put the claimant 'so far as money can do it ... in the same situation ... as if the contract had been performed' (*Robinson v Harman* (1848)). Explain how this principle operates in practice, and discuss any exceptions that there may be to it.

Answer plan

This essay will be largely descriptive. In explaining the general principle, you should describe the manner in which the courts go about compensating the claimant for loss of what is generally known as the 'expectation interest'. The exceptions which should then be discussed include:

- the remoteness rules, mitigation and contributory negligence;
- the use of the 'reliance' interest as an alternative to the expectation interest (as, for example, in *Anglia Television v Reed* (1971)); and
- restitution, as a further alternative.

The question also provides an opportunity for a discussion of the problems of calculating exactly what the measure of compensation should be, even when the basis of the award is the expectation interest, as illustrated by the House of Lords' decision in *Ruxley Electronics v Forsyth* (1995).

Answer

The general principle of contractual damages is as stated in *Robinson v Harman*, and is in contrast to the position in tort, where the approach is normally to put the claimant in the position he would be in if the tortious act had not taken place. The contract approach is generally described as protecting the claimant's 'expectation interest'. This means that the claimant can recover for lost profits on the transaction, as well as consequential losses flowing from the breach.[1] Such profits will often arise from some further contract. Partial recovery for lost profits may be made even if they were not certain to be made. In *Simpson v London and North Western Rly Co* (1876), for example, the plaintiff had contracted for some specimens to be delivered to a trade exhibition by a specific date. They arrived late, and the plaintiff was allowed to recover damages for the lost profits on sales he might have made had the specimens arrived on time.

The claimant will not necessarily recover, however, every loss which, *as a matter of fact*, flows from the breach by the defendant. The rules of remoteness, mitigation and contributory negligence act as controls over the amount of damages. To the extent to which they operate, they will mean that the claimant is not being put in precisely the position he or she would have been in had the contract been performed satisfactorily.

Looking first at the rule of remoteness, this is designed to prevent a claimant recovering losses which are adjudged to be inappropriate to attribute to the defendant. Suppose, for example, I book a taxi to take me to the railway station by 3 pm, and the taxi is 20 minutes late. As a result, the potential business colleague who I am supposed to be meeting at the station at 3 decides that I am unreliable, and refuses to go through with a multi-million pound deal which we had been negotiating. It is clear that, in this situation, my loss of the deal flows directly from the taxi firm's breach of contract. Nevertheless, I would be very unlikely to be able to recover from the firm for this loss, because of the rule of remoteness.

The rule derives from the case of *Hadley v Baxendale* (1854), where there was delay in the transport of a broken mill shaft which resulted in considerable loss for the mill owner. The court held that the carrier was not liable for the full extent of these losses because they were too remote. The rule was expressed as being that the defendant will only be liable for those losses which flow as a natural result of the breach, or which were within the reasonable contemplation of the parties at the time of the contract as the probable result of such a breach. Although this appears to establish a two-part rule, the common view now, as a result of the decisions in *Victoria Laundry (Windsor) Ltd v Newman Industries* (1949) and *The Heron II* (1969), is that there is just one rule. The situation must be looked at through the eyes of the reasonable defendant, with that defendant's state of knowledge at the time of the contract. The defendant will be presumed to contemplate the normal sorts of losses which would flow from the breach; as regards anything more unusual, it will have to be established that the defendant had sufficient knowledge to be aware of the risk. So, in *Victoria Laundry v Newman*, the fact that the defendant did not know about the existence of a particularly valuable contract which was lost as a result of breach meant that he was not liable for that particular loss.[2]

The second limiting factor is mitigation. The claimant is not entitled to sit back once a breach of contract has occurred and watch the losses accumulate. Reasonable steps must be taken to mitigate the loss: *British Westinghouse Electric Manufacturing Co Ltd v Underground Electric Railways of London Ltd* (1912). For example, if the seller defaults in a sale of goods contract, the buyer will be expected to go into the market and attempt to obtain equivalent goods. If the buyer can do so at or below the contract price, then only nominal damages will be recoverable. If there is an available market in the goods which the buyer fails to enter, then the court will assess damages on the basis that other goods could have been obtained at the prevailing market price.[3] The claimant, however, need only take such steps as are reasonable in all the circumstances. In *Wroth v Tyler* (1974), the plaintiff's lack of resources was held to be a reasonable ground for his failure to make an alternative purchase.

The third limiting factor is contributory negligence. This can only arise where the defendant's liability is based on negligent performance rather than strict liability: *Barclays Bank v Fairclough Building Ltd* (1994). Where this is the case, however, a claimant who has been contributorily negligent will be liable to have his or her damages reduced to take account of this, applying the principles under the Law Reform (Contributory Negligence) Act 1945 (which in effect allows for apportionment of losses): *Vesta v Butcher* (1986).[4]

In addition to these limiting factors, which may prevent the claimant recovering his or her full losses, in certain situations, damages may be calculated on a different basis altogether. First, where the profits which might have resulted from the contract are so speculative that it is in practice difficult to give them any value at all, the claimant may prefer to seek compensation for the expenses incurred towards the contract up to the time of breach. This approach is described as protecting the claimant's 'reliance interest'. A good example is the case of *Anglia Television v Reed* (1971). The plaintiff had contracted with Reed, an actor, to play a leading role in a television film. At a late stage, Reed was unable to take part and the project was abandoned. Anglia sued Reed for breach of contract. It did not seek lost profits, because it was unclear what its profit would have been had the film been made. Instead,

Anglia sought compensation for its expenses paid out in reliance on the contract. The Court of Appeal held that the plaintiff was free to choose whether to seek the expectation or the reliance interest, although of course both could not be recovered. In the later case of *C & P Haulage v Middleton* (1983) it was made clear, however, that the claimant will not be allowed to claim the reliance interest simply because he or she has made a bad bargain on which no profit was likely to be made.[5]

Secondly, in certain situations, for example where there has been a total failure of consideration (*Whincup v Hughes* (1871)), the claimant may simply wish to recover money that has been paid to the other side without seeking any further damages. This is what is known as the 'restitutionary interest'. This kind of action more commonly arises, however, where for some reason no contract was ever in fact made between the parties.

Thirdly, it has recently been recognised by the House of Lords that, in some exceptional situations, it may be appropriate to order the defendant to make an 'account of profits' acquired by the breach of contract. In *AG v Blake* (2000), a convicted spy who had escaped to Russia had written his memoirs, dealing with his time as a member of the British security services. It was held by the House of Lords that publication of these memoirs constituted a breach of his contract with the British government. The British government suffered no financial loss from the publication. Nevertheless, the House of Lords felt that in the exceptional circumstances it was appropriate that any profit made by the spy from the publication should be paid to the government. The scope of this exception is left indeterminate by the decision in *Blake*, but it clearly opens the door to a wider range of situations where a contractual action may enable a claimant to recover damages even though no financial loss has been suffered.

In all these ways, the claimant may end up receiving something different from the full expectation interest, and therefore end up not in exactly the position he would have been in had the contract been performed. A House of Lords decision suggests that, in certain circumstances, even where none of the above considerations comes into play, the claimant may still not recover damages which would give him exactly what he contracted for. In *Ruxley Electronics and Construction Ltd v Forsyth* (1995), the contract was for the construction of a swimming pool, at a cost of £70,000. When it was completed, it was found that it was, at its deepest point, six inches shallower than specified in the contract. The only way to remedy this, and to provide the plaintiff with exactly what he had contracted for, would have been to reconstruct the pool, at a cost of £20,000. The House of Lords held that this would be unreasonable, and the basis of the award in this situation should be the difference in value between what was contracted for and what was supplied. Since the trial judge had held that there was no difference in value, the plaintiff was left with recovering a nominal sum for 'loss of amenity'.[6]

It can be seen from the above discussion that, while the general principle set out in *Robinson v Harman* (1848) remains at the centre of the issue of the calculation of contractual damages, there are a number of other factors which may come into play in appropriate circumstances, and which will mean that the claimant will not always be put exactly into the position he or she would have been in had the contract been performed satisfactorily. These operate principally to guard against overcompensation of the claimant. In general, it may be concluded that the scheme of compensation for breach of contract works satisfactorily, in that it enables the courts to do justice between the parties on the basis of appropriate criteria.

Notes

1 Subject to the rules of remoteness which are outlined later in this answer.

2 Some reference might also be made to *Parsons v Uttley Ingham* (1978), but the Court of Appeal disagreed about the grounds of their decision, and the case is, as a result, rather unclear in its effect. In particular, Lord Denning's attempt to draw a distinction between physical and economic loss in the remoteness context has not been picked up by other judges.

3 Other examples which could be used here include *Brace v Calder* (1895) (offer of reasonable alternative job after termination of contract of employment) and *Payzu v Saunders* (1919) (breach of contract of sale, followed by offer to supply at below the market price).

4 Although the statements of the Court of Appeal in this case are strictly *obiter*. See also *Gran Gelato v Richcliff* (1992) on the application of contributory negligence to liability under s 2(1) of the Misrepresentation Act 1967.

5 See also *CCC Films (London) Ltd v Impact Quadrant Films Ltd* (1984).

6 The sum was in fact £2,500.

Question 42

(a) How do the courts decide whether to grant an order of specific performance? Are the criteria used sensible?

(b) Paperfine Ltd is a printing business. It makes a contract with Mekanix Ltd to repair one of its printing machines, at a cost of £200. Mekanix's employee negligently reassembles the machine incorrectly, so that the first time it is used a drive shaft breaks, and the machine is then beyond repair. The cost of replacing it is £7,500, and Paperfine is unable to obtain a replacement for three weeks. During this period it is estimated that the lack of the machine has reduced the firm's profits by £500 per week. Moreover, the firm misses out on the chance to bid for a very lucrative contract, which would have produced a profit of £6,000.

Advise Paperfine Ltd as to the damages it can claim for Mekanix's breach of contract.

Answer plan

The two parts of this question are entirely distinct. While both are concerned with remedies, they raise totally different issues, and so need to be tackled virtually as two short questions rather than one long one.

Part (a):

- The first part of this answer will be purely descriptive. Following a brief introduction explaining the nature of the remedy, it is simply a question of outlining the bases on which the courts will exercise their discretion to grant an order, such as the adequacy, or otherwise, of damages, and the requirement of mutuality. Some critical analysis of these criteria must then be made. This is probably most easily done by making comments on each of the criteria as it is discussed, and then giving a brief summing up at the end. The quality of the argument, rather than the specific points made, will be most important here.

Part (b):

- This is concerned with the issue of remoteness. It will be necessary to outline the principle from *Hadley v Baxendale* (1854), and describe its development through the cases. There is little doubt that the cost of the replacement, and some lost profits, will be recoverable. The main issue is whether the chance to bid for the lucrative contract can be taken into account. If Mekanix have actual knowledge of this, or it is within their reasonable contemplation, then the issue becomes one of assessing the value to be placed on the 'loss of a chance' (as in *Chaplin v Hicks* (1911)).

Answer

Part (a)

The order of specific performance is an equitable remedy, whereby the court orders one of the parties to perform his or her side of the contract. Disobedience to the order will result in the party being in contempt of court, and thus liable to fines or imprisonment. The fact that the remedy developed in the courts of Chancery means that it is intended to complement the common law remedy of damages. It also means that it is a discretionary remedy. The claimant cannot claim specific performance as of right (unlike damages); it is up to the court to decide whether the remedy is appropriate.

In exercising this discretion, the courts have developed a number of guiding principles, which form the 'criteria' referred to in the question. The first of these is the question of the adequacy of damages, as held in *Harnett v Yielding* (1805). As has been mentioned, the common law remedy of damages is available as of right, but it will not always provide a just result. If, for example, the contract concerns a valuable original painting, a disappointed purchaser will not be properly compensated by money.[1] Conversely, if the seller has failed to supply goods which are easily available elsewhere, even if at a higher price, the claimant buyer is unlikely to be granted an order of specific performance. The provision of damages in the form of money to buy equivalent goods will be a perfectly adequate remedy.

Another example where damages may be inadequate is if there is no real financial loss, so that only nominal damages are available. This will apply where, for example, the benefit of performance is to be received by a third party. This was the position in *Beswick v Beswick* (1968), where the nephew was ordered to perform the contract made with his uncle, for the benefit of his aunt.[2]

The principle of considering the adequacy of damages is clearly sensible. It is questionable, however, whether the way it is applied in relation to contracts for the sale of land is justifiable. The courts take the view that each piece of land is unique, so that specific performance is always available for this type of contract. It is hard to see that this really applies in relation to a standard plot on a housing development, for example. In many cases, it is submitted, a disappointed purchaser could be adequately compensated by damages, though it is admitted that there would be many others where an order for performance would be appropriate.

A second criterion for exercising the discretion is whether or not the performance will require close supervision. If it will, then the court will be reluctant to grant the order, as in *Co-operative Insurance Society Ltd v Argyll Stores (Holdings) Ltd* (1998), which concerned a covenant to keep a supermarket open during specified hours.

Nor will the court normally grant an order in relation to a contract for personal services. This basic principle is sensible, in that there is no point in trying to get people to work together if they are clearly incompatible. In some circumstances, however, for example where the breach of contract is not a result of any breakdown of the relationship between the parties, an order may still be appropriate. This was the case in *Hill v Parsons* (1972) (dismissal as a result of union pressure) and *Powell v Brent LBC* (1987) (defect in appointments procedure). This principle is therefore acceptable, provided that it is not applied rigidly.

The courts also look to 'mutuality' in deciding whether to make an order. This means that they will be reluctant to order performance against the defendant, unless such an order would also be available against the claimant. This might arise, for example, where the claimant is a minor. The time to assess the position, however, is at the time of trial (*Price v Strange* (1978)), and if the claimant has by this stage performed (even though he or she could not have been compelled to do so), the order may be granted.

Disproportionate hardship to the defendant as a result of the making of an order will result in the discretion being exercised against it. Thus, in *Denne v Light* (1857), the making of the order in relation to the sale of a piece of land would have left the defendant without any access to his plot.[3] Specific performance was therefore refused.

Finally, the origin of the remedy in the Chancery courts inevitably means that it will only be used where it is 'equitable' to do so. In addition to the above criteria, some of which may also be said to be concerned with 'doing equity', there is a general requirement that the claimant has acted equitably. As the equitable maxim puts it, 'he who seeks equity must do equity'.[4] Thus, a claimant who has made unfair use of a strong bargaining position (*Shell v Lostock Garages* (1977)), or who has taken advantage of the defendant's ignorance or mistake (*Walters v Morgan* (1861)), will not be granted an order for performance. This flexibility which the courts allow themselves to do justice on the facts of the case seems entirely sensible, though as with any such approach, it carries with it a lack of predictability of the outcome of any particular set of facts.

Overall, then, the rules relating to the use of the remedy of specific performance are satisfactory. The only area where there is room for criticism is in relation to contracts for the sale of land. Here, in contrast to the flexible approach taken elsewhere, a rather rigid rule applies, for which there is little obvious justification.

Part (b)

Mekanix are in breach of contract, as a result of their employee's negligence, and Paperfine is seeking damages. The basic objective which the courts will generally try to achieve is to put the innocent party into the position he or she would have been in had the contract been performed properly (*Robinson v Harman* (1848)). This 'expectation interest' is what Paperfine will be seeking.[5] The difficulty is in deciding exactly what should come under this heading, particularly in the way of lost profits.

Taking the most straightforward issue first, we are told that the defective assembly has led to the machine needing to be replaced. If that is right, then there seems little doubt that Mekanix will have to pay for the replacement. This loss is a direct result of their employee's negligence. Paperfine will of course be under an obligation to mitigate its loss: *British Westinghouse Electric Manufacturing Co v Underground Electric Railways Co of London* (1912). This means that it must take reasonable steps to acquire the cheapest replacement machine of equivalent quality, as quickly as possible. It is assumed that the price of £7,500 is the best deal available, and that therefore Mekanix will be liable to pay this amount.

We must then consider the losses which follow as a consequence of this breach, that is, the lost profits. Such losses are recoverable, provided that they are caused by the breach and are not too remote. Looking first at the loss of £500 per week, there appears to be little argument that this has been caused by the breach. Is the loss too remote? The contractual rules of remoteness derive from the case of *Hadley v Baxendale* (1854), which concerned a delay in the delivery of a drive shaft. The principle to be applied was said to be that the defendant was liable for all losses which flowed from the breach in the natural course of events, plus those which may reasonably be supposed to have been in the contemplation of the parties at the time of the contract as the likely consequence of a breach. Subsequent interpretation of this rule in *Victoria Laundry (Windsor) v Newman* (1949) and *The Heron II* (1969) shows that there is in effect one test: given the parties' state of knowledge at the time of the contract, was the loss one which should reasonably have been within their contemplation as a consequence of the type of breach that has occurred? Knowledge of everyday matters will be assumed, but where the loss results from some particular intricacy of the claimant's business, awareness of this will not be assumed. Thus, in *Balfour Beatty Construction (Scotland) Ltd v Scottish Power plc* (1994), it could not be assumed that the defendant would be aware of the fact that the claimant's construction project required a 'continuous pour' of concrete, and that disruption of this halfway through would mean that it would have to start again from the beginning.

Applying this to the problem, the fact that a machine being put out of service would result in some loss to Paperfine's profits was surely within the reasonable contemplation of the parties at the time of the contract. As long as some loss under this heading is contemplated, the precise figure does not have to be foreseen (*Parsons v Uttley Ingham* (1978)). Mekanix will therefore have to pay the £1,500 lost profits for the period until the replacement machine is obtained.

The loss relating to the missed chance to bid for a very lucrative contract is more remote. In *Victoria Laundry (Windsor) v Newman* (1949), the plaintiffs were not allowed to recover for some particularly lucrative contracts of which the defendants were unaware. The possibility of recovery under this heading, then, will depend on the knowledge of Mekanix at the time of the original contract.[6] Did they know that Paperfine had a chance of this special deal? If, as seems likely, they did not, then Paperfine will not be able to recover under this heading. Even if Mekanix did know about the deal, Paperfine will not be able to recover the full £6,000 that it might have made on it. We are told that it missed out on the 'chance to bid'. Courts are prepared to award compensation for the 'loss of a chance'. In *Chaplin v Hicks* (1911), the plaintiff was prevented from taking part in an audition for a show. She was awarded a proportion of what she might have earned, had she been successful. So, here, the best that Paperfine will be able to do is to recover some proportion of the £6,000, assessed according to the court's view of its chances of actually landing the contract.

Paperfine will be likely, therefore, to recover a total of £9,000: £7,500 to replace the machine, and £1,500 for lost profits. It is unlikely that it will be able to recover any part of the £6,000 on the special contract, unless Mekanix knew about this when the original contract to repair the machine was made.

Notes

1 Unless, perhaps, the sole reason for the purchase is investment.

2 The fact, however, that damages are nominal because equivalent goods are easily available at or below the contract price will not be a reason for granting specific performance.

3 A more recent example is *Patel v Ali* (1984).

4 Or, 'he who comes to equity must come with clean hands'.

5 In contrast to the 'reliance' interest, or restitution.

6 Note that knowledge at the time of the breach is not enough.

Question 43

In January 2002, Peggy made a contract with the Regency Hotel in Leighborough, booking it for the wedding reception of her daughter, Samantha, to be held on 10 August 2002, at a price of £6,000. Samantha particularly wanted the reception to be at the Regency because of its extensive grounds, enabling much of the reception to take place out of doors. Two weeks prior to the wedding, when Peggy rang the Regency to check on certain arrangements, she was told that there had been a mistake over the dates. When Peggy made the contract, the hotel had in fact already been booked for another event on 10 August. On learning this, Peggy immediately attempted to find another location for the reception. The only two possibilities were a local public house, the King George, which could offer a function room and limited catering for £4,500, and the Majestic Hotel in the middle of Leighborough. The Majestic was able to offer an equivalent provision to the Regency, but at a price of £7,500. Peggy booked the Majestic, and the reception took place there. It went smoothly, but Samantha was very disappointed at the change in venue because the Majestic had no grounds, and the whole event had to take place indoors. As a result of all the worry and extra work caused by the change of venue, Peggy suffered a breakdown, and three months later was still receiving treatment for depression.

Advise Peggy, on the basis that the Regency Hotel has accepted that the mistake over the booking was entirely its fault.

Answer plan

Since the Regency Hotel has admitted that it is at fault, the issue that needs to be considered here is the extent of the damages which Peggy may be able to recover. The two main issues which need discussion are the questions of mitigation and non-pecuniary loss. As regards mitigation, the principles set out in *British Westinghouse Electric Manufacturing Co v Underground Electric Railways Co of London* (1912) will need consideration. On non-pecuniary losses, the most important authority is the recent House of Lords decision in *Farley v Skinner* (2001).

The suggested order of treatment is:

- statement of the general principles relating to damages;
- consideration of whether the 'extra' £1,500 paid to the Majestic is recoverable; this will in part depend on whether Peggy could be said to

have taken reasonable steps to mitigate her losses. Should she, for
example, have taken the cheaper alternative offered by the King George?;

- statement of general principles relating to non-pecuniary loss;
- consideration of whether Peggy can recover for Samantha's
  disappointment – this will include the question of recovering damages on
  behalf of another – see *Jackson v Horizon Holidays* (1975);
- consideration of whether Peggy can recover damages for her breakdown
  and continuing depression – applying the principles set out in *Farley v
  Skinner*;
- conclusion.

Answer

The Regency Hotel has accepted that the mix-up over the bookings was its
fault. It is therefore in breach of contract in failing to provide the reception
which it had promised in its contract with Peggy of January 2002.[1] The
question is then what damages Peggy can recover as a consequence of this
breach.

The general principle of contract damages is that they are intended to put
the innocent party into the position that would have resulted had the contract
been performed properly – *Robinson v Harman* (1848). So in this case we need
to look at what the position would have been had the Regency Hotel
performed its contract, and the extent to which Peggy is worse off as a result
of its failure to do so.

The first way in which Peggy has suffered a loss is that she has had to pay
the Majestic Hotel £7,500, whereas she would only have had to pay the
Regency £6,000. It is assumed in this discussion that the Regency has repaid
any deposit that Peggy may have paid. If not, then this should be included in
the loss. Subject to this, Peggy's loss appears to be £1,500. The right to claim
contract damages is, however, subject to an obligation on the innocent party
to mitigate the loss. Allowing the loss to increase without taking steps to limit
it, or taking action which contributes to its size, is not permitted. Any loss
which is attributable to a failure to mitigate will not be allowed. The
principles were set out in *British Westinghouse Electric Manufacturing Co v
Underground Electric Railways Co of London* (1912), where it was stated that the
claimant is under a duty to take reasonable steps to limit the losses flowing
from a breach of contract. What is the relevance of this to Peggy's claim? It is
possible that the Regency Hotel may wish to argue that Peggy should have
taken the cheaper alternative that was available to her – that is, the offer of
the King George public house to provide the reception for £4,500. If that

argument was successful, then Peggy's economic loss would be reduced to nil. She could have obtained alternative provision for less than the contract price. It is important to remember, however, that the obligation is to take reasonable steps to mitigate. The question is therefore whether it would have been reasonable for Peggy to take the King George's offer. It is likely that the function room at a public house would provide less elegant surroundings for the reception than could be provided by a hotel. Moreover, it seems that the King George could only offer 'limited catering'. This suggests, again, that it would not be providing something equivalent to what the Regency had offered. The Majestic, on the other hand, was able to provide an 'equivalent' service. For this reason, Peggy's action in deciding to reject the offer from the King George would be likely to be regarded as reasonable. She should, therefore, be able to recover the full £1,500 additional payment that she has had to make.

The facts do not reveal any other financial losses flowing from the Regency's breach, so this seems to be the total of the damages that Peggy can claim under this head.

The other losses for which Peggy may wish to claim fall into the category of 'non-pecuniary losses' – that is, the disappointment, including that of her daughter, in having to change the venue, and her breakdown and continuing mental illness. The recovery of this type of loss in a contractual action is generally regarded as being exceptional – contracts are concerned with economic transactions, and compensation for the resulting economic losses is the limit of what should be recoverable. Particularly in commercial contracts, the view is taken that the disappointment or distress that may result from a breach is irrecoverable – as stated in *Addis v Gramophone* (1909). This approach has been modified, however, in some circumstances, particularly in relation to contracts involving consumers. The current position was recently reconsidered by the House of Lords in *Farley v Skinner* (2001).

In *Farley v Skinner*, the House of Lords confirmed that there were two types of situation where non-pecuniary losses (other than those arising from consequential physical injury resulting from a breach of contract) could be recoverable. The first category is where the object of the contract, or a significant part of it, is to provide 'pleasure' or 'enjoyment' to the other party. Thus, where the contract is to provide a holiday, as in *Jarvis v Swans Tours* (1973) or *Jackson v Horizon Holidays* (1975), damages may be recoverable for the disappointment resulting from the fact that the defendant's breach of contract meant that the holiday did not match expectations. A case bearing some resemblance to the problem is the Scottish decision in *Diesen v Samson* (1971), where damages were recovered under this head for the failure to take photographs of a wedding. In *Farley v Skinner* itself, this was extended to the failure of a surveyor to take proper steps in relation to a specific contractual obligation to investigate whether a house which the claimant was planning to buy was affected by aircraft noise.

Applying this to the problem, there seems little doubt that a contract to provide a wedding reception would come into the category of contracts to provide pleasure and enjoyment. It seems, therefore, that Peggy will be able to recover compensation for any disappointment she may have suffered as a result of the enforced change of venue. The person most affected in this way, however, seems to be Samantha. She, of course, is not a party to the contract between Peggy and the Regency. It has been recognised, however, that in certain types of case, a claimant who has made a contract designed to provide pleasure to a group of people may be able to recover compensation for the disappointment of the rest of the group. This was the view of the House of Lords in *Woodar v Wimpey* (1980), in explaining the Court of Appeal's decision in *Jackson v Horizon Holidays* (1975) where a father was allowed to recover damages for the disappointment suffered by the rest of the family in relation to an unsatisfactory holiday. One of the examples given in *Woodar v Wimpey* was that of a person booking a meal in a restaurant. It would seem likely that the situation of booking a wedding reception would be treated in the same way, and that the disappointment of the bride in particular should be able to be taken into account in assessing damages.

The second category of situations where non-pecuniary damages can be recovered is where some physical inconvenience causes discomfort or distress. In *Farley v Skinner* (2001), for example, it was held that the claimant could claim compensation for the fact that his occupation of the house he had bought was adversely affected by the noise of aircraft. It does not seem, however, that this will apply here. As was made clear in *Farley v Skinner*, there can be no recovery under this heading, even if the claimant has suffered a complete mental breakdown, if there is no physical discomfort arising directly from the breach of contract. The failure to provide the wedding reception has not involved discomfort of this kind. As regards Peggy's breakdown and mental illness, therefore, it seems that recovery for this will only be possible if it can be attached to the first category of non-pecuniary loss – that is, that it is a consequence of her unhappiness at the effect that the breach of contract has had on the wedding arrangements. In the circumstances, it seems likely that a court would look sympathetically on such an argument.

Whichever category of non-pecuniary loss is involved, this will, of course, be subject to the normal 'remoteness' rules. That is, was a loss of the type suffered within the reasonable contemplation of the parties at the time of the contract as a likely consequence of the breach: *The Heron II* (1969). Again, it is likely that a court would find this test to be satisfied in this case. The late cancellation of wedding arrangements is very likely to cause distress to all involved.

Finally, there is the question of the amount recoverable for non-pecuniary losses. In *Ruxley Electronics v Forsyth* (1996), the plaintiff was awarded £2,500 for 'loss of amenity' when his swimming pool was built to the wrong depth. In *Farley v Skinner* (2001), £10,000 was awarded for the problems relating to the aircraft noise. In both cases, the House of Lords, while upholding the awards, suggested that they were on the high side. In general, awards for non-pecuniary loss in contracts will be modest. Given the overall cost of the contract in this case, an award in hundreds rather than thousands of pounds would be most likely.

In conclusion, therefore, Peggy should be able to recover £1,500 for the economic loss involved in having to find an alternative venue for her daughter's wedding reception. As regards the non-pecuniary losses which they have suffered, some recovery should be possible under this heading as well, but the sum involved is likely to be small.

Note

1   It might be pointed out here that it is strictly speaking an 'anticipatory breach' – in that the Regency Hotel indicates before performance is due that it will not be able to perform its obligations. On the facts, however, this does not seem to raise any particular problems in relation to remedies. For further discussion of this type of breach, see Stone, *The Modern Law of Contract*, 5th edn, 2002, pp 449–50.

CHAPTER 13

QUASI-CONTRACT AND RESTITUTION

Introduction

The topic of quasi-contract, or, as it is more commonly known nowadays, restitution, is on the margins of contract law, and many courses will not touch on it, although it is a topic which is of increasing practical importance. By definition, the situations are ones where there is no contract governing the relationship. This will generally be either because a contract which was made is ineffective, as a result of a mistake or illegality, or some other vitiating factor, or because the parties, while negotiating towards a contract, never in fact managed to formalise their agreement.

Both questions in this chapter raise similar issues, though the first does so in essay form, and the second by way of a problem. The issues that are likely to come up in any question relating to this area are:

- the ways in which money can be recovered, where it has been paid in pursuance of an ineffective contract; and

- the extent to which compensation can be recovered for work which has been done outside the framework of a contract (the *quantum meruit* claim).

The area is not an easy one, because the basis of the law has never been very clear, and it tends to stray across other topics, such as mistake and frustration. The fact that in some respects the law is in a process of development adds to the uncertainty. If, however, the main types of action and the basic authorities are grasped, there is no reason to shy away from answering a question on this topic.

One of the reasons why this topic is often not dealt with in a contract course is that the law of 'restitution' is now emerging as a topic in its own right. This follows the pioneering work done in this area by Lord Goff and Professor Gareth Jones in their book, *The Law of Restitution*, 5th edn, 1998, and developed subsequently, in particular by Professor Peter Birks (for example, in *An Introduction to the Law of Restitution*, 1989).

Checklist

You should be familiar with the following areas:

- Definition of 'quasi-contract' and 'restitution'.
- Historical development of the area.
- Situations currently governed by the two concepts.
- Recovery of money on the basis of a total failure of consideration.
- Recovery of money paid on the basis of a mistake (including the change in the position relating to mistakes of law resulting from the case of *Kleinwort Benson Ltd v Lincoln City Council*).
- Availability of compensation on a *quantum meruit* basis, in particular, where a contract has failed to materialise.

Question 44

'It is clear that any civilised system of law is bound to provide remedies for what has been called unjust enrichment, or unjust benefit, that is, to prevent a man from retaining the money of, or some benefit derived from, another which it is against his conscience he should keep.' (Lord Wright in *Fibrosa Spolka Akcyjna v Fairbairn Lawson Combe Barbour Ltd* (1943).)

How does English law attempt to provide such remedies? Does it do so satisfactorily?

Answer plan

This is a very broad essay question, which requires you to summarise the main rules relating to 'quasi-contract' or 'restitution', and to make some critical comments about them. There are two aspects which need consideration:

- actions to recover money (paid to either the defendant or a third party); and
- actions to recover compensation for some benefit conferred on the defendant (that is, a *quantum meruit* claim).

The best way to tackle this is to give a brief outline of each possible action, and then to describe some examples from the cases.

The commentary on the area is likely to raise difficulties arising from the fact that this is still a developing area of law, and one within which, as a result, there are still uncertainties about exactly how it applies and which situations it covers.

Answer

English law has been slow to develop remedies of the kind mentioned by Lord Wright. This is in part because the kinds of situations in which such remedies are necessary do not fall easily into the categories of either contract or tort, though they may have some connection with either or both. Where money has been paid under a contract which turns out to be void, for example, no action on the contract is possible, because no contract exists. Similarly, work done in prospect of an agreement which has been promised, but does not materialise, again cannot be compensated for by a contract since, by definition, no contract has ever been finalised. Moreover, in the absence of fraud or, in some circumstances, negligence, no tortious action will be possible either. Certain remedies do exist, however, and there is a growing acceptance amongst both judges and academic writers that this area is best regarded, for the purposes of analysis, as falling outside both tort and contract, and under a separate heading of 'restitution'.[1] What are the remedies that have so far been recognised? We need to look at them under two headings. First, remedies to recover money which has been paid. Secondly, remedies to compensate for benefits conferred.

In respect of the recovery of money paid, one clear example of a situation where the courts will allow recovery is where there is a contract, but there has been a total failure of consideration. This was the situation in *Fibrosa Spolka Akcyjna v Fairbairn Lawson Combe Barbour Ltd* (1943), where the contract was frustrated. The House of Lords held that, because the plaintiffs had received no part of what they had contracted for, they were entitled to reclaim all the money they had paid towards the contract. This approach has been applied controversially in relation to sale of goods contracts where the seller has no title to the goods. In *Rowland v Divall* (1923), the plaintiff was a car dealer who bought a car from the defendant. Neither party knew that the car had previously been stolen. The plaintiff resold the car to X from whom, after some months, the true owner reclaimed it. The plaintiff repaid the purchase price to X and sued the defendant for the price he had paid to him. Despite the fact that the car was now valued at considerably less than the plaintiff had paid, he was allowed to recover the full amount, because there had been a total failure of consideration. The essence of the sale of goods contract was the transfer of legal title to the goods, and this the defendant had failed to do. The decision, which was to some extent understandable on the basis that the plaintiff, as a dealer, was primarily interested in rights of ownership which he could resell, was applied in a different situation in *Butterworth v Kingsway Motors* (1954). In this case, the plaintiff was a private individual who had used the car for nearly a year before it was discovered that it had been sold in breach of a hire purchase agreement. The defendant, who was again innocent of the defect in title, was nevertheless compelled to repay the full purchase price to the plaintiff. The plaintiff had thus had the free use of the car for nearly a year.

Money will also be recoverable where it is paid under a mistake of fact. The mistake must be as to a fact which, if true, would have obliged the claimant to pay the money: *Aiken v Short* (1856). Contracts which are void for a common mistake of fact will come into this category. The rule will apply more generally, however, as is shown by *Norwich Union Fire Insurance Society Ltd v Price Ltd* (1934). An insurer paid out on a claim in the belief that a cargo of fruit had been damaged at sea. In fact, it had been sold because it was becoming overripe. The insurer was able to recover the payment as having been made on the basis of a mistake of fact. Of course, recovery will not be possible if the person making the payment is aware of the mistake, but it seems that the fact that they perhaps *should* have been aware of it is not enough. This is illustrated by *Kelly v Solari* (1841), where an insurance company paid out on a life policy, having overlooked the fact that the final premium had not been paid. The company was allowed to recover its payment.

Although, in general, the cases on mistake of fact have involved legal obligations, it seems that this may not be necessary. In *Larner v LCC* (1949), it was held that payments made under a mistake of fact which if true would have created a 'moral' rather than a legal obligation to pay could be recovered.[2]

Until recently, it was the position that there could be no recovery in relation to money paid under a mistake of law. This has now changed as a result of the decision of the House of Lords in *Kleinwort Benson Ltd v Lincoln City Council* (1998). The House could see no reason why there should not be recovery where the recipient would otherwise be unjustly enriched. If the recipients of the money had changed their position in reliance on the payment, this might preclude recovery. On the other hand, the fact that the mistake was based on a view of the law, which appeared to be settled at the time, but which the courts later ruled was incorrect, would not prevent recovery. The only subsequent reported decision on the application of this new principle, however, *Nurdin and Peacock plc v DB Ramsden & Co Ltd* (1999), involved payments made on the basis of incorrect legal advice.

A further situation where recovery of money may be possible is where the claimant has paid money to a third party for which the defendant is liable. In *Exall v Partridge* (1799), for example, Exall paid the arrears of rent owed by Partridge, in order to prevent Exall's carriage, which he had left on Partridge's premises, being seized by bailiffs.[3] The money must be paid under an obligation or constraint, rather than voluntarily, for this action to succeed: *Macclesfield Corp v Great Central Rly* (1911). Moreover, the defendant must have been under a legal obligation to pay the money. In *Metropolitan Police District Receiver v Croydon Corp* (1957),[4] a police authority had paid the wages of an injured policeman, as it was obliged to do under statute. The policeman sued and recovered damages for negligence from the defendants. These damages did not include any element for lost wages, because these had been paid by the police authority. The police authority sought to recover the amount of the wages from the defendants. It was held that they could not succeed, because the defendants had no legal liability as regards the wages of the policeman, only as regards his losses. Since he had been paid his wages, he had suffered no loss in this respect.

We must now turn to the situation where the claimant is trying to recover, not a particular sum of money paid, but compensation for some benefit conferred on the defendant. The claim will be for a *quantum meruit* payment, that is, a sum equivalent to the value of the benefit conferred. Such a claim may, of course, arise within a contract where no price has been fixed for work to be done. Generally, the defendant will be expected to pay a 'reasonable' price.[5] A *quantum meruit* claim can have a wider scope than this, however, and has been recognised in some cases as existing independently of any contract. A good example is *Planché v Colburn* (1831). The plaintiff had agreed to write a book for the defendant. After the plaintiff had done a considerable amount of work, the defendant pulled out of the project. It was held that, independent of any contract,[6] the plaintiff should be able to recover on a *quantum meruit* basis. There was no longer any contract in existence, and the plaintiff should not be deprived of the 'fruit of his labour'. A payment of 50 guineas was ordered.

A further situation where such a sum may be recovered is where services have been performed under a void contract. It was noted above that money paid under such a contract is recoverable. It is, therefore, not surprising that an action for compensation for work done may also be successful. An example of this is the case of *Craven-Ellis v Canons Ltd* (1936). The plaintiff had been appointed managing director of a company under a procedure which was invalid. He sought to recover either the money due under his contract with the company, or on a *quantum meruit* basis. It was held that he could not recover under the contract, since it was void, but he was allowed to recover reasonable remuneration for the work he had done.

By analogy with this, it has also been recognised in more recent cases that work done under an anticipated contract which never actually comes into existence may be compensated in a similar way. In *British Steel Corp v Cleveland Bridge and Engineering Co* (1984), Robert Goff J[7] held that the plaintiffs were entitled to reasonable compensation for work done, at the defendants' request, in manufacturing items which were to be used in the construction of a building. Although there had been extensive negotiations, no contract had ever been finalised. The action succeeded as a restitutionary *quantum meruit* claim.[8]

The above outline shows that in a number of areas English law has found sufficient flexibility to provide compensation so as to avoid unjust enrichment or unjust benefit. To this extent, it is fulfilling the requirement that Lord Wright laid down for 'any civilised system of law'. It cannot be said, however, that the result is wholly satisfactory. The area has developed piecemeal and, as is inevitably the case with the common law, in response to particular problems. As a result, there are gaps and inconsistencies in what it provides. The actions for recovery of money paid, for example, are much better developed than those for compensation for work done. There is also only a very slow development of general principles to provide a framework for future development. Only when this has been achieved will it be possible to say that the law in this area is 'satisfactory'.

Notes

1   The seminal work by Goff and Jones, *The Law of Restitution*, 5th edn, 1998, has been very instrumental in pointing the way forward.

2   Cheshire, Fifoot and Furmston suggest that, as a result of this, the test is not whether there would have been a legal obligation to pay, but rather whether the mistake was 'sufficiently serious': *Law of Contract*, 13th edn, 1996, p 675; cf Stone, *The Modern Law of Contract*, 5th edn, p 465.

3   The landlord was seizing property on the premises in order to exercise his right to 'distrain' for the overdue rent.

4   Heard together with *Monmouthshire v Smith* (1957).

5   This is given statutory force by s 15(1) of the Supply of Goods and Services Act 1982.

6   The contract action probably failed because it was for a specific sum payable on completion of the book.

7   Relying on the decision in *William Lacey (Hounslow) Ltd v Davis* (1957), which in turn relied on *Craven-Ellis v Canons Ltd* (1936).

8   The decision in *Trentham v Archital Luxfer* (1993) means that situations of this kind are now more likely to be dealt with in contract.

Question 45

In January 2002, Exmouth University acquired a large site, containing a derelict factory, on which it proposed to build a new hall of residence. In connection with this project, it took the following steps:

(a) it engaged a firm of architects, Shark & Co, to draw up plans for the new building. The contract price was to be £12,000, with a deposit of 7.5% payable immediately. Dim, the University's finance officer, incorrectly calculated the deposit as £1,800 instead of £900 and paid the larger amount to Shark;

(b) it offered the job of clearing the site to tender. The lowest tender (£28,000) was received from Crush & Co, and the University decided to contract with it. Negotiations on the details of the contract were slow, but in the meantime the University allowed Crush onto the site to start work; and

(c) it bought 20,000 used bricks from Facers Ltd, at a price of £20,000. Several hundred of the bricks were used immediately to repair buildings on the University's main site. The rest were to be used for the warden's accommodation at the new hall.

In June 2002, Shark, whose business was in difficulties, terminated its contract with the University, having produced only an outline sketch of the hall. Crush's work was proceeding so slowly (though 25% of the site had been cleared) that the University told it to leave the site, as it was going to offer the clearance contract to another firm. Finally, the bricks turned out to have been stolen (though Facers was ignorant of this) and were reclaimed by the true owner. The market price of such bricks is now 80 p per brick.

Discuss.

Answer plan

There are three main elements to this rather complicated problem, relating to the three different contracts. All raise issues of quasi-contract, or restitution. The matters for consideration are:

- can the University recover the deposit paid to Shark on the basis of a total failure of consideration (as in the *Fibrosa* case)? If not, can it recover the £900 overpayment, as money paid under a mistake of fact (*Kelly v Solari*)?;

- can Crush recover any compensation for the work it has done in clearing the site, on a *quantum meruit* basis (*BSC v Cleveland Bridge and Engineering Co Ltd*)?; and

- can the University recover the price of the bricks from Facers, on the basis that as it had no title to sell, there was a total failure of consideration (*Rowland v Divall*)?

Answer

The problems with the three arrangements or contracts which the University has entered into in connection with its new hall of residence all raise issues relating to the area of quasi-contract, or restitution.

Looking first at the contract with Shark, since its business is in difficulties, suing for damages for breach of contract may well not be worthwhile. Instead, the University may wish simply to try to recover the money that it has paid, that is, the £1,800. It is well established in English law that, in appropriate circumstances, money paid towards a contract which is terminated may be recovered. In *Fibrosa Spolka Akcyjna v Fairbairn Lawson Combe Barbour Ltd* (1943), for example, a contract for the manufacture of machinery was frustrated by the outbreak of war. The plaintiffs were allowed to recover all the money they had paid, because it was held that they had received nothing of what they had contracted for, and therefore there had been a total failure of consideration. If, however, there has been some performance which has conferred a benefit on the other side, then the action will fail. In *Whincup v Hughes* (1871), the fact that one year of a six year apprenticeship contract had been served before the master died, prevented the recovery of a premium paid by the apprentice. In the problem, then, the difficulty for the University is that, although the full drawings required have not been produced, Shark has provided an outline sketch. It would seem likely that, although this may not be of much value to the University, it is sufficient to prevent the action for recovery on the basis of a total failure of consideration being successful.

If this is the case, the University may alternatively wish to recover the overpayment of £900 which resulted from the miscalculation of the finance officer. Again, it is well established that a payment made on the basis of a mistake of fact is recoverable. In *Cooper v Phibbs* (1867), for example, the plaintiff had paid money in relation to the rent of property which in fact already belonged to him. He was allowed to recover. In this case, there is clearly a mistake of fact as to the amount of money due. The only query is whether the University is entitled to rely on this, since it results from the mistake of one of its officers. The answer would seem to be 'yes'. In *Kelly v Solari* (1841), the careless oversight by an insurance company of the fact that an instalment of the premium had not been paid was nevertheless held to allow the company to recover the money which it had paid out on the policy.

The carelessness of the finance officer in miscalculating the amount due would therefore seem to be irrelevant. The University should be able to recover its £900.

The next agreement to consider is that with Crush. The problem here is that, although the two parties are negotiating towards an agreement, no contract has ever been made. Nevertheless, Crush has done 25% of the work required, and may well feel that it should receive some compensation, such as 25% of the £28,000 which it tendered. Crush's claim would be a quasi-contractual one for a *quantum meruit* payment. The courts have insisted that 'an agreement to agree' does not give rise to legal obligations: *Courtney & Fairbain v Tolaini Bros (Hotels) Ltd* (1975).[1] A *quantum meruit* claim has, however, been recognised as possible where services have either been requested or have been freely accepted by the other party, as in *William Lacey (Hounslow) Ltd v Davis* (1957). In that case, the plaintiffs had prepared plans and estimates on the assumption that they would receive a building contract.[2] This work went beyond what would normally be expected, and was done at the defendant's request. The plaintiffs were allowed to recover a reasonable sum for the work done. Similarly, in *British Steel Corp v Cleveland Bridge and Engineering Co Ltd* (1984), the plaintiffs were allowed to recover on a *quantum meruit* basis for the manufacture and delivery of a number of steel nodes, required for the construction contract by the defendants. No contract was ever finalised, and moreover the defendants claimed that there were problems with the time and order of delivery of the nodes. The plaintiffs were, however, allowed to recover a reasonable sum for the work they had done.[3] Can Crush similarly claim for the work it has done in clearing the site? For Crush to succeed, the work will have had to be of some benefit to the University, and either done at the University's request or have been freely accepted by it. Despite the fact that the work has been done very slowly, 25% of the work has been done. It will now presumably cost the University less to have the work completed.[4] We are also told that the University 'allowed Crush onto the site to start work'. This indicates at least free acceptance of what was being done, if not that the work was done at the University's request. It seems, then, that Crush will be able to claim some compensation. What it receives need not have any necessary connection to the contract price, but 25% of £28,000 (that is, £7,000) is presumably in practice going to be the most likely sum to be awarded.

The third problem arises with the contract for the bricks. They turn out to be stolen, and are reclaimed by the true owner. It is well established in the cases on the sale of goods where the seller has no title that the buyer can generally claim repayment of the purchase price, on the basis that there has been a total failure of consideration. This was held to be the case in *Rowland v Divall* (1923), and was followed in *Butterworth v Kingsway Motors* (1954). In both cases, the contracts concerned cars which were sold between two innocent parties who were in ignorance of the fact that earlier the car had been stolen, or sold in breach of a hire purchase agreement. The eventual buyer was allowed to recover the full purchase price even though there was a considerable lapse of time between the contract and the discovery of the defect in title. On this basis, it would seem that, although Facers sold the bricks to the University in good faith, because it had no title to them, it would be liable to repay the full £20,000. The University would then apparently be able to buy a similar load of bricks for £16,000, and thus end up £4,000 better off. There is a problem, however, in that some of the bricks have already been used to repair buildings on the main site. One of the conditions for using the *Rowland v Divall* approach is that the buyer should be in a position to return the goods. If, by his actions, the buyer has made it impossible for them to be returned, then this right of action will be lost. In this case, it would seem unlikely that the bricks already used in the repairs could be returned. If that is so, then the University would not be able to succeed in its claim to recover the £20,000. What is its position if it is sued in conversion by the true owner of the bricks? It will have to return those bricks that it can, and pay compensation for having converted the rest (or simply compensate the owner for the conversion of the full 20,000). The University will, however, be able to recover a contribution from Facers under the Civil Liability (Contribution) Act 1978.

To summarise the position, then, the most likely outcomes of the three situations would be: (a) that the University would be able to recover simply the £900 overpayment from Shark; (b) that Crush would be able to recover on a *quantum meruit* basis for the work which it has done in clearing the site; and (c) that the University will be liable to the true owner of the bricks, but will be able to recover a contribution towards any compensation paid from Facers. The University is unlikely, however, to be able to reclaim the full purchase price of the bricks from Facers.

Notes

1   Confirmed in *Walford v Miles* (1992).

2   Like Crush & Co, they had submitted the lowest tender.

3   The defendant's counterclaim in relation to the late delivery and the fact that the nodes were delivered in the wrong order was not successful. The two parties may not, therefore, be in an equal position as regards a restitutionary claim of this kind.

4   It might be worth considering here what the effect on Crush's claim would be if the University could not get the rest of the work done without paying out at least another £28,000. Would Crush's work then be of any benefit to it? To put it another way, would there be any 'unjust enrichment' at Crush's expense?

CHAPTER 14

AGENCY

Introduction

A full blown consideration of the topic of agency is more properly the concern of a commercial law course, rather than one on the general law of contract. It is not uncommon, however, to find some treatment of agency in contract law. There are probably two reasons for this. One is that the concept is an important exception to the doctrine of privity. It will often be dealt with in this context. Another reason is that the basic concepts of agency are used in other areas of the law (company law is a good example) and so some basic understanding of them is desirable. Even within the mainstream of contract, cases such as *The Eurymedon*, which involve the use of agency concepts, such as ratification, are difficult to understand properly without some grasp of the essence of agency itself.

The main issues dealt with in two of the questions in this chapter (that is, 46 and 48) relate to the decision of when a principal will be liable, or be able to sue, on a contract made by the agent without authority. The concepts which need to be understood are:

- the different types of authority, and in particular ostensible authority (also commonly known as 'apparent authority'); usual or customary authority may also be important in some situations; and

- ratification – what it means, when it can be used and what its effects are.

In both areas, the effect of s 36C of the Companies Act 1985, on the rights and liabilities of promoters of as yet unincorporated companies, needs to be noted.

Question 47 concentrates on the rather different issue of an agent's rights and liabilities vis à vis the third party. The concept of the undisclosed principal is important here. The roles of the collateral contract and the implied warranty of authority also need to be noted.

Checklist

You should be familiar with the following areas:

- General concept of agency, and its relationship to the doctrine of privity.
- The concepts of implied, usual and ostensible authority.

- The concept of the 'undisclosed principal'.
- Ratification: its availability and effects.
- Duties of the agent as regards the principal.
- Rights and obligations between agent and third party.
- Implied warranty of authority.

Question 46

Albert is the manager of a supermarket owned by Bertha. In January, he is told by Bertha not to buy biscuits from a new company, Crunch & Co, because she has heard that its products are of poor quality. On 18 February, Smooth, a representative of Crunch & Co, visits the supermarket and, as a result, Albert orders £100 worth of biscuits. Smooth is unaware of Bertha's instruction to Albert. When, later in the day, Bertha discovers what Albert has done, they have an argument and Albert resigns. The following day, Albert goes to Drinkit Ltd, Bertha's regular supplier of wines and spirits, and purchases six cases of whisky on credit in Bertha's name. He then absconds with the whisky.

Advise Bertha as to her liability to Crunch & Co and Drinkit Ltd.

Answer plan

This question is concerned with the issue of an agent's authority, and in particular the extent to which a principal can be bound by contracts which the agent has made without authority.

The two contracts concerned here raise different points, though there is some possibility of overlap. In relation to the contract with Crunch, there is the possibility of Bertha being liable on the basis of 'usual' authority, as in *Watteau v Fenwick* (1893). This will involve looking at what is the usual authority of a supermarket manager.

The contract with Drinkit, on the other hand, will only be binding on Bertha if Albert can be said to have 'ostensible' authority. This is sometimes referred to as 'apparent' authority, or 'agency by estoppel'. It involves the principal having made a representation of the agent's authority which is then acted on by the third party. *Freeman & Lockyer v Buckhurst Park Properties (Mangal) Ltd* (1964), which is one of the leading authorities on this area, will need discussion, although the case of *Summers v Solomon* (1857) is closer to the facts of what happened in the problem.

The overlap arises from the fact that it might also be possible to treat the contract with Crunch & Co as being binding on the basis of ostensible authority, if it can be established that there was some representation of authority by Bertha on which Crunch & Co could rely.

Answer

An agent frequently has the power to make contracts which are binding on his or her principal. Problems arise, however, where the agent exceeds the authority given. In what circumstances can the principal still be liable? There are two main situations. First, if it is customary for an agent of a particular type to have certain authority, then restrictions on that authority will be ineffective unless the third party knows about them. This is also referred to as 'usual' authority or, sometimes, 'implied' authority.[1] An example of this type of authority which will be discussed below is the case of *Watteau v Fenwick* (1893). The second type of extended authority which we will need to consider is 'ostensible' authority, which arises where the principal has made some representation of the agent's authority on which the third party has relied. An example of this is the case of *Freeman & Lockyer v Buckhurst Park Properties (Mangal) Ltd* (1964). We will need to examine whether either type of authority will lead to Bertha being bound to either of the two contracts made by Albert.

In relation to the contract with Crunch & Co, the most obvious type of authority to consider here is usual authority. In *Watteau v Fenwick* (1893), the defendants owned a beerhouse which was managed by a man named Humble.[2] Humble was under instructions not to buy cigars for the business from anyone other than the defendants. In breach of this instruction, Humble bought cigars on credit from the plaintiff. At the time of the contract, the plaintiff thought that Humble was the owner of the beerhouse. When he discovered the truth, however, he sought payment from the defendants. The defendants resisted on the basis that Humble had had no authority to bind them to this contract. On the contrary, he was acting in breach of express instructions not to act in this way. The court nevertheless found the defendants liable. It said that it was within the usual authority of the manager of a beerhouse to be able to buy cigars from any source. The fact that Humble had been instructed not to do so was irrelevant, since the plaintiff was unaware of this restriction. He was entitled to rely on Humble's usual authority, and thus the defendants were obliged to pay for the cigars. The issue of what constitutes usual authority is a question of fact, which will have to be decided in each case. The decision in *Watteau v Fenwick* can, for example, be contrasted with the earlier case of *Daun v Simmins* (1879), where it was held that where a public house was 'tied' to a particular brewer, the third party should have realised that the freedom of the manager to purchase would be restricted.

Watteau v Fenwick has been the subject of considerable criticism, in that it applied this approach to a situation where the third party was unaware that he was dealing with an agent.[3] This, however, does not detract from the general principle. Even if it only applies where the principal is disclosed, it is still a type of authority which can bind the principal, even where the agent has exceeded his or her actual authority.

Applying this to the problem, we find that Albert, the manager of a supermarket, has, like Humble in *Watteau v Fenwick*, failed to follow an express limitation on the contracts he is entitled to make. It is not clear whether Smooth knew that he was dealing with an agent. If he did not, it is possible that the court would refuse to apply *Watteau v Fenwick* on the basis that, despite what happened in the case itself, the concept of usual authority should not be applied to situations involving an undisclosed principal. It seems more likely, however, that Smooth would have realised that he was dealing with a manager rather than the owner of the supermarket. In that case, the next issue to decide is the limits of the usual authority of the manager of a supermarket. As indicated above, this is a question of fact, not of law. In other words, it would be necessary to look at evidence as to what was normally accepted as being within the scope of the authority of someone like Albert. If it was found that such managers usually had authority to purchase goods from suppliers chosen at their own discretion, then Bertha will be likely to be found liable for this contract. If the opposite is found, or if it is not possible to determine any particular usual authority for such managers, then Crunch & Co will probably have to pursue Albert rather than Bertha. The only other possibility is if Crunch & Co could argue for the existence of ostensible authority. Consideration of this point, however, will be left until after the discussion of the position as regards Drinkit Ltd.

In respect of the contract for the whisky, there is no possibility of using usual authority, because Albert is no longer an agent when he makes the contract. The only possibility here will be for Drinkit Ltd to argue that Albert had ostensible authority[4] to make this contract. As defined by Diplock LJ in *Freeman & Lockyer v Buckhurst Park Properties* (1964), this requires a representation by the principal,[5] intended to be acted on by the third party, and in fact acted on, that the agent does have authority to make the contract.[6] The representation need not be in the form of words; conduct will be sufficient. In *Freeman & Lockyer v Buckhurst*, a person had been allowed to act as managing director of a company by the other directors, although he had never been appointed as such in the manner required by the company's Articles of Association. It was held that the directors' actions in allowing him to act in this way amounted to a representation to the outside world that he had authority to do so. The company was therefore bound by his actions. The case which is closest to the facts of the problem, however, is *Summers v Solomon* (1857). Solomon owned a jewellers shop, and employed a manager to run it. Solomon regularly paid for jewellery that had been ordered by the manager from Summers. After the manager had left Solomon's employment, he ordered jewellery in Solomon's name from Summers, and then absconded with it. It was held that Solomon was bound to pay for the jewellery. His previous conduct in paying for the jewellery had amounted to a representation of the manager's authority. That representation had not been contradicted or withdrawn, and so Summers was still entitled to rely on it.

At first sight, this decision would seem clearly to mean that Bertha will have to pay Drinkit Ltd for the whisky. There are, however, two questions that need to be asked. We are told that Drinkit Ltd is Bertha's regular supplier. What we do not know, however, is what the usual ordering procedures were. In particular, was it usual for goods to be ordered on credit? And, if so, did Albert follow the usual procedures in placing this order and immediately taking the goods away? If the answer to either of these questions is no, then Bertha may escape liability. If it was not usual for goods to be ordered on credit, then there is less in the way of a representation of authority for what Albert has done in this case. Secondly, if Albert has not followed the normal procedures, should not Drinkit have been put on notice that something unusual was happening, and therefore made some attempt to confirm that Albert was acting with authority? If, however, these issues are not resolved in Bertha's favour, then it seems certain that she will be bound by Albert's ostensible authority, and will have to pay for the whisky.

The final point to consider is whether the contract with Crunch could fall under the heading of ostensible authority as well. The problem here is that of finding a representation. We are told that Crunch & Co is a new company, and therefore there will have been no previous dealings. It might be argued, however, that simply by employing Albert as a manager, Bertha is representing that he has authority to do all the things that a supermarket manager would normally do, including, perhaps, making contracts to buy biscuits. This was the kind of approach adopted in *United Bank of Kuwait v Hamoud, City Trust v Levy* (1988), where it was held that a firm that employed X as a solicitor was representing to the world that X had authority to engage in all transactions on the firm's behalf which came within the normal scope of a solicitor's responsibilities.[7] If this was followed here, it would be another argument for making Bertha responsible for Albert's contract with Crunch & Co.

The advice to Bertha in relation to these two contracts must be that she is on fairly weak ground. The doctrines of usual and ostensible authority, taken together, mean that it is very likely that she will have to meet the obligations under the contracts with both Crunch & Co and Drinkit. Her only remedy then will be to try to trace Albert, and attempt to recover her losses from him.

Notes

1   Although it is probably preferable to restrict 'implied' authority to filling out the relationship between principal and agent, as in *Waugh v Clifford* (1982), rather than as indicating the extent to which the agent may bind the principal to a third party despite a clear breach of the authority given by the principal.

2   Humble had, in fact, previously been the owner of the beerhouse.

3   See, for example, Stone, *The Modern Law of Contract*, 5th edn, 2002, p 161.

4   As noted in the answer plan, the phrases 'apparent authority' and 'agency by estoppel' are also used to describe this concept.

5   It was confirmed in *Armagas v Mundogas* (1986) that the representation must be by the principal. A representation by the agent will not be sufficient.

6   Note also *Rama Corp Ltd v Proved Tin and General Investments* (1952), where Slade J identified the need for: (i) a representation; (ii) reliance on the representation by the third party; and (iii) an alteration of position resulting from such reliance.

7   This approach, if used widely, would of course render the concept of usual authority virtually redundant. Cf also *Gurtner v Beaton* (1993).

Question 47

To what extent is it true to say that, once an agent has brought his principal and a third party into a contractual relationship, the agent drops out, and has no rights or liabilities as against the third party?

Answer plan

This question requires you to know and explain the exceptions to the general rule that an agent is neither liable under, nor entitled to enforce, a contract he makes on behalf of his principal.[1] It goes a little further than that, however, in that there are some actions which may be taken by the third party against the agent which are not strictly speaking based on the contract. Examples are liability on a collateral contract, or liability for breach of the implied warranty of authority. The issues to be discussed are:

- intention to contract personally;
- custom;

- undisclosed principal;
- principal non-existent;
- collateral contract; and
- implied warranty of authority.

It may also be useful to say a little about the power of the third party to choose whom to sue in a situation where both principal and agent may be potentially liable.

Answer

There is no doubt that it is true to say that in the normal course of events, once the principal and third party have made a binding contract, the agent has no further rights or liabilities against the third party. The agent may of course have outstanding claims on, or obligations towards, the principal, but that is a separate issue, arising from their continuing relationship rather than the specific contract which has resulted from the agent's activities. It is also true, however, that in certain situations the agent will have rights and liabilities either alongside, or in place of, the principal, and it is to those exceptions which we now turn. Some of them relate to rights and liabilities on the contract itself; some are independent of the contract.

The first exception which must be considered is where the parties themselves intend that the agent should have personal rights or liabilities. At one time, much stress seemed to be placed on the exact form in which the contract was signed, for example, to sign 'as solicitors' left the agent liable,[2] whereas to sign 'on behalf of' or 'per pro' was taken to indicate an intention that the agent should not be liable. The more recent approach, set out by Brandon J in *The Swan* (1968), suggests that it is a question of looking carefully at the contract and the surrounding circumstances to try to determine the intention of the parties.[3] *The Swan* involved a one-man company, JD Rodger Ltd, which had hired a boat belonging to JD Rodger himself, who was a director of the company. The company gave instructions, through JD Rodger, for repairs to be carried out. It was held that, in all the circumstances, although the order for the work had been signed simply as 'Director' (which carried no implication of personal liability),[4] JD Rodger, the agent, was personally liable. It was natural for the ship repairers to assume that the shipowner would accept personal liability.

It is also clear that if there is a custom or trade usage that agents are personally liable or entitled, the courts will give effect to it, provided that it is consistent with the express terms of the contract and the surrounding circumstances.[5]

Where the principal is undisclosed, then it is only fair that the third party, who thinks that the agent is the other party, should be able to take action against the agent.[6] Once this is established, it must also be fair to allow the reciprocal right to the agent.

There may also be rights and liabilities where there is in fact no principal standing behind the agent. This might occur in two ways. It may be that the agent is in fact the principal and is simply pretending to act as an agent. Secondly, the principal may not be in existence at the time the contract is made.

If the agent is simply pretending to be acting for a principal (real or imaginary), while really acting on his own behalf, then there is no doubt that he will be liable on the contract. He will also be able to enforce the contract provided that he gives due notice of the fact that he was acting on his own behalf, and the contract is not one where the personal characteristics of the other party are important, as they would be, for example, in an employment contract or an underwriting contract: *Collins v Associated Greyhound Racecourses Ltd* (1930).[7]

More difficulty can arise where the principal was not in existence at the time of the contract. This can happen in relation to contracts made on behalf of a company which has yet to be incorporated. The common law approach was demonstrated by *Kelner v Baxter* (1866), where it was held that the promoters were personally liable for the contract. This has now been given statutory force by s 36C(1) of the Companies Act 1985. The terms of the section deal only with liability, rather than ability to enforce. At common law, the only authority in this area was *Newborne v Sensolid* (1954), where the decision against allowing the agent to enforce turned on a very pedantic argument about the precise form of the signature on the contract.[8] This kind of technical argument has been disapproved of in later cases, and in particular by the Court of Appeal in *Phonogram v Lane* (1982). The balance of opinion seems to be that following the statutory intervention noted above, the agent should be able to sue as well as being liable, where a contract is made on behalf of a company not yet incorporated. That was also the view taken by the majority of the Court of Appeal in *Braymist Ltd v Wise Finance Co Ltd* (2002), though with the limitation that the third party may have a right to escape from the contract if the identity of the other contracting party is important.

The situations we have looked at so far have involved the agent being liable on the contract itself. There are two situations, however, in which the agent may have a separate type of liability to the third party. The first is where there is a collateral contract between the agent and the third party. The kind of situation where this could arise is exemplified by the case of *Andrews v Hopkinson* (1957). The plaintiff wanted to acquire a car on hire purchase. The dealer said, 'It's a good little bus. I would stake my life on it'. The plaintiff entered into a hire purchase contract with a finance company for the car, arranged through the dealer. When the car turned out to be defective, it was held that the plaintiff, although at first sight having no contractual remedy against the dealer, could in fact sue him on the basis of a collateral contract. At the time, the dealer was held not to be the agent of the finance company, but that has now been changed by statute.[9] The case illustrates how a statement made by an agent which encouraged the third party to enter into the contract could make the agent liable for breach of a collateral contract.

The final way in which the agent may be liable to the third party is for breach of the implied warranty of authority. This will occur where the agent has held himself out as having authority from the principal, when in fact he does not. Of course, in some circumstances, the principal may nevertheless be liable for the contract on the basis of usual or ostensible authority. If the principal is not liable, however, the agent will be liable for breach of this implied warranty. The remedies that the third party will be able to recover, however, are limited to what could in practice have been recovered from the principal. Thus, if the principal is insolvent, it may not be worth suing the agent for breach of the implied warranty.

The existence of the warranty does not depend on the agent's awareness of the lack of authority. This was established in *Collen v Wright* (1857) and taken to its logical extreme in *Yonge v Toynbee* (1910). In the latter case, the warranty was held to operate against a solicitor who had continued to act for a client who, unknown to the solicitor, had become mentally incapacitated (which had the automatic effect of terminating the solicitor's authority). The fact that the solicitor had acted in good faith throughout was regarded as irrelevant.

A final issue which may need consideration is the position where the third party has the possibility of suing either the agent or the principal. Judgment cannot, of course, be enforced against both, but suppose judgment has been obtained against the principal, who turns out to be unable to pay. Can the third party then sue the agent in respect of the same loss? Or does he have to make a choice at an earlier stage? The rules are not very clear. It used to be the case that once judgment has been obtained against either principal or agent, that precluded any action against the other. That was changed, however, by the Civil Liability (Contribution) Act 1978, so that there is no longer any automatic effect of this kind. In all situations now, the test is whether the third party has 'elected' to sue one party. If so, this will bar any action against the other. The problem is in deciding what amounts to an 'election'. In *Clarkson Booker Ltd v Andjel* (1964), it was held that what was required was a 'truly unequivocal act'.[10] It might have been thought that the institution of proceedings was such an act, but the Court of Appeal thought that this was only *prima facie* so. The election to be binding must be made with knowledge of all relevant facts. In the case before them, the third party had issued a writ against the principal, but had subsequently discovered that the principal was insolvent. It was held that, because they were not in possession of the full facts, the issue of the writ against the principal was not a binding election. Proceedings could be started against the agent. The question of the precise requirements for an election remains unclear.

As we have seen, there is a variety of ways in which the agent may have rights against and liabilities towards a third party. Most of the rules seem to operate in a reasonably satisfactory way. Some criticism might be made, however, of the rather strict approach to the implied warranty of authority. Moreover, as has just been pointed out, the rules relating to 'election' are in considerable need of clarification.

Notes

1   Stone, *The Modern Law of Contract*, 5th edn, 2002, pp 169–71.

2   *Burrell v Jones* (1819).

3   The test is, as in most other areas of contract law, objective, that is, the question is not what the two individuals actually intended, but what 'two reasonable businessmen making a contract of that nature, in those terms, and in those surrounding circumstances, must be taken to have intended' (Brandon J in *The Swan* (1968)).

4   It did nothing to avoid liability, either.

5   For example, *Fleet v Murton* (1871).

6   *Sims v Bond* (1833).

7   In this case, the problem was that an undisclosed principal wanted to take over the contract, but there is no reason why it should not also apply where the agent is wanting to step into the shoes of the supposed principal.

8   It was taken to have been signed in the name of the company, that is, 'Leopold Newborne (London) Ltd'.

9   That is, s 56 of the Consumer Credit Act 1974.

10   This approach was confirmed in *Chesterton v Barone* (1987).

Question 48

Sasha has decided to start a new business selling high quality dresses by mail order. She has asked her friend, Kristen, who is a designer, to assist her. Sasha goes to Venture Finance Ltd to seek funding for her project. She makes an appointment to see Colin, Venture Finance's regional manager. She has approached Colin in the past for support for other business ideas, and knows that he can approve loans of up to £60,000 without approval from his superiors. Sasha visits Colin with Kristen. They initially ask for £60,000, but realise, in working through the project with Colin, that more capital is needed. Sasha eventually applies for £80,000. Three weeks later, Sasha receives a letter from Colin, in which he says that he can confirm that the loan will be available. A copy of this letter is sent by Colin to Kristen. As a result, Kristen sells £5,000 worth of shares which she has promised Sasha she will contribute to the business. Sasha and Kristen use this money to buy equipment for the business.

Two weeks later, however, Sasha receives a letter from the Head Office of Venture Finance telling her that Colin had not sought the proper approval for her loan, and that the money will not be paid.

Advise Sasha and Kristen.

Answer plan

The matters to be discussed in answering this problem are:

- usual authority, that is, can Sasha rely on Colin's 'usual authority' as a regional manager to enforce the loan agreement against Venture Finance?;
- ostensible authority, that is, what was Colin's ostensible authority as regards the loan of £80,000?; and
- if the agreement cannot be enforced against Venture Finance, what remedies might Sasha and Kristen have against Colin himself, for example, for misstatement, or under the implied warranty of authority?

Relevant cases include:

- on ostensible authority: *Freeman & Lockyer v Buckhurst Properties (Mangal) Ltd* (1964), *Armagas v Mundogas* (1986) and *First Energy (UK) Ltd v Hungarian International Bank Ltd* (1993); and
- on the implied warranty of authority: *Collen v Wright* (1857) and *Penn v Bristol and West Building Society* (1997).

Answer

This question is concerned with the extent to which agents, who act beyond their actual authority, can still bind their principals. It also raises the issue of the remedies available against the agent for those who have acted on a false representation of authority.

Sasha and Kristen presumably wish to continue to set up and run their new business. Ideally, therefore, they will wish to argue that Venture Finance is bound by the offer of the loan made by Colin in his letter to Sasha. If this is not possible, however, they will then wish to explore remedies against Colin personally.

Colin did not have authority to approve loans of over £60,000, and so has clearly acted in excess of his actual authority. Can Sasha argue that Venture Finance is nevertheless caught by Colin's 'usual' or 'ostensible' authority?

'Usual' authority arises where the principal puts the agent in a position to which it can be said that certain authority attaches. A solicitor, for example, can be said to have usual authority to compromise a claim, as in, for example, *Waugh v Clifford* (1982). Is it possible to argue that Colin, as 'regional manager', would be taken to have usual authority to approve the loan to Sasha? There are two difficulties with this. First, it is by no means clear that it would be possible, as a matter of fact, to establish what the 'usual' authority of a regional manager of a finance company would be. It is, in any case, unlikely that it would include authority to make loans without some limit on their value. Secondly, and even more importantly in these circumstances, it is clear that Sasha is aware of the limits on Colin's actual authority, as a result of her previous dealings with him. It would therefore be very difficult for her to argue that she was relying on his 'usual' authority when he wrote to her confirming that the loan was approved.

What about the possibility of 'ostensible' authority? The requirements for this were laid down in *Freeman & Lockyer v Buckhurst Park Properties (Mangal) Ltd* (1964). There must be a representation (by words or conduct) from the principal to the third party, which is relied on by the third party and which leads to an alteration of position by the third party. There is no doubt here that Sasha has assumed that Colin had authority, and changed her position by entering into the agreement for the loan. The more difficult question is whether the assumption was created by any representation from Venture Finance to Sasha. There was clearly an implied representation of authority in the letter from Colin to Sasha. Is this enough to bind Venture Finance? The difficulty with such an argument is that the representation of authority must normally come from the principal (that is, Venture Finance) rather than the agent (that is, Colin). This was emphasised by the House of Lords in *Armagas v Mundogas* (1986). In this case, a vice president of a company had indicated that he had authority to agree a deal for the sale and charter back of a ship. His plan was to make a secret profit out of the transactions. When his deceit came to light, the third party argued that the shipowners were bound by the vice president's ostensible authority. The House of Lords disagreed, holding that there was no representation of authority from the principal as opposed to the agent, and that therefore ostensible authority could not arise.

Applying this approach to the facts of our problem would suggest that Sasha cannot rely on Colin's ostensible authority, since the only representation was contained in a letter from Colin himself. The subsequent decision of the Court of Appeal in *First Energy (UK) Ltd v Hungarian International Bank Ltd* (1993) may, however, lead to a different answer. In this case, a branch manager of a bank had, in contravention of limitations on his actual authority, agreed arrangements with a third party for the provision of credit facilities to customers of the third party's business. The third party knew that the manager had no personal authority to enter into such arrangements on behalf of his principal, but assumed, from a letter written by the manager, that the appropriate approvals had been obtained. Although this appeared to amount to a representation by the agent, and therefore to fall foul of the decision in *Armagas v Mundogas*, the Court of Appeal felt able to distinguish the earlier case. It held that an agent who does not have ostensible authority to enter into a particular transaction may nevertheless have ostensible authority to communicate to a third party that such a transaction has been approved. Part of the reason for this was a feeling that it would be unreasonable to expect a third party to have to check in such situations whether the board, or whatever body within the principal company was appropriate, had in fact given approval to the transaction. If this approach were to be applied here, it would be of assistance to Sasha. The argument would be that it would have been unreasonable for her to have had to check that Colin had in fact sought the approval of his superiors as required. She ought, therefore, to be able to rely on his ostensible authority, as indicated in his letter, and enforce the loan agreement against Venture Finance.

What, on the other hand, is Sasha's position if the *First Energy* approach is not adopted by the court here, and it is held that there was no ostensible authority for Colin to agree to the loan? Although the loan cannot then be enforced, Sasha will clearly be looking to recover compensation from Colin himself. There are two ways in which this might be possible. First, there is the possibility of an action in tort for deceit, or negligent misstatement under the *Hedley Byrne v Heller* (1964) principle, as modified in *Caparo v Dickman* (1990).[1] If Colin is found to have made a statement as to the fact that the transaction had been authorised, which he knew was false or which he made without proper care, this could give rise to an action for damages.

Secondly, Sasha may seek to rely on the 'implied warranty of authority' which is given by all agents when they purport to contract on behalf of a principal (as in, for example, *Collen v Wright* (1857)). This might enable her to recover all the losses which she has suffered as a result of the fact that Colin was acting without authority. It is possible to obtain either expectation or reliance damages under this action. It is available even if the representation of authority is innocent, or completely inadvertent. Thus, in *Yonge v Toynbee* (1910), it applied where the principal had become a certified lunatic, thus ending any authority, even though the agent was quite unaware that this had happened. It is therefore quite a powerful remedy, which Sasha may well be able to use.

What about Kristen? She has sold her shares in reliance on Colin's letter, and used the money to buy equipment. This may well have resulted in some loss to her (if, for example, the shares have subsequently increased in value). It would seem that she could bring an action in deceit (assuming that Colin's misstatement was deliberate or reckless), since it is clear that Colin's misrepresentation was made to her and she acted on it. Similarly, an action for negligent misstatement would also be possible, provided that Kristen could be said to be owed a duty of care by Colin, under the principles of *Caparo v Dickman*. This would not seem to be too difficult on the facts. Colin's letter was copied to Kristen and she was, therefore, within the group whom Colin could have expected to rely on the statements contained in it. Provided that Kristen's action in selling her shares could be said to be reasonably foreseeable, she will be able to claim for damages for her losses consequent upon this.

Could Kristen also claim under the breach of the implied warranty of authority? It might be thought that this would not be applicable, since Kristen was not in the end someone whom Colin was purporting to bring into a contractual relationship with his principal. The decision in *Penn v Bristol and West Building Society* (1997), however, suggests that this may not be an obstacle. In this case, a solicitor agent's innocent misrepresentation of authority to a building society was held to give rise to liability for breach of the implied warranty, even though the building society's loss resulted not from attempting to contract with the solicitor's principal, but from lending money to someone who was entering into such a contract. It was held to be sufficient that the representation of authority had been made to the building society and that it had acted on it to its detriment. Applying that to the situation in the problem, the representation of authority was clearly made to Kristen, and she has acted on it to her detriment by selling her shares. On this basis, Kristen, like Sasha, could seek damages for breach of the implied warranty of authority from Colin.

The possibilities for Sasha and Kristen, therefore, look good. Sasha may well be able to rely on Colin's ostensible authority, and so enforce the loan agreement with Venture Finance. If, however, this is not possible, she will be able to recover compensation from Colin either in tort or for breach of the implied warranty of authority. Kristen will not be able to enforce the loan, but if Colin has acted without authority, she will have the same possibilities of action against him as are available to Sasha.

Note

1   An action under the Misrepresentation Act 1967 would not be possible here, since that only applies as between the parties to a contract, and there is no contract between Sasha and Colin.

CHAPTER 15

SALE OF GOODS

Introduction

As with agency, the full consideration of the topic of sale of goods belongs more properly in a commercial law (or perhaps a consumer law) course. We have already seen, however, that it is difficult to escape the Sale of Goods Act 1979, and aspects of it have already been touched on in the questions on exemption clauses (Question 23).

Within a contract course, the most likely topic to be discussed is liability under the implied terms in ss 12–15. The Sale of Goods Act 1979 is regularly used as an example of statutorily implied terms, and this discussion may well lead into a general consideration of the content of those terms. The terms concerning title (s 12) and sale by sample (s 15) will be considered less frequently than the terms relating to quality. If sale of goods is part of your contract course, you are likely to need to have a good understanding of:

- s 13 (compliance with description);
- s 14(2) (satisfactory quality); and
- s 14(3) (fitness for a particular purpose).

It is important to understand the relationship between these three sections, and to remember that s 13 is the only one which applies to sales which are not in the course of a business. In particular, it is important to remember that, although 'fitness for purpose' is referred to by s 14(2B) as one of the factors which is relevant in deciding whether goods are of 'satisfactory quality', this is quite distinct from the 'fitness for a particular purpose' covered by s 14(3). There is considerable case law on ss 13 and 14(3) which needs to be understood; the case law on s 14(2) is less helpful because it is all concerned with the concept of 'merchantable' quality which was used prior to 1994, when it was replaced with 'satisfactory' quality, with an amended definition. Some knowledge of the pre-1994 cases will nevertheless be useful.

The other area which you may be asked about, and which is covered in Question 49, is the 'passing of property'. The rules relating to this are of considerable practical importance as the answer to Question 49 indicates. Providing you are familiar with ss 16–20 of the Act, and apply them carefully, there should be no difficulties with questions in this area. There is less case law than on the implied terms, so it is easier to deal with the most important authorities (for which, see the answer to Question 49).

Checklist

You should be familiar with the following areas:

- The scope of the implied terms under ss 12–15 of the Sale of Goods Act 1979.
- Meaning of 'sale by description': s 13.
- Meaning of 'satisfactory quality': s 14(2).
- Meaning of 'fitness for a particular purpose': s 14(3).
- Remedies for breach.
- Passing of property: general principles (ss 16–20) and the importance of determining when property passes.
- The special rules for passing of property under s 18.

Question 49

When, according to the Sale of Goods Act 1979, does ownership of goods pass under a sale of goods contract? Why is it important to pinpoint this time?

Answer plan

To answer this question, you will need to know your way around ss 16–20 of the Sale of Goods Act 1979 and the related case law. Ownership is of course described as 'property' in the Act, so we are dealing with the rules for the 'passing of property'. The main features are:

- goods must be 'ascertained': s 16;
- intentions of the parties are important: s 17; and
- in the absence of express intentions, the rules contained in s 18 apply, so that, for example, in a contract for the sale of specific goods, property will often pass at the time of the contract (r 1). If the contract is for unascertained or future goods, however, property will not pass until there has been an 'unconditional appropriation' of relevant goods to the contract (r 5).

Not all the rules in s 18 will need to be discussed in detail. The answer should, however, demonstrate that you have a general grasp of their scope and provisions.

The second part of the question asks why it may be important to pinpoint the time when property passes. There are three main reasons:

- if one of the parties becomes insolvent, it may be vital to discover who owns the goods;
- if goods are lost or damaged, generally speaking, it will be the owner who will be able to take action against anyone responsible, or alternatively will have to bear the loss: s 20 (passing of risk); and
- it is only when the property has passed that an action for the price can be maintained: s 49.

Answer

The Sale of Goods Act 1979 uses two words to denote rights of ownership, namely, 'title' and 'property'. 'Title' is mainly concerned with the right to sell the goods, as in the implied condition in s 12.[1] Where the transfer of ownership rights is concerned, the Act refers to the 'passing of property'. The rules relating to this are set out in ss 16–18 of the Act.

Section 16 states that property cannot pass unless the goods are 'ascertained'. This means that, if the contract is, for example, for the purchase of '5,000 size four widgets', no property will pass until the widgets relevant to the contract are 'ascertained'. Similarly, if you go into an electrical store and order a particular model of washing machine, property cannot pass until the actual machine which you are going to buy has been identified. The way in which this will operate is discussed further below in connection with s 18, r 5.

Where goods are ascertained, that is, it is clear at the time of the contract which particular items are being sold or are specific, as in, for example, the sale of a second hand car, then s 17 says that property will pass when the parties intend it to pass. Thus, the intentions of the parties are paramount and will override any other rules. The intentions must, however, be expressed prior to the time when the contract was made.

In *Dennant v Skinner* (1948), the successful bidder in an auction wanted to pay by cheque. The seller agreed, provided that the buyer signed a document saying that property would not pass until the cheque was cleared. It was held that this expression of intention as to the passing of property came too late, since the contract was concluded when the auctioneer knocked the lot down to the buyer.

In many cases, of course, the parties do not bother to express any intention as to when property should pass, and in that situation the Act provides a set of rules, set out in s 18, to determine what should happen. There are five rules in all.

Rule 1 deals with the situation where the contract is for the sale of specific goods in a deliverable state.[2] It states that in this case property passes when the contract is made. The time of payment or delivery are irrelevant. If, for example, a person agrees to buy a second hand car on a Monday, which is to be collected and paid for on the Wednesday, property passes on the Monday, and the buyer becomes the owner of the car from that point. This becomes even more important when the position as to 'risk' (discussed below) is considered.

Rules 2 and 3 again deal with specific goods, but relate to the situation where something further needs to be done, either to put the goods into a deliverable state (r 2) or to determine the price (r 3). In both cases, property will not pass until what is required has been done, and the buyer has notice of that fact. So, for example, if the contract is for a load of grain in a ship, it may need to be put into bags to be deliverable (r 2). Or if the load is bought at a price per tonne, it will be necessary to weigh it to determine the exact contract price (r 3).

Rule 4 deals with the particular problems of sales which are on an 'on approval' or 'sale or return' basis. It provides guidelines for deciding when it should be deemed that the goods are going to be retained. Once it is clear that the goods are to be kept by the buyer, property will pass immediately. This presumably means, for example, that if several cases of wine are bought on a sale or return basis for use at a party, the property in each bottle will pass as soon as it is opened.

The final rule, r 5, deals with the problem of unascertained or future goods. It thus covers both the order for generic goods which are already in existence (as in the '5,000 size four widgets' mentioned above) and goods which have to be manufactured, or grown, for the contract. Rule 5 says that property passes when goods matching the contract description, and in a deliverable state, are 'unconditionally appropriated' to the contract by either party 'with the assent' of the other. There are two problems which may arise with this rule. First, what is meant by 'unconditional appropriation'? Secondly, what is meant by 'assent'?

Looking first at 'unconditional appropriation', there is a further provision in the second part of r 5, which indicates that this may be satisfied by delivery of the goods to a carrier. The goods will need also to be 'ascertained' at this stage, however, in order to fulfil the requirements of s 16. Thus, in *Healey v Howlett & Sons* (1917), the contract was for 20 boxes of fish. The seller put 190 boxes onto a train, with instructions that 20 were to be delivered to the seller. It was held in this case that delivery to the carrier did not amount to an unconditional appropriation. Such appropriation could only occur when the defendant's 20 boxes were separated from the rest of the 190.

Other than this, the Act gives no guidance on what amounts to unconditional appropriation. In *Carlos Federspiel & Co SA v Charles Twigg & Co Ltd* (1957), it was emphasised that the assignment of the goods to a particular contract had to be intended to be irrevocable. Moreover, it was relevant to ask whether the seller had done the 'last act' which he was obliged to do. Thus, in *Aldridge v Johnson* (1857), grain had been bagged in accordance with the buyer's order and was awaiting collection by the buyer. Property was held to have passed. In the *Carlos Federspiel* case, however, although the goods had been packed, the seller had the obligation to ship them. Since the seller had not taken this last step, it was held that property had not passed.

As to assent, this may be express or implied, and may be given before or after the appropriation has taken place. It is clearly not necessary for the other party to be notified and to agree specifically. In fact, the approach seems to be that provided that what has been done is what was reasonably to be expected, then assent will be implied.

We must now turn to the second issue raised in the question, that is, why is it important to fix the time at which property passes? There are a number of reasons.

First, it may be that one of the parties becomes insolvent. If the seller becomes insolvent prior to delivery, or the buyer after delivery but before payment, the other party will be in a much stronger position if they can establish a proprietary claim over the goods. The problem has arisen most commonly in relation to the insolvency of the buyer, and s 19 specifically recognises the seller's right to 'reserve the right of disposal' of the goods until payment has been made. Such a reservation by the seller is taken to be an indication that property is not to have been intended to pass. This works satisfactorily where the goods are still in their original state in the hands of the buyer or seller. More difficulties arise where the goods have been resold or have been used in some manufacturing process. Here, there have been elaborate attempts to protect the seller's position by so called *Romalpa* clauses.[3] These cannot be discussed in detail here, but their development indicates the importance of the issue 'when does property pass?'.

The second reason why it may be important to identify when property passes is that, as a result of s 20 of the Sale of Goods Act 1979, 'risk' usually passes with property. Thus, if goods are lost or damaged, it is the owner who will be responsible, and will have the obligation of insuring them. If property has not passed to the buyer, then the seller will have to provide the buyer with replacement goods. If property has passed, the buyer will be obliged to pay for the goods, and will have to bear the loss of repairing or replacing them. Moreover, if someone else (such as a carrier) can be identified as being at fault, only the owner of the goods will have a right to take a tortious action against them: *Leigh & Sillivan Ltd v Aliakmon Shipping Co Ltd (The Aliakmon)* (1986).[4]

Finally, s 49 of the Act makes it clear that it is only where property has passed that the seller may maintain an action for the price against the buyer.

The rules relating to the transfer of ownership in a sale of goods contract are fairly clearly defined by the Sale of Goods Act 1979 provisions. Some uncertainties, such as what exactly is meant by 'unconditional appropriation', remain, but generally the parties in a sale of goods contract will know where they stand. This is important, since, as has been indicated, the issue of if and when property has passed can be of vital importance in determining the rights and liabilities between buyer and seller.

Notes

1   See also s 21 which sets out in statutory form the rule of *nemo dat quod non habet* (a person cannot pass property in something they do not own).

2   It also states that the contract must be 'unconditional', but this seems to be of very little practical significance.

3   Named after the case of *Aluminium Industrie Vaasen BV v Romalpa Aluminium Ltd* (1976). The proper discussion of *Romalpa* clauses is outside the scope of a basic contract course.

4   One of the parties is, of course, likely to have a contractual action against the carrier.

Question 50

Suppliers plc makes three contracts to sell 5,000 widgets each to Alpha Ltd, Beta Ltd and Gamma Ltd, at a contract price of £3,000. Advise Suppliers if:

(a) the widgets delivered to Alpha were described on the packaging as 'British made'. Alpha has now discovered that they were in fact made in Japan, and wishes to reject them;

(b) the widgets delivered to Beta prove unable to stand up to use in the continuous process for which Beta required them; and

(c) the widgets destined for Gamma were stolen en route and sold to Kappa Ltd, who knew nothing of the theft. Gamma is suing for non-delivery.

The market price of 5,000 widgets is now £4,000.

Answer plan

The first two parts of this question deal with the implied terms as to the quality of goods contained in ss 13 and 14 of the Sale of Goods Act 1979. The issues to discuss are:

(a) for s 13 to apply, there has to be a sale by description. If the description only comes to the attention of Alpha Ltd after the contract is made, then it will be irrelevant. Moreover, there must be some reliance on the description: *Harlingdon & Leinster Ltd v Christopher Hull Fine Art Ltd* (1990); and

(b) the relevant implied terms are s 14(2) 'satisfactory quality', and s 14(3) 'fitness for a particular purpose'. Both should be described, though s 14(3) is more likely to be relevant. The main issue here will be whether Suppliers knew what the widgets were to be used for.

The third problem, (c), is slightly different. It is mainly concerned with the passing of property and the remedies for failure to deliver. It will be necessary to discuss, first, whether property has passed at the time of the theft, applying the provisions of ss 16–18 of the Sale of Goods Act 1979. If the property in the goods has already passed to Gamma Ltd, then Suppliers has no problems (note that it is only Suppliers which you are asked to advise). If it retains the property, then it will want to recover the widgets from Kappa Ltd. This it should be able to do, unless Kappa can rely on one of the exceptions to the *nemo dat* rule. Suppliers may still, however, have to pay damages of £1,000 to Gamma, if Gamma has terminated the contract for failure to deliver (s 51).

Answer

The three elements in this problem are all concerned with provisions of the Sale of Goods Act 1979 (the Act). They raise different issues, however, and so each will be looked at separately.

Part (a)

Alpha Ltd is presumably wishing to reject the goods on the basis of a breach of the implied condition as to compliance with description in s 13 of the Act. That section says that, where there is a sale by description, there is an implied condition that the goods will correspond with that description. The first point to make is that there seems no doubt that statements on the packaging of goods can be part of the description. Thus, a person selecting goods in a supermarket will rely on the statements on the outside of a packet as describing its contents. If a packet of biscuits described on the outside as coconut rings turns out on being opened to contain ginger nuts, there is no doubt a breach of s 13. It is important to note, however, that the provision only applies to a sale by description. In the problem, it is not clear when the description came to the attention of Alpha, but it seems it may not have been until the widgets were delivered. If so, then Alpha has no cause of action against Suppliers, because the words 'British made' cannot have been part of the contractual description. Even if Alpha was aware of these words before the contract, this does not necessarily mean that there is a breach of s 13. Although, in some cases, the courts' approach seemed to be to treat the most minor non-compliance as leading to a breach,[1] more recently the view has been expressed that only those parts of the description that are important in identifying the goods should fall within s 13 (*Ashington Piggeries v Christopher Hill* (1972); *Reardon Smith Lines v Hansen Tangen* (1976)). Section 15A, which was added to the Act in 1994, reinforces this trend by removing from business purchasers the right to reject for slight breaches of the implied conditions. Moreover, in *Harlingdon & Leinster Ltd v Christopher Hull Fine Art Ltd* (1990), it has been held that there must be some reliance on the description before failure to comply with it gives rise to a remedy. For Alpha to succeed under s 13, therefore, it will have to be shown that it was aware of the description before the contract was made, that it was important to Alpha in identifying what it was buying, and that it relied on the description. If all this is established, then Alpha will be able to reject the goods, reclaim the purchase price (if it has been paid), and recover damages for any losses. Since the market price is now £4,000, it should at least recover £1,000 (s 51 of the Act).

Part (b)

In this case, Beta Ltd is complaining about the quality of what has been supplied, that is, that the widgets do not stand up to use. There are two provisions of the Act to consider here, namely, s 14(2), which implies a condition of 'satisfactory quality', and s 14(3), which implies a condition of 'fitness for a particular purpose'.

Satisfactory quality in s 14(2A) requires goods to meet the standard that a reasonable person would regard as satisfactory, taking account of all relevant circumstances, including the description of the goods and the price. This very broad definition is supplemented by s 14(2B), which indicates some factors which may be relevant in applying the test. The two which are of particular relevance here are, first, the fitness of the goods for all the purposes for which goods of that kind are commonly supplied[2] and, secondly, the durability of the goods. As to the first issue, the question will be whether the widgets supplied are of a kind which are commonly used for continuous processes of the sort which Beta is operating. Secondly, the problem here seems to be one of 'durability'. The question will, therefore, be whether it was reasonable to expect these widgets to be sufficiently durable to withstand the needs of Beta's processes. Both of these questions are essentially issues of fact, on which evidence of the expectations and understanding of those involved in buying and selling widgets will be very important. If Suppliers can show that Beta's process was unusual, and not the kind of situation in which widgets of the kind supplied would normally be used, then it may well be able to sustain an argument that the goods are of 'satisfactory' quality under s 14(2).

If this is the case, then the possibility of liability under s 14(3) must be considered. This provides that, where goods are required for a particular purpose which has been made known to the seller, there is an implied condition that the goods will be fit for that purpose. This will not apply if the buyer did not rely, or it was unreasonable for the buyer to rely, on the seller's skill and judgment in supplying the goods. It should be noted that s 14(3) can apply even if the goods only have one purpose: *Priest v Last* (1903) (hot water bottle). It will also operate even if there is only partial reliance on the seller: *Cammell Laird & Co Ltd v Manganese Bronze & Brass Co Ltd* (1934).[3] An example of a case where the plaintiff failed because insufficient information was given to the seller is *Griffiths v Peter Conway* (1939), where the purchaser of a Harris Tweed coat contracted dermatitis from wearing it. The seller was held not to be liable because the buyer had not revealed that she had particularly sensitive skin.

In relation to the problem, two questions therefore need to be asked. First, did Beta make known to Suppliers the exact purpose for which the widgets were intended? Secondly, if so, was it reasonable for it to rely on Suppliers' skill and judgment in providing the widgets, and did it so rely to any extent? We cannot discover the answers to these questions, but if the answer to both of them is 'yes', then Suppliers will be liable under s 14(3). Since Beta appears to have used some of the goods, then it may well not be able to terminate the contract (s 11(4)), but Suppliers will simply have to compensate it with damages.

Part (c)

Suppliers' position as regards Gamma depends, in part, on whether the property in the goods had passed at the time they were stolen. The rules as to the passing of property are contained in ss 16–18 of the Act. They state that, for property to pass, the goods must be ascertained: s 16. In relation to specific or ascertained goods, property will pass when it is intended to pass:

s 17. If, however, the parties have not expressed any intention, then the rules in s 18 will apply. It is assumed here that there is nothing in the contract between Suppliers and Gamma about the passing of property. If that is so, it seems almost certain that at the time of the contract the goods will be unascertained,[4] and so the relevant provision will be r 5 of s 18. This states that property in such goods will pass when goods meeting the contract description are 'unconditionally appropriated' to the contract with the assent of the other party. Part 2 of r 5 states that delivery to a carrier will be regarded as unconditional appropriation. So, if Suppliers has delivered Gamma's widgets to a carrier, and they do not form part of a larger load (as in *Healey v Howlett* (1917)), then it will be able to claim that the property had passed to Gamma before the goods were stolen.[5] Gamma will therefore have to sort out the question of what happens to the goods with Kappa.

If the answer to the passing of property issue is, however, that the goods still belonged to Suppliers when they were stolen, the position will be different. Suppliers will probably be able to recover the goods from Kappa. Since Kappa bought the goods after they had been stolen, it will have been unable to obtain a good title to them, unless it can bring itself within one of the exceptions to the *nemo dat* rule, as set out in ss 21–25 of the Act. None of these seems likely to apply on the facts. Suppliers may still have to pay damages for non-delivery to Gamma, however, assuming Gamma has terminated the contract before Suppliers can recover the goods from Kappa. The measure will be *prima facie* the difference between the contract and market prices, that is, £1,000 (s 51).

Notes

1   Cases such as *Arcos v Ronaasen* (1933) and *Re Moore & Co and Landauer & Co* (1921) could be cited here. They are discussed in the answers to Questions 38 and 39.

2   The position prior to 1994 was that to be 'merchantable' goods had to be fit for just *one* of the purposes for which they were commonly bought: *Aswan v Lupdine* (1986).

3   *Ashington Piggeries v Christopher Hill* (1972) might also be cited here.

4   A contract for 5,000 widgets is almost certainly a contract for generic goods sold by description.

5   Note also s 32 of the Act, which deems delivery to a carrier to equal delivery to the buyer.

INDEX

Acceptance. 1–5
  See also Offer
  advertisements 19–21
  electronic communications 1
  fax, by. 4
  meaning 2–5
  not matching offer 1
  postal rule 4–5
  relationship with offer 1
  silence as 1, 21–23
  telephone 7–10
  telexes. 5
Account of profits. 213
Advertisements,
  acceptance 19–21
  invitations to treat. 14–18, 20
  offer. 1, 15, 20
  rewards. 20–21
  websites 15
Agency. 111, 235–49
  apparent authority 235
  authority. 236–40
    apparent. 235
    awareness of lack of
      authority. 243
    implied 235, 237,
      243, 248–49
    ostensible. 235, 236,
      239–40, 246–47
    usual. 236, 237–39,
      246
  collateral contract 235
  deceit. 247
  election to sue party 243–44
  estoppel, by 236
  implied warranty of
    authority 237, 243,
      248, 248–49
  negligent misstatement 247–48
  ostensible authority. 235, 236,
      239–40, 246–47
  principal or agent,
    suing. 243–44
  privity. 235
  ratification 235

third parties. 240–44
undisclosed principal. 235, 241–44
usual authority 236, 237–39, 246

Banks,
  undue influence 147–51, 152–56
Bilateral contracts. 1
Blue pencil test 168
Breach of contract,
  conditions 196–97, 204–07
  intentions of parties 205
  repudiatory 202
  termination after. 204–07

Capacity. 67–80
  intoxication 67, 76–80
  mental incapacity 67, 76–80
  minors. 67, 68–71
    See also Minors
  types 67
Collateral contracts. 89, 94–95
  agency. 235
  exclusion clauses. 114
Common mistake 120, 123–26, 134
Competition law. 157
Conditions. 82
  breach of contract 196–97, 204–07
  consumer contracts. 197–98
  delay, effect of 197
  meaning 195
  performance of contract. 195–98
  test for. 195–96
  warranties distinguished 193,
    194–95
Consideration 25–48
  adequate. 25
  basic rules 25
  benefit. 29
  detriment 29, 30
  economic value 29, 30
  existing obligations 25, 29–30,
    46–48
  fundamental nature 29

mutual exchange. 30
past 25, 30–31
public duty,
    performance of 46–47
requirements 29
sufficient. 25
value. 25, 29, 30
variation of contracts 25, 40–41

Construction,
exclusion clauses 100–01,
    109, 113

Contents of contract. 81–95

Contra proferentem rule. 100–01

Contributory negligence,
damages. 212

Counter offer,
meaning 3

Damages. 211–14, 218–19,
    220–24
account of profits 213
contributory negligence. 212
disappointment. 223
discomfort or distress. 223
expectation interest 209, 211, 213
general principle. 211, 214
losses. 221–22
misrepresentation. 120, 122, 133
mitigation. 212
non-pecuniary losses 209, 222–24
objectives 210, 218, 221
principles 209
reliance interest. 209, 212–13
remoteness 209, 211, 211–12,
    218–19, 223–24
restitutionary interest. 213
speculative profits 212

Debts,
part payment. 26, 36–39
remission 48

Deceit 120, 247

Disappointment damages. 223

Distance selling. 17–18

Duress,
basis 135
common law origins. 138, 148
criminal offences. 135, 137, 139
disadvantage. 139
economic 141, 142–44
industrial action 137
meaning 135
operative threat. 135
physical violence. 148–49
reasonable alternative
    to compliance 135, 137,
    139, 143
remedies. 135
threat. 135, 137, 139, 143
unconscionability 139–40
undue influence and 136–40
unlawful acts. 137
voidable contracts. 138

EC law,
restraint of trade 157

Electronic communications,
acceptance 1, 6
offer. 1, 6

Employment contracts,
exclusion clauses. 110
restraint of trade 173–75
unfair contract terms 110

Estoppel, promissory,
See Promissory estoppel

Exclusion clauses 97–116
See also Unfair contract terms
business liability 101
collateral contracts 114
construction. 100–101, 109, 113
contra proferentem rule 100–01
effectiveness. 107–11
employment contracts 110
fair and reasonable test 101
implied terms 114–15
incorporation 99–100, 108–09,
    113–14
industry practice. 101
misrepresentation. 113–14

negligence 101
privity 51, 110–11
reasonable notice 108–09
sale of goods 251
statutory controls 102–06

Exclusive dealing 170, 171–72

Expectation interest,
   damages 209, 211, 213

Formation of contract,
   acceptance, *See* Acceptance
   battle of the forms 10–13
   consideration,
      See Consideration
   intention, *See* Intention to
      create legal relations
   internet 14–18
   offer, *See* Offer

Fraud,
   misrepresentation 120

Frustration 177–92
   common law
      position 177, 179–80,
                              181, 184, 188
   concept 179
   consequences 179–81, 183–87
   destruction of
      subject matter 181–83, 189
   effect 179–80
   event, frustrating 177, 179,
                              180, 191
   government intervention 182–83,
                              190–91
   just result 181, 189
   meaning 179, 188
   operation of rules 180
   radically different
      contracts 181–82
   recovery of benefits
      conferred prior to 180, 189
   self-induced 177, 182–83,
                              191–92
   statutory provisions 177, 179–80,
                              181, 185–87,
                              188, 189

total failure of
   consideration 180
valuable benefit 189–90
war time, requisitioning
   of property during 182

Fundamental breach 98

Guarantees, manufacturers',
   unfair contract terms 105

Identity,
   misrepresentation 122, 128
   mistake 119, 120,
                              127–30
'if' contracts 7

Illegality 157–75
   bargaining position 165
   basic rule 165
   class-protecting statutes 166
   exceptions to general
      principle 165
   executory contracts 165
   immoral purposes,
      contracts for 159–61
   meaning 157
   not carried out, purposes 165
   oppression 165
   ownership of goods 165, 166
   restraint of trade,
      See Restraint of trade
   solus agreements 170, 171–72
   title, contract to
      purchase a 165

Immoral purposes,
   contracts for 159–61

Implied terms 81, 82–85
   approaches to 81–82, 83–85
   business efficacy 83
   common law 81–82, 83–85
   fact, implication of 83
   incomplete agreements 84
   law, in 84
   Moorcock test 81, 83
   officious bystander test 81, 84

reasonableness 83
sale of goods 81, 84–85
statutory.................. 81, 84–85

Incapacity, *See* Capacity

Incorporation,
exclusion clauses 99–100, 108–09,
113–14
terms of contract........... 82, 87–88

Industrial action,
duress........................ 137

Injunctions...................... 209

Innominate terms 82

Intention to create
legal relations
basic rules 25
commercial agreements 25, 28–29,
45–46
consideration................... 28
domestic agreements....... 25, 28–29,
45–46
family arrangements 28
social and domestic
arrangements............... 28–29

Internet,
acknowledgment of orders 18
distance selling 17–18
formation of contract 14–18

Intoxication 67, 76–80

Invitations to treat,
advertisements 14–18, 20

Lock out agreements 92–93

Mental incapacity........... 67, 76–80

Minors,
anomalies in law.............. 68–71
beneficial contracts
of service 69
capacity 67, 68–71
dealings with................. 68–71
guarantors 70
necessaries.......... 69, 70, 71, 72–77
risks of dealing with.......... 69–70

rules protecting............... 68–71
third party, adult 70
voidable contracts................ 69

Misrepresentation 81, 88–89,
94, 117–34, 150
damages............... 120, 122, 133
deceit......................... 120
fraudulent 120
identity.................. 122, 128
inducement of
contract.............. 120, 132, 133
innocent 120
intention, statement of.......... 119
meaning 119, 132
mistake and 117, 121–22
negligent 120, 133–34
operative factor................ 120
opinion, statement of 119, 132
partial reliance.................. 132
reliance....................... 120
remedies.................. 120, 133
remoteness..................... 120
rescission 120, 122
silence........................ 132
statutory............... 120, 133–34
third party rights 120
undue lapse of time 120
unreasonable reliance 120
verification.................... 132

Mistake...................... 117–34
case law 117
common.................. 120, 121,
123–26, 134
equitable rules 117, 123,
126–27
fact, of..................... 124, 228
fundamental 129
identity 119, 120,
.........................127–30
misrepresentation and 117,
121–22
mutual................... 120, 121,
123–26, 134
nullifying agreement 123
outline........................ 120
quality........................ 127

remedies 130
restitution 228
subject matter 121, 123–26
test 124
third party rights 125–26
types 120
unilateral 119, 120,
                                    121, 134
value 125
void contracts 121

Mitigation,
damages 212

Moorcock test 81, 83

Mutual mistake 120, 121,
                                    123–26, 134

Necessaries 69, 70, 71

Negligence,
exclusion clauses 101
misrepresentation 120, 133–34
privity 52, 57–62
unfair contract terms 105, 107–11

Negligent misstatement 81, 247–48

Offer 1
See also Acceptance
advertisements 1, 15, 20
contents 3
electronic communications 1
invitation to treat
    distinguished 2
lapse 6
meaning 2–5
relationship with acceptance 1
requirement 3
revocation 1
withdrawal,
    See also Revocation of offer
    email 15–16
    instantaneous
        communications 16
    telegram 16
    timing 21
    unilateral contracts 8–9

Officious bystander test 81, 84
Opinion, statement of 119, 132

Part payment of debts 26, 36–39
Passing of property 251, 252–56,
                                    259–60
Performance of contract,
conditions 193, 195–98
contract price, earning 199–203
entire contracts 193, 199–203
innominate terms 193
sale of goods 201–02
severable contracts 193, 199–203
substantial performance 201
warranties 193
Postal rule 1, 4–5, 8, 16–17
avoidance 7–11
recalling posted
    acceptance 22
Pre-contractual
statements 81, 86–90
Privity 51–66, 97
agency 235
consideration and 51
exclusion clauses 51, 110–11
imposition of obligations 51
Law Commission Report 51, 54
meaning 51, 54
negligence 52, 57–62
traditional doctrine 51, 54, 63
Tulk v Moxhay, rule in 53, 56–57
Promissory estoppel 25, 31–36
                                    40–44
basic elements 26
limitations 26, 34–35
modern form 41–42
origins 26
part payment of debts 26, 36–39
requirements 33–35
single debts 48
variation of contract 42–43
Public interest,
restraint of trade 161

Quasi-contract, *See* Restitution

Recovery of money paid 227–29
Reliance interest,
  damages 209, 212–13
Remedies 209–24
  damages, *See* Damages
  duress 135
  misrepresentation 120, 133
  mistake 130
  specific performance,
    See Specific performance
  undue influence 135
Remoteness,
  damages 209, 211,
                            211–12, 218–19
Repudiation of contract 202
Rescission,
  misrepresentation 120, 122
Restitution 225–34
  academic interest 225
  anticipated contract,
    work done under 230
  compensation for benefit
    conferred on defendant 229
  development 227
  flexibility of law 230
  importance 225
  meaning 227
  mistake 228
  overpayments 232–33
  quantum meruit basis
    of recovery 229, 233
  rationale 227
  recovery of money paid 227–29
  services performed under
    void contract 229
  total failure of
    consideration 232–33, 233–34
Restraint of trade 161–63, 166–69
  activity, restricted 162
  area 162
  blue pencil test 168

competition law 157
EC law 157
employment contracts 173–75
exclusive dealing 170, 171–72
legitimate interest,
  protection of 166, 167,
                            171, 172, 173
length of restriction 168, 172
meaning 157
public interest 161, 163,
                                166, 169
reasonable 157, 161, 162–63,
                        166, 167, 172, 173–74
requirements 161
severance 168
solus agreements 170, 171–72
valid interest requiring
  protection 161–62
worldwide restrictions 167
Revocation of offer 1
  communication 16
  third party 22
  timing 16
  unilateral contract 7–11
Rewards,
  advertisements 20–21

Sale of goods 251–60
  durability 259
  exclusion clauses 251
  fitness for purpose 258–59
  implied terms 81, 84–85,
                                251, 256–60
  passing of property 251, 252–56,
                                259–60
  performance of
    contract 201–02
  quality of goods 257–58
  satisfactory quality 258–59
  unfair contract terms 97
Severable contracts 193
Silence,
  acceptance, as 1, 19–23
Solus agreements 170, 171–72

Specific performance 216–17
 adequacy of damages. 216
 appropriate uses 209
 basis of award 209
 criteria. 216
 discretionary nature 216
 disproportionate hardship 217
 mutuality 217
 nature of remedy 216
 origins. 217
 sale of land. 217–18
 supervision of
  performance. 217
Subject matter,
 mistake 121, 123–26
Surety 150–51
 undue influence 150–51, 154

Telephone,
 acceptance 7–10
Telexes,
 acceptance 5
Terms of contract,
 conditions, *See* Conditions
 implied, *See* Implied terms
 innominate, *See* Innominate terms
 representations and 82
 warranties, *See* Warranties
Tulk v Moxhay, rule in 53, 56–57

Undue influence,
 actual 135, 137, 138,
                  144–47, 149
 advice, proper 154–55
 automatic presumption
  of influence 135
 banks and. 147–51, 152–56
 constructive notice 150–51, 154
 continuing relationships 139
 development 135
 disadvantage 135, 138
 duress and 136–40
 equitable origins 138, 148
 essence of 137–38
 lending 147–51, 152–56

operative 135
presumed 135, 137, 138,
            139, 144–47, 149
 remedies. 135
 surety 150–51, 154
 unconscionability 139–40
 voidable contract 138
Unfair contract terms 97, 102–06,
               107–11
 See also Exclusion clauses
 business 102–06, 113
 consumer, dealing as a. 103–06
 contractors 105
 contractual liability. 105
 employment contracts 110
 enforcement of liability,
  restrictive or onerous 115
 guarantees, manufacturers'. 105
 implied terms 114–15
 manufacturer's guarantees 105
 negligence 105, 107–11
 reasonableness 110, 114–16
 sale of goods 97
 written standard terms
  of business,
  contracting on 105, 114
Unilateral contracts 1, 6–10

Variation of contract,
 consideration. 25, 40–41
 promissory estoppel. 42–43
 remission of debt 48
Void contracts 117
 See also Mistake;
 Restraint of trade
Voidable contracts. 117
 See also Duress; Misrepresentation;
  Undue influence

Warranties. 82
 breach, effect of 196–97
 conditions distinguished 193,
                 194–98
 consumer contracts. 197–98
 meaning 195